Trade and Growth
in the Philippines

AN OPEN DUAL ECONOMY

Trade and Growth
in the Philippines

AN OPEN DUAL ECONOMY

George L. Hicks *and*
Geoffrey McNicoll

Cornell University Press | ITHACA AND LONDON

865559

First published 1971

International Standard Book Number 0–8014–0612–9
Library of Congress Catalog Card Number 73–139507

PRINTED IN THE UNITED STATES OF AMERICA
BY KINGSPORT PRESS, INC.

Acknowledgments

This study of the postwar Philippine economy in the analytical framework of open dualism was originally prepared as part of the Philippine Project of the Center for Development Planning, National Planning Association, Washington, under a contract with the Agency for International Development. That version of the report, submitted to AID in October 1968, has since been substantially revised and brought further up to date. We are grateful for the research opportunity offered by the NPA project, while stressing that the views expressed here are those of the authors alone.

We wish to acknowledge the useful criticism of a number of economists who read the earlier draft report; in particular, the comments of Bruce Glassburner, Benjamin Higgins, Lovell Jarvis, Gerardo P. Sicat, and Jeffrey G. Williamson were most helpful.

We are grateful also for the cooperation and assistance of members of the faculty of the School of Economics, University of the Philippines, during two years (1966–1967) of field work for the NPA Philippine Project.

A basic debt is to our colleagues at the National Planning Association, especially to Richard W. Hooley and Forrest E. Cookson; many of the ideas in this study originated in our joint discussions. John C. H. Fei kindly gave us the benefit of his advice on some questions of model-building. Finally, the encouragement and frank criticism of Douglas S. Paauw, Director of the NPA's Center for Development Planning, have been of great help to us. In substance and presentation few parts of this work have not gained from his suggestions, although on specific points and attitudes we may often have differed.

GEORGE L. HICKS
GEOFFREY McNICOLL

Singapore and Berkeley
February 1971

Contents

Acknowledgments   v

Introduction   1

1. Development of the Open Dual Economy   6
   Dualism and Exports   10
   Approaches to Trade and Development   16
   Problems of Open Economy Growth   25
   Analytical Framework   33

2. The Philippine Experience   38
   Categorization Problems: Sectoral Divisions   38
   Statistical Survey of the Philippines   43
   Land Surplus or Labor Surplus?   76
   Traditional Sector Responses   98
   Investment and Import Dependence   104
   Summary of the Philippine Experience   117

3. A Theory of Open Economy Growth   121
   Traditional Sector Output   123
   Agricultural Surplus   131
   Modern Sector   135
   Intersectoral Relationships   146
   General Model   154
   Philippine Parameters   162
   Economic Implications of the Model   167

4. Exports and Resources: Some Modern Dilemmas of
   Growth   178
      Dualistic Analysis of Export Sector   179
      Dynamics of Export Growth   185
      Problems of Reducing Resource Content of Exports   187
      Productivity and Natural Resources   195
      Past Growth and the Future of Philippine Exports   217

5. Toward Stagnation?   221

   Bibliography   232
   Index   241

Figures

1. Investment allocation and trade   12
2. Population distribution and trade   15
3. Structural framework for an open dual economy   36
4. Philippine exports by major category, 1950–1968   48
5. Regression of harvested area on labor force employed in agriculture, Philippines, 1950–1968   78
6. Harvested area per person in the agricultural labor force (in hectares)   81
7. Traditional sector production function: pure land surplus   126
8. Traditional sector production function: slowing of land expansion   130
9. Determination of total and exportable agricultural surpluses   134
10. Modern sector production function with fixed coefficients: (a) pure labor-saving technical progress, (b) labor-saving bias   138
11. Formal determination of intersectoral terms of trade   153

Tables

1. Major indices for selected countries in Southeast Asia, 1960   9
2. Contribution of change in harvested area and change in yield to growth in output of cereals, selected countries in Southeast Asia, 1952/1956–1961/1965   32

3. Sectoral distribution of gross national product, Philippines, 1950–1968   44
4. Recorded Philippine exports and imports as percentages of totals estimated from statistics of major trading partners   46
5. Philippine exports by major category, 1950–1968   49
6. Philippine imports by major category, 1950–1968   50
7. Sectoral distribution of employed labor force, Philippines, 1950–1968   52
8. Traditional sector indices, Philippines, 1950–1968   57
9. Distribution of traditional sector output by demand use, Philippines, annual averages, 1950–1968   60
10. Selected ratios for major industry groups in modern sector, Philippines, 1961   63
11. Returns to factors, propensity to invest, and average payrolls in Philippine manufacturing, selected years, 1956–1966   65
12. Manufacturing sector indices, Philippines, 1950–1968   68
13. Intersectoral terms of trade, Philippines, 1950–1968   73
14. Philippine land/labor ratios by major region, 1954–1968   80
15. Unemployment rates in the experienced labor force by sex and major industry group, Philippines, 1960   84
16. Characteristics of surplus labor in the Philippines, selected years, 1958–1967   85
17. Real daily wage rates in agriculture and industry, Philippines, 1950–1968   91
18. Characteristics of postwar interregional migration in the Philippines   96
19. Apparent per capita direct absorption of cereals, Philippines, 1910–1965   101
20. The financing of Philippine imports, 1951–1967   106
21. Indices of imports and domestic production of durable equipment, Philippines, 1955–1967   110
22. Philippine growth and structural change in the framework of the open dual economy model   163
23. Effect of bias in modern sector technical progress and level of innovation intensity in agriculture on modern sector growth and labor absorption: hypothetical data using naive model   166

24. Average yield indices for major crops, Philippines, 1939/1941 and 1954–1968   197

25. Rice yields for selected regions, Philippines, 1950–1968   199

26. Rice yields, costs, and returns: improved and traditional varieties, Rizal Province, Philippines, 1967 dry season   207

27. Land utilization in Mindanao, 1952 and 1963   213

28. Past and projected average annual growth rates of Philippine log exports, 1955–1985   215

29. Crude rates of natural increase of population implied in official population projections, Philippines, 1960–1980   219

Trade and Growth
in the Philippines

AN OPEN DUAL ECONOMY

Introduction

A major objective of this study is to analyze at the aggregate level the process of economic development in the context of openness. Our thesis is that trade makes a fundamental difference to the growth process and should play a central role in the pure theory of development. Although having nothing new to say about the specific role of trade in development, we have attempted to incorporate it in a theory of growth of a dual economy and to draw out some of the implications of observed growth patterns which then follow. The theory makes no claim to be generally relevant. Indeed, it is now widely agreed that the diversity of underdeveloped countries effectively precludes the possibility of a generally applicable theory of development. In the present study we are concerned with the export-oriented, land surplus, dual economy.

The significance of treating an open economy is that it allows us to recognize the fact that most countries must rely heavily on imported capital equipment for their industrial growth. For all but a few countries, the assumption commonly made in closed economy approaches that industrial goods can be used indifferently as consumer goods or investment goods (or that the latter can be produced domestically at will) is inadequate and disguises what may well be an important constraint on growth.

We consider the land surplus economy in contrast to the labor surplus case of studies in the Lewis tradition in the belief that the former is a more accurate description of many developing countries. An examination of the sources of recent growth of agricultural output in Southeast Asia as well as in extensive regions of Africa and Latin America suggests that a major portion of this growth may be accounted for by simple expansion of cultivated area. Here, the emphasis of much development theory on how to utilize a surplus or underemployed agricultural labor force to develop an industrial sector should be replaced by a more rigid connection between a labor transfer out of agriculture and a decline in the potential agricultural surplus. (The justification for the nearly exclusive attention the labor surplus economies have received is that although constituting a numerical minority of countries they contain over half the world's population.) The distinction between these two types of economy cannot be pursued too far, since the absence of an organized labor market in premodern societies (and of other conditions necessary for applying conventional labor force concepts) may permit the existence in the same country of both labor "surpluses" and "shortages." Population growth, of course, will eventually transform a land surplus economy into a labor surplus form unless there is large-scale labor absorption by industry.

The third characteristic of the type of economy in which we are interested is its dualistic nature. The term "dualism" is used in the literature in a number of different senses. In this study we use it to characterize two fundamental features of the economy: a substantial labor productivity differential between a traditional agricultural sector and a relatively modern industrial sector, and differing patterns of resource use and consequently of growth dynamics in the two sectors. The latter feature is seen in a basic asymmetry of the sectoral production functions, with capital playing a significant role in the modern industrial sector but a much less important (and often negligible) role in traditional agriculture.

The particular example of an open, land surplus, dual economy towards which most of this study is directed is the Philippines. We believe that it is also relevant to economies such as Thailand, Burma, and Malaysia, which share many of the same essential characteristics. However, we have not attempted to argue formally for this more general application, or to take examples from outside the restricted region of Southeast Asia.

In Chapter 1 we describe in general terms the main features of open economy growth that will be stressed in the remainder of the study. We are interested in only a few of the large number of ways in which trade is thought to influence development. The countries of Southeast Asia are taken to illustrate both the diversity of economic structures and development patterns and the underlying similarity of some of the serious obstacles to sustained growth. Indeed, an analysis of some of these recent patterns of growth even suggests that they may represent a case of temporary success leading in the longer run to economic stagnation. The contrast between this deviant type of growth and the probable successful patterns is the major focus of this study. What we regard as an ultimately unsuccessful growth pattern is that characterized by excessive or "hothouse" import substitution and resource-intensive export growth.

Excessive import substitution, among other things, effectively discourages the export of manufactured goods and the growth of a domestic investment goods industry. As a result, the economy remains dependent on the import of capital goods and therefore on exports needed to pay for them. Partly because of the emphasis on import-dependent industrialization, traditional agriculture remains relatively stagnant although the growing modern sector is heavily dependent upon it. Without increasing productivity, the exportable agricultural surplus is eroded by the twin pressures of eventual diminishing returns at the margin combined with the rising share of the nonagricultural population which must be fed. Countries with suitable natural resources such as minerals and forests can supplement traditional agricultural exports with these "extractive" exports, but this type of export, as with traditional agriculture, tends to be resource-using and ultimately resource-exhausting. The dual flaw of this open economy growth pattern stems from excessive import substitution linked to natural resource using and traditional exports. Combined, but not singly, they lead to eventual cessation of industrial growth.

This thesis is hardly novel—indeed, it is basically the received doctrine. What we attempt in Chapters 2–4, however, is to formalize the theory and present a complete case study. The Philippines is an example of this unfavorable pattern of growth, showing short-run gains in output but not accompanied by the structural and institutional changes which would lay the foundation for long-run development. Chapter 2 endeavors to document this assertion by establishing the validity and relevance of the analytical framework proposed and the absence of indications of significant structural shifts which might render the framework obsolete.

Based on this empirical study and the descriptive model implicit in the discussion, Chapter 3 sets out a formal model of an open dual economy. It has elements in common with the closed dual economy models of Fei and Ranis and Jorgenson, and also with the several traditions of model-building which recognize capital specificity. As with other aggregative models, its purpose is neither accurate description nor to serve as a basis for policy prescriptions. Rather, it is to set out clearly and rigorously the implications for future development goals of a few simple but fundamental economic relationships which we believe reflect certain rules of growth in many open dual economies.

The present model serves, *inter alia,* to highlight the close connection between the growth rates of industry and of exports. Even a cursory examination of the sources of postwar export growth in Southeast Asian countries, however, suggests that prospects for future growth in exports are in many cases bleak. Chapter 4 investigates these prospects in more detail. While we take the major Philippine export industries as examples, these are in fact fairly typical of the region as a whole. They face the same problems of inelastic foreign demand, resource exhaustion, and the difficulties of raising agricultural productivity.

Among the conclusions we draw from the analysis, perhaps the most important is the obvious but often disregarded fact that the past growth performance of an economy may not be a reliable indicator of future growth prospects. In the Rostovian idiom, an economy that has been cruising down the runway at a rapid rate is generally assumed to have an excellent chance of "taking off" in the near future. In fact, of course, the inner dimensions of development are hardly measured at all by indices such as GNP. What is required is an examination of the sources and quality of that growth. For this purpose we believe that the theoretical model of open economy growth is a useful framework of analysis, offering some important insights into economic relationships and future development prospects which may be obscured at a more disaggregated level. Based on the case study of the Philippines, we see that Philippine growth diverges substantially from what is postulated as an ideal pattern, and the major policy problem is seen in Chapter 5 as one of changing direction in order to bring about an eventual convergence of the actual and ideal. This involves policies which change the industrial structure to encourage exports of manufactured goods and backward integration to reduce import dependence. Equally important is an internal redirection of resources which raises productivity in the traditional sector and reduces the resource-using bias of the export sector.

CHAPTER 1

Development of the
Open Dual Economy

Openness and dualism are two basic features common to the majority of underdeveloped countries. The only major exceptions would be on the one hand the underdeveloped giants such as India and Brazil, which produce a sizeable share of their capital goods and raw materials requirements and to that extent are independent of many (though by no means all) of the constraints of reliance on foreign trade, and on the other hand the few agrarian economies which are effectively without an industrial sector so that the term "dual" is inapt. In choosing to emphasize these features in a study of the Philippines, therefore, we are concerned with developmental problems of a wide generality.

Analyses of the dual economy have formed an important part of modern development theory, but in contrast the role of trade in the growth process is comparatively neglected. It is interesting to reflect on how the latter situation has come about. It is possible that modern study of the very different nineteenth-century development experience and the anticolonial reaction to the exploitative foreign-created export economies has succeeded not only in greatly advancing knowledge of the various trading problems facing the developing countries (adverse terms of trade, instability of earnings, etc.) but also, on a less conscious level, in largely suppressing serious thought on the

6

issue of the role of trade in economic development. A less speculative factor which has accentuated the closed economy approach of development theory is the dominance in much of the literature of empirical studies and examples based on India and Pakistan and models of development drawing their inspiration from these particular cases. The ratio of foreign trade to total product is lower for India and Pakistan than for almost any other underdeveloped economy and hence the assumption of a closed economy presumably does less violence to the reality. In recent years even these countries have experienced severe foreign exchange shortages with consequent unfavorable impact on their rates of growth.

Recognition of the importance and pervasiveness of foreign exchange (and other trade-related) constraints on growth is reflected on a theoretical level in the development of "two-gap" growth models, and on a more general and practical level in the rapidly growing literature on "aid through trade." Discussion of the latter has been stimulated and often dominated by the influence of the United Nations Conference on Trade and Development. The present study, while it makes use of the two-gap concept and touches some of the issues raised by UNCTAD, is oriented more toward the nature of the domestic economy in the underdeveloped country. It is concerned with the significance of trade for dualistic growth, treating the international situation as part of the environment.

In this introductory chapter we begin by giving a brief and somewhat assertive overview of growth in the open dual economy. Two variants of this type of economy are identified—one in which modern export industries are dominant, the other where exports mainly originate in the traditional sector. Since a major point of emphasis is the role of trade in the growth process, we devote some space to an examination of the various means by which trade is thought to help or hinder development, isolating those which seem particularly relevant for the present treatment. Trade is seen as an essential factor in dual economy growth, but also as providing a means by which the economy can avoid, at least in the short term, some of the basic structural and institutional changes which are concomitants of long-run development. In the final section of the chapter, as a foundation for the subsequent empirical and formal analysis, we outline a simple and highly aggregated accounting system for the open dual economy. While some such system is implied in any attempt at describing aggregative development patterns, its explicit statement is helpful both in clarifying the assumptions being made and also in drawing a sharp distinction between changes in the level of flow variables within the framework and the more fundamental structural shifts which can undermine the relevance of the framework itself. The importance of this latter distinction is apparent when the particular obstacles facing the Philippine economy are investigated at greater length in following chapters.

While much of the discussion in this chapter could be cast in terms of most of the small or medium-sized underdeveloped countries around the globe, it has seemed preferable to draw our examples in the main from the countries of Southeast Asia, the regional context of the Philippines. Although their trade ratios vary substantially, for all the countries in this area the role of trade is a vital one. Specialized in production, they export a limited range of primary products and import a wide range of consumer goods, raw materials, and virtually all their durable capital equipment. Without trade these economies could hardly exist in their present form and their prospects for further growth would be dim. With the exception of the city-state of Singapore, they are also dualistic economies in the sense defined in the Introduction. Traditional agriculture gives employment for well over half the economically active population, while accounting for a much smaller share of total product. The countries are nevertheless highly diverse with respect to size, economic structure, level of development, and historical experience. Some of the relevant economic indices are given in Table 1 for selected countries in the area.

Table 1. Major indices for selected countries in Southeast Asia, 1960

Country	Population (millions)	Per capita income (U.S. $)	Per capita exports (U.S. $)	Exports as percentage of gross domestic product	Share of income originating in agriculture (per cent)	Share of labor force in agriculture* (per cent)
Burma	22.3	70	10.0	14.2	45	n.a.
Indonesia	94.2	80	8.9	10.8	57	72
Malaysia†	6.9	235	98.1	41.9	44	57
Philippines	27.4	140	20.4	14.8	33	60
Thailand	26.4	100	15.3	15.1	39	82

Sources: United Nations, *Demographic Yearbook, Economic Survey of Asia and the Far East,* and *Yearbook of National Accounts Statistics;* International Labour Office, *Yearbook of Labour Statistics* (various issues).
*Ca. 1960.
†West Malaysia only.

DUALISM AND EXPORTS

In each of these countries, as in virtually all underdeveloped countries, exports originate both from modern, capital-intensive production or processing industries and from industries employing traditional, labor-intensive technologies. It is useful (and natural in a dual economy analysis) to classify economies according to which of these categories of exports dominates. We shall refer to the two classes respectively as *modern sector dominant* and *traditional sector dominant,* while recognizing that some economies lie close to midway between them. Malaysia, whose economy is based chiefly on its mines and plantations, would lie in the first group; Burma and Thailand, with their reliance on traditional agriculture, in the second. The Philippines in the postwar period has been moving from traditional to modern sector dominance.

Sectoral allocation of individual industries is generally straightforward. Rice farming throughout the region is clearly traditional in form, while logging and copper mining in the Philippines, the petroleum industry in Indonesia, and tin mining in Malaysia would not be possible on such a scale without the application of capital-intensive methods of production. The plantation industries of such importance in Indonesia and Malaysia are less easy to classify, but in most cases must also be regarded as "modern."[1]

Aside from any export industries which may be included in the modern sector of the economy, this sector also contains industries primarily oriented towards domestic consumption. The modern factories which process food, brew beer, and manufacture cigarettes and textiles are obvious examples, as also are those specializing in assembly of imported equipment. Central to several of the major issues discussed in this study is the extreme difficulty experienced by most underdeveloped coun-

[1] A more detailed treatment of this classification problem with reference to the Philippines is given in Chapter 2. The important Philippine sugar industry, it is argued there, is "traditional" in character.

tries in exporting manufactures such as these on any substantial scale. Without access to the foreign sector in its capacity to transform the output of consumer manufactures into investment goods through trade, we in effect have a situation of capital specificity in the modern sector. Unlike the export industries the output of which is freely transformable between investment and consumption uses, the capital stock in an important segment (sometimes the whole) of the modern sector is "specific" to the production of consumer goods.

It is possible to overstate the prevalence of this capital specificity. Most underdeveloped countries have at least some industries whose output can be directed towards either consumption or investment. The construction industry would be the best example. Their production of durable capital equipment, however, is often either negligible or based entirely on assembly industries. Some relevant data on the import content of investment are noted below, together with two of the likely explanations in terms of economies of scale and over-rapid import substitution.

In distinguishing between exportable commodities (mostly raw materials) and effectively nonexportable manufactured goods in modern sector output, we are immediately faced with an investment allocation choice. This can perhaps best be discussed in terms of a highly simplified contrast between typical colonial and postcolonial policies in the modern sector dominant economy. The colonial powers generally preferred to invest resources in producing goods for export, while postwar independent governments have shown a clear preference for the home market. Very little investment has found its way into traditional agriculture, which appeared an equally unattractive outlet to both colonial and independent governments.

The contrast between these differing investment priorities is shown schematically in Figure 1. PQ represents total investment, all of which is assumed to be allocated between modern industry for domestic consumption and modern exports such as the products of mines, plantations and logging enterprises. As a smaller share of resources invested in export industries would mean less export volume, the export schedule slopes down to the right. Import requirements, however, probably do not change significantly with a reallocation of investment since investment is heavily import-dependent in both parts of the modern sector. Both mining equipment and textile machinery must be imported.

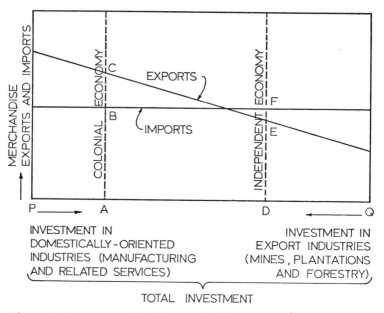

Figure 1. Investment allocation and trade

In this example the colonial economy invests an amount *PA* in modern manufacturing for the domestic market and *AQ* in export industries. Exports are high and the trade surplus *BC* is used to finance the profit outflow typical of the colonial economy. In contrast, the independent economy invests the bulk of its resources (*PD*) in domestic manufacturing and has an adverse balance of trade (*FE*) which is financed by various forms of invisible earnings, such as foreign aid and foreign military expenditure. A major objective of the independent economy is to build a modern manufacturing sector and escape from the colonial export economy. Investment in manufactures is therefore at a maximum consistent with the inevitable balance of payments constraint. Unless an economy is fortunate in having a favorable invisibles account, it will be unable to maintain for long a level of imports in excess of exports, and the equilibrium position will tend to lie close to the intersection of the import and export schedules. (We assume for simplicity that the traditional agricultural sector of this economy makes no contribution to exports—for example, it might produce just enough food to feed the country as a whole. The modifications for more general cases are obvious.)

The constraints on growth in such an economy are very clear. The modern manufacturing sector grows through additions to capital stock, an important part of which has to be imported.[2] Imports are paid for primarily by exports, which in turn can only grow through investment in modern, capital-intensive mining, plantation, and forest industries—in effect, operating as capital goods producers.[3] For a given investment allocation the balance of payments constraint thus sets a ceiling on the rate of growth of manufacturing which may be below that permitted by domestic savings.

The identification of separate foreign exchange and savings-investment constraints is now, of course, a familiar part of modern development theory. As they arise here, they are not in-

[2] The first half of this statement is of course more controversial than it appeared during the long sway of Harrod-Domar. The present study, however, is aimed mainly at stressing necessary conditions for growth (and, by inference, sufficient conditions for nongrowth) so that there is less need to insist on identifying growth with increase of capital stock.

[3] The apparent close analogy here with the two sector Soviet growth models analyzed by Findlay and others is pursued in Chapter 3. The breakdown of this analogy (resulting from the resource-using character of these "extractive" export industries) has far-reaching consequences for the development process in these economies. Ronald Findlay, "Optimal Investment Allocation between Consumer Goods and Capital Goods," *Economic Journal*, 76 (1966), 70–83.

dependent of each other: a higher average propensity to invest would make possible more investment in both parts of the modern sector. The foreign exchange constraint is in fact a consequence of the investment constraint taken together with the existence of capital specificity. Without capital specificity the foreign exchange constraint could not exist, as domestically produced goods could always be substituted for capital goods imports. For this economy, however, regardless of the propensity to invest, consumer goods or raw materials cannot be used interchangeably with capital goods.

Economies whose exports are primarily "traditional" in character face somewhat different allocation problems from those described above. We consider the extreme case of traditional sector dominance in which all exports originate in this sector. Capital is assumed to play a minor or even negligible role as a factor in their production. The examples of the rice economies of Burma and Thailand were noted earlier; they perhaps come closest to this type of economy among the group of Southeast Asian countries listed in Table 1. Rice cultivation requires little or no imported inputs but large quantities of land and labor. The contrast could hardly be greater between this factor mix and the mining industry which requires negligible land, relatively little labor, and large quantities of (mainly imported) capital inputs. Although unproductive by Western standards or those of Japan and Taiwan, these two economies produce enough rice to feed both the rural and urban sectors and leave a substantial amount for export. International trade makes it possible to convert this agricultural surplus into the raw materials and capital equipment needed for the modern manufacturing sector.

While the amount of capital in traditional agriculture (apart from the labor-intensive investment over long periods of time in bunds and irrigation works) is small, its marginal product may be—and almost certainly is—quite large. The explanations as to why the traditional sector has not attracted the investment which might be expected according to the usual neoclassical allocation criteria must be sought in its elaborate and change-resistant institutional structures, especially those relating to land tenure and credit. This is not, however, the focus of the present study.

The factor of production of which the sectoral allocation vitally affects the level of trade in this economy is of course

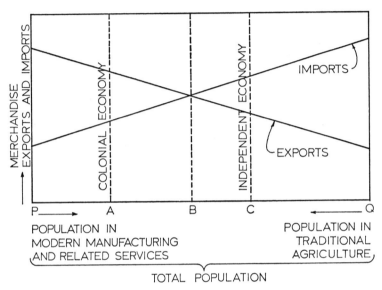

Figure 2. Population distribution and trade

labor. Figure 2 sketches the import and export schedules as functions of the sectoral population shares. In the absence of surplus labor we have the rough argument (which will be re-stated more precisely in Chapter 3) that the larger the proportion of the population in the agricultural sector, the greater will be the total agricultural output, the smaller will be the urban population requiring to be fed, and the greater will be the agricultural surplus available for export. As a consequence, the export schedule slopes down to the right. Modern manu-facturing is highly import-dependent, but traditional agricul-ture is not, hence the import schedule has the opposite gradient.

A colonial economy such as prewar Burma traditionally had a trade surplus and was not interested in developing an industrial sector. Its position might therefore be represented by the vertical line through the point *A*, with *PA* and *AQ* denoting the modern and traditional sector populations respectively. The prime objective, at least in theory, of the independent economies has been to industrialize and shift the sectoral distribution of population away from agriculture. If successful in this then their population distribution could be defined by the point *B*, if they are forced to balance their trade accounts, or further to the right (*C*), if a deficit in merchandise trade can be sustained. As with the previous example of modern sector dominance the apparent trade constraint reflects underlying capital specificity. Rice can be transformed into machines only through trade. An obvious growth dilemma faced by this type of economy is that to industrialize at a more rapid rate it is necessary to import more capital equipment and this entails more exports. But exports are drawn from the total agricultural surplus which must also feed the population. If both per capita food consumption and agricultural productivity are constant then the attempt to move people out of agriculture would result in a fall in the exportable surplus.

APPROACHES TO TRADE AND DEVELOPMENT

The discussion of the role of trade in development in the previous section has centered on a single aspect of this complex relationship: the function of trade in overcoming the constraints on growth caused by capital specificity. While in much of what follows it is this aspect which receives greatest attention, it is worth pausing here to view the interconnections in a wider perspective.

We noted at the outset of this chapter that the greater part of development theory, and specifically that concerned with the dual economy, all but ignored foreign trade. Similarly, it is true that trade theory largely avoids the issues of development, taking as parameters or exogenous variables what development theory seeks to explain.[4] There is a substantial literature tracing causal relationships from trade to growth, but on the whole it cannot compare in analytical rigor with the main body of theory either in trade or development—and perhaps as a result it has had relatively little impact.

This literature on development through trade is so often surveyed that a summary of the arguments is hardly necessary.[5] Because of the heterogeneous nature of the material, surveys almost inevitably adopt a taxonomic approach, cataloging the arguments for trade, against it, and the few more or less neutral.[6] In sharp contrast with most of trade theory and even development theory, the polemical element is strong. Writers who support the pro-trade case stress comparative advantage, markets, specialization, and technological change. The opponents argue that, in one form or another, underdevelopment is in part a consequence of the international trading system. Nurkse is one writer who takes an intermediate position, allowing that trade was a successful engine of growth in the nineteenth century but arguing that it cannot be expected to perform the same role in the twentieth century—and hence that

[4] The literature on the effect of growth on trade is surveyed by Richard E. Caves, *Trade and Economic Structure* (Cambridge, Mass.: Harvard University Press, 1960), chapter 14; and W. M. Corden, *Recent Developments in the Theory of International Trade* (Princeton: Princeton University Press, 1965), chapter 3.

[5] See, in particular: Gerald M. Meier, *The International Economics of Development: Theory and Policy* (New York: Harper and Row, 1968), chapter 8; J. E. Haring, "Dynamic Trade Theory and Growth in Poor Countries," *Kyklos*, 16 (1963), 371–391; Shu-Chin Yang, "Foreign Trade Problems in Economic Development," *Scottish Journal of Political Economy*, 11 (1965), 116–135; and C. W. Hultman, "Exports and Economic Growth: A Survey," *Land Economics*, May 1967, pp. 148–157.

[6] Caves describes these arguments as "dynamic fragments, patches of analysis compatible with any number of complete models" (*Trade and Economic Structure*, p. 244). A major addition to this literature since the publication of Caves' book, however, is the further elaboration by Baldwin of his theory of export technology and economic development. (See Note 8.)

countries must now largely rely on industrial expansion for the home market.[7]

For our present purposes, a more useful classification of these arguments than the division into pro- and anti-trade theories is a division into theories which are focused on the domestic economy and those which, in contrast, are externally oriented. The first are those claiming that the impact of trade on development depends on the structure and behavior of the domestic economy. The emphasis in this approach is on the nature of the domestic production function. The second group of theories largely ignores the conditions prevailing in the domestic economy and focuses on external issues such as terms of trade, price stability, and all the favorable and unfavorable effects (e.g., technology) that trade is said to carry in its wake.

The domestically oriented theories, those associated, for example, with the names of North, Myint, and Baldwin,[8] tend to be rather specific in their application. They have been applied to fairly clearly defined countries and historical circumstances, often only to explain a given historical outcome. In this sense, they are somewhat narrowly conceived. By limiting the range

[7] Ragnar Nurkse, *Patterns of Trade and Development* (Oxford: Basil Blackwell, 1961).

[8] Douglass C. North, "Location Theory and Regional Economic Growth," *Journal of Political Economy*, 63 (1955), 243–258; Hla Myint, "The 'Classical Theory' of International Trade and the Underdeveloped Countries," *Economic Journal*, 68 (1958), 317–337; and Robert E. Baldwin, "Export Technology and Development from a Subsistence Level," *Economic Journal*, 73 (1963), 80–92, and *Economic Development and Export Growth: A Study of Northern Rhodesia, 1920–1960* (Berkeley: University of California Press, 1966).

Theories of enclave dualism associated with the work of Higgins and others also emphasize the importance of the domestic economy. The failure of trade to stimulate growth is explained in terms of the structure of the domestic economy and the nature of the production functions. This approach is directed towards the special case of nongrowth and is therefore less helpful as a guide to understanding the process of development. Benjamin Higgins, "The 'Dualistic Theory' of Underdeveloped Areas," *Economic Development and Cultural Change*, 4 (1956), 99–115.

of their applicability, they are able to encompass more of the
institutional and factual framework than is possible in more
general theories. Hence, each in its own ground has considerable realism and historical explanatory power. Another feature
of this approach is its low level of aggregation in contrast to the
more general theories. Much of the discussion takes place at the
commodity level rather than that of broad sectors. This disaggregation, together with the institutional factors incorporated
and the considerable variety of their assumptions and behavioral relationships, means that these theories tend not to be
amenable to mathematical treatment or to inclusion as part of
a wider general equilibrium model of trade and growth.

The "staple" and "export base" theories are examples of this
approach to economic development. The staple theory was first
developed by Innis, who showed the importance of the export
staple in the development of the Canadian economy.[9] In a later
elaboration, North demonstrated how regional development in
the American economy was often dependent on the successful
expansion of an export base.[10] He stressed not only the effect of
the initial increase in income that followed successful development of a regional export but also the subsidiary industries that
were likely to arise—for example, those that buy from or supply
the export industry. Thus, North foreshadows subsequent discussion of backward and forward linkages and indirectly shows
the significance for development of an industry's production
function.

Baldwin presents a development theory "for an initially
backward, subsistence economy into which a substantial for-
eign-financed and foreign-directed export industry is introduced."[11] His major case study is of Northern Rhodesia, which
has a modern, capital-intensive mineral industry together with
traditional agriculture. The key feature of this theory is the

[9] See, inter alia, Harold A. Innis, *Essays in Canadian Economic History*
(Toronto: University of Toronto Press, 1956).
[10] North, "Location Theory and Regional Economic Growth."
[11] Baldwin, *Economic Development and Export Growth.*

technological nature of the production function. If the factor requirements for a given industry fit the existing relative factor conditions, then the input of the industry is favorable from the viewpoint of generating domestic demand. For example, tea and coffee are labor-intensive and generate income which is largely spent domestically. On the supply side, however, the effect is less favorable: because the industry fits the existing factor conditions, there is little need to train and upgrade the labor force. The opposite holds with an industry such as copper mining, which on the supply side facilitates the training of skilled labor but, because it fails to generate much domestic demand, has little impact on the wider economy.

Myint, like Baldwin, lays considerable emphasis on the role of the production functions in the domestic economy as the main determinants of the impact of trade on economic development. Explaining the historical process of growth in peasant export production, Myint argues as follows:

Where the export crop happened to be a traditional crop (e.g., rice in Southeast Asia), the expansion in export production was achieved simply by bringing more land under cultivation with the same methods of cultivation used in the subsistence economy. Even where new export crops were introduced, the essence of their success as peasant export crops was that they could be produced by fairly simple methods involving no radical departure from the traditional techniques of production employed in subsistence agriculture.

Thus, instead of a process of economic growth based on continuous improvements in skills, more productive recombinations of factors and increasing returns, the nineteenth-century expansion of international trade in the underdeveloped countries seems to approximate to a simpler process based on constant returns and fairly rigid combinations of factors.[12]

In a more recent publication, Myint elaborates this argument and draws out the implications for future growth. In expanding export production, the peasants "took full advantage of the market opportunities available to them; but this

---

[12] Myint, "The 'Classical Theory' of International Trade," p. 321.

does not mean that they took full advantage of the technical opportunities to improve their productivity. Peasant holdings in rice production, for example, have remained approximately the same, and the same combinations of land, labor, and capital have been used throughout half a century of rapid expansion of rice exports from Southeast Asia. . . . If this is true, then peasant export production continuing on the same basis as before is bound to come to a stop sooner or later, even if the demand conditions continue to be favorable. Sooner or later the extension of cultivation will press against the limits of cultivable hinterland, and thereafter population growth will outstrip export expansion."[13]

Although not explicitly discussed, a production function for peasant agriculture is clearly implicit and it plays a central role in linking exports to economic growth. Myint mentions three factors of production: land, labor, and capital. Virtually the whole of the discussion, however, is centered on land and labor; apparently capital is minor—and unmeasurable. He observes that these factors are combined in fairly constant proportions although it is not clear whether he means to imply technologically fixed factors or merely a constancy in the ratio in which they have historically been combined. An observed constancy in factor proportions does not of course imply a zero elasticity of substitution. Another important aspect of the production function postulated by Myint is that there is no significant technological change over time. If we assume that the land is all of roughly equal quality, then production per farmer remains constant and the area under cultivation increases for a time *pari passu* with population. The assumption of surplus cultivable land is part of the "vent-for-surplus" theory of the classical economists (notably Adam Smith) which Myint has popularized.[14]

[13] Myint, *The Economics of the Developing Countries* (London: Hutchinson, 1964), p. 51.
[14] Myint, "The 'Classical Theory' of International Trade." The essence of vent-for-surplus is the existence of unemployed resources. Caves argues that the Lewis model of unlimited labor can also be classified as a vent-

It is clear that no satisfactory analysis of the impact of trade on the development process can ignore the role of the production functions in the domestic economy. The observed differences in the impact of trade on different countries and on different sectors within the one country can to a large extent be explained by the differences in domestic economic structure and behavior. Myint's approach, while not openly specifying a production function and leaving a number of loose ends, is obviously pertinent to an analysis of the land surplus open economy. Baldwin states explicitly that his theory hinges on the nature of the production function, although he too does not specify analytically the function implied (nor does he provide the data on inputs and output that would help to indicate its form). Nevertheless, this emphasis on the relation of the domestic economic (and, implicitly, social and political) structure to the issues of trade and development is a novel and important advance.

The second broad group of theories relating trade to development we have termed "externally oriented" since, in contrast to those discussed above, they place little emphasis on the conditions prevailing in the domestic economy. They are generally assumed to hold true regardless of time and place. Although both pro- and anti-trade arguments can be distinguished, it is the former which are presently of most interest.[15]

---

for-surplus model. With Lewis, the opportunity cost of employing additional labor can be assumed zero, while with Myint the same holds for land. This highlights the essential difference between the labor surplus India-Pakistan type economy and the land surplus economies typical of Africa and most of Southeast Asia. Myint draws all his examples from the latter two regions. R. E. Caves, " 'Vent for Surplus' Models of Trade and Growth," in *Trade, Growth, and the Balance of Payments: Essays in Honor of Gottfried Haberler* (Chicago: Rand McNally, 1965).

[15] The anti-trade arguments of this school appear to have lost ground in recent years. MacBean has shown that the importance of export instability has been grossly exaggerated. A. I. MacBean, *Export Instability and Economic Development* (London: George Allen and Unwin, 1966). The adverse terms of trade hypothesis has never won widespread support. Baldwin, for example, concludes that it is on "shaky ground both theo-

The case for trade as a stimulus to development was argued quite fully by John Stuart Mill and modern statements have added surprisingly little. There was first the Ricardian lesson that specialization according to comparative advantage results in an increase in real income. Mill also approved of the still older doctrine of Adam Smith that trade induces an increase in total productivity. Following Smith, he noted "the tendency of every extension of the market to improve the process of production. A country which produces for a larger market than its own can introduce a more extended division of labor, can make greater use of machinery, and is more likely to make inventions and improvements in the process of production."[16] Finally, he stressed the favorable effects of the introduction of "foreign arts" and foreign capital and the stimulating effect of trade in generating new ideas and new wants.

Modern statements of the case for trade mostly echo these arguments. While few of the ideas have been rigorously formulated, a number have strong a priori plausibility.[17] In his well-known Cairo lectures Haberler gives a concise summary:

---

retically and empirically" (see Baldwin, *Economic Development and Export Growth*, pp. 8–9). Other theories such as Myrdal's "backwash effect" appear to have limited empirical content.

[16] John Stuart Mill, *Principles of Political Economy* (1848), ed. W. J. Ashley (London: Longmans, Green, 1909), p. 581.

[17] For example, the idea of trade as an "engine of growth" has not been presented rigorously. The same applies to the concept of trade as a "leading," "lagging," or "balancing" sector. See C. P. Kindleberger, *Foreign Trade and the National Economy* (New Haven: Yale University Press, 1962). Corden (*Recent Developments in the Theory of International Trade*, p. 41) has remarked on this point with reference to Kindleberger's approach. Even less clearly formulated are a series of arguments, stemming in the main from Mill, which credit trade with something like metaphysical qualities. Cairncross, for example, argues that trade allows an economy "to be permeated with the ideas that are the seed of true development" and that "trade is no mere exchange of goods . . . as often as not it is trade that gives birth to the urge to develop, the knowledge and experience that make development possible." A. K. Cairncross, *Factors in Economic Development* (London: George Allen and Unwin, 1962), p. 364.

First, trade provides material means (capital goods, machinery and raw and semifinished materials) indispensable for economic development. Secondly, even more important, trade is the means and vehicle for the dissemination of technological knowledge, the transmission of ideas, for the importation of know-how, skills, managerial talents and entrepreneurship. Thirdly, trade is also the vehicle for the international movement of capital especially from the developed to the underdeveloped countries. Fourthly, free international trade is the best antimonopoly policy and the best guarantee for the maintenance of a healthy degree of free competition.[18]

The first two of these points are of chief concern to us here. The argument that capital formation in most underdeveloped countries relies heavily on imported machinery and equipment was noted earlier in this chapter where it underlay our assumption of capital specificity. The data on the issue are examined in the following section. The role of trade as a carrier of technological change is less amenable to analysis, although it follows in part from the high level of the import content of investment. Countries which import modern equipment automatically import technological advances. (The comparative intractability of the mathematics of embodied technology, however, is a sufficient reason for our reverting to the disembodied case in the analysis of Chapter 3.)

We may conclude this very brief review of trade and development theories by drawing out three elements which appear of particular relevance to our study of dual economy growth. The classical vent-for-surplus model (in its original Smithian form and as applied by Myint) is of major importance in an understanding of the traditional sector in a land surplus economy, both in the colonial and the postcolonial periods. To a lesser extent, the emphasis given by Baldwin to the fit between factor supply and factor demand is helpful in studying the role of modern sector extractive industries: this is pursued further in Chapter 4. Lastly, the function of trade in providing essential

[18] Gottfried Haberler, *International Trade and Economic Development*, National Bank of Egypt Fiftieth Anniversary Commemoration Lectures (Cairo, 1959), p. 11.

capital equipment and raw materials is perhaps the main reason for arguing the significance of openness in the study of development.

PROBLEMS OF OPEN ECONOMY GROWTH

Two basic, related obstacles to sustained growth in the open dual economy are the reliance on capital goods imports on the one hand and the resource-intensive bias of export industries in the face of limited resources on the other. The rather dismal outlook for many of these economies would be transformed if this dependence of the modern manufacturing sector on imported inputs could be reduced or if new sources of foreign exchange were found. In practice, the open economies of Southeast Asia and of most of the underdeveloped world have proved quite unable to produce for themselves the raw materials and capital goods required to reduce import dependence. It is worth examining both the facts of and possible reasons for this state of affairs.

One of the marked features of the development process, at least in the early stages, is the apparent difficulty of investment goods substitution in contrast with the ease of consumer goods substitution. The literature on import substitution is almost entirely concerned with the latter, but it is instructive to apply the same approach to capital goods.[19] The empirical evidence on investment goods substitution has been analyzed in some detail by Maizels, Adams, and Kuznets.[20] According to Adams' cross-section data, the ratio of capital goods imports to gross domestic capital formation ranges from 41.4 per cent for coun-

[19] Following Chenery, import substitution is said to occur when the ratio of imports of a product to total supplies of that product declines.

[20] Alfred Maizels, *Industrial Growth and World Trade* (Cambridge: Cambridge University Press, 1963), pp. 264–270; Nassau A. Adams, "Import Structure and Economic Growth: A Comparison of Cross-Section and Time-Series Data," *Economic Development and Cultural Change*, 15 (1967), 143–162; and Simon Kuznets, "Quantitative Aspects of the Economic Growth of Nations: IX. Level and Structure of Foreign Trade: Comparisons for Recent Years," *Economic Development and Cultural Change*, vol. 13, no. 1, part 2 (1964).

tries with annual per capita incomes of less than $100 to 27.1 per cent for countries with per capita incomes greater than $700. Adams points out that this level of aggregation disguises an important difference between large and small countries. The decline in import dependence for capital goods is strongly marked only among the large countries, for which the ratio falls from 41.1 per cent in the lowest income group to 8.6 per cent in the highest.[21] This suggests that substantial import substitution for capital goods occurs only among the large developed countries.

Maizels reaches the same general conclusion but by a slightly different route and in substantially more detail. He points out that world production of capital goods is highly concentrated in a few countries and that this degree of concentration did not change significantly over the period 1938–1959. As an example, he cites the world production of metal goods, of which 84 per cent of the total both in 1948 and in 1955 was produced in France, Germany, Italy, Japan, the United Kingdom, and the United States. "This heavy concentration of output in the large industrial countries implies that in all other countries, industrial as well as nonindustrial, there is a high degree of dependence on imports for supplies of producers' durables."[22] Maizels' estimates show convincingly that only the large industrial countries have a low import content of investment.[23] The five large countries (excluding Japan) had an import content of investment averaging 7 per cent in 1957–1959. The small industrial countries averaged 59 per cent over the same period, while the underdeveloped countries were higher still at about 80 per cent.

[21] Adams, "Import Structure and Economic Growth," p. 148.

[22] Maizels, *Industrial Growth and World Trade*, p. 265.

[23] Maizels' definition of the import content of investment differs from that of Adams. Maizels' refers to the ratio of imported machinery and transport equipment to gross investment in these items. Adams' estimates are lower because they apply to the ratio of capital goods imports to gross domestic capital formation. A significant part of the latter is necessarily of domestic origin.

Kuznets' approach is very similar to Maizels'. He estimates the proportion of producers' equipment imports to producers' equipment capital formation. For the large developed countries he obtains a ratio of 12.5 per cent compared to Maizels' 7 per cent. (As the relevant period is the same, the difference is apparently because of the inclusion of Canada in Kuznets' sample.) His estimate of the import dependence of the developed small countries, 59 per cent, is the same as Maizels'. Underdeveloped countries also averaged 59 per cent, with the small countries substantially more import-dependent than the large ones. Small countries with a high trade ratio had an import content of investment of 85 per cent.[24]

These results are of considerable importance, suggesting as they do that throughout its development the small economy must expect to remain highly dependent on imports of capital goods. During the course of growth from the lowest to the highest income group, the import content of investment in producers' equipment for the small economy might be expected to fall from about 80 per cent to around 60 per cent. The underdeveloped countries, whether large or small, produce few capital goods; but among the highly developed countries the crucial factor is size. The United States and Canada have similar per capita incomes, but the former has an import content of investment of 3 per cent in contrast to the latter's 68 per cent.[25] In the terms used by these writers the Southeast Asian countries listed in Table 1 (with the exception of Malaysia) would usually be classed as "large"—although, excepting Indonesia, they are at the lower end of the spectrum.

Time series support of this cross-section finding is quite limited. Maizels could not find comparable data for the prewar years, but Adams has long series for a small sample of countries. Between the late nineteenth century and the midfifties the import content of investment fell substantially only

[24] Kuznets, "Quantitative Aspects of the Economic Growth of Nations: IX," pp. 64–65.
[25] Maizels, *Industrial Growth and World Trade*, p. 266.

in Japan. For the other (small) countries in Adams' sample—Denmark, Sweden, Canada, and Australia—there is no similar marked long-run trend in the ratio.[26]

In part, these results can be explained in terms of the large economies of scale found in many investment goods industries. Among the few attempts to quantify the role of economies of scale in industrial development are those of Maizels and Chenery,[27] and these writers reach somewhat different conclusions. Maizels' data indicated that economies of scale are significant only in the metals industry where a "ten per cent variation in population size between different countries tends to be associated with a difference of about four and one-half per cent in metal production per head after allowing for differences in per capita income levels."[28] Chenery, however, found significant economies of scale in most investment and intermediate goods industries but not in consumer goods industries. A probable reason for the difference is that Chenery's sample includes the highly developed countries while Maizels' only the semi-industrial countries. It may be that economies of scale are nonlinear over the income range and more significant at the higher levels. Basic metal industries, which both writers agree are characterized by large economies of scale, account on average for only 4 per cent of output at the $100 per capita income level.

A further but more speculative explanation for the difficulty most underdeveloped countries face in building an investment goods industry can be inferred from the interesting empirical finding of Maizels that there is an inverse correlation between the degree of "success" in import substitution and the over-all growth rate of the economy.[29] The process of substituting domestically produced manufactured consumer goods for the

[26] Adams, "Import Structure and Economic Growth," p. 157. In Japan the ratio fell from 31.2% in 1903–1907 to 4.2% in 1955–1958.

[27] Maizels, *Industrial Growth and World Trade*, pp. 53–54; and Hollis B. Chenery, "Patterns of Industrial Growth," *American Economic Review*, 50 (1960), 624–654.

[28] Maizels, *Industrial Growth and World Trade*, p. 54.

[29] *Ibid.*, pp. 139 ff.

imported product is one of the most striking features of twen-
tieth-century industrial growth. The underdeveloped countries,
however, have pursued this policy at a rate very much faster
than did the industrial countries at a similar stage of their development.[30] Forced import substitution, induced by high tariff
barriers, can result in the growth of inefficient industries and
waste of scarce resources.[31] Such high cost industries supply the
domestic market but are unable to compete in world markets.
Despite decades of "successful" import substitution, for example, the large Latin American countries have negligible exports of industrial goods. Trade, in these cases, does not provide
a means for overcoming the limitations on growth imposed by
domestic demand and for realizing economies of scale. Of more
immediate relevance in the present context is the argument,
adduced notably by Power and Hirschman, that the tariff policies adopted to encourage import substitution serve specifically
to discourage the establishment of industries with backward
linkages.[32] This would directly inhibit the development of
domestic investment goods production.

[30] According to Maizels' findings, opportunities for the underdeveloped
countries to expand further by means of import substitution had been
virtually exhausted by 1959 (*ibid.,* p. 140). This process can explain
the similarity (observed by Kuznets, "Quantitative Aspects of the
Economic Growth of Nations: IX," p. 64) in the structure of imports
between developed and underdeveloped countries based on cross-section
data. The latecomers undertook the most rapid import substitution,
with the result that by the late 1950's most countries, irrespective of
their level of development, had a high share of capital goods and a low
share of consumer goods in total imports.

[31] Tariff barriers are very much higher in countries which have
recently experienced drastic import substitution. Among Maizels' semi-
industrial countries, Brazil, India, and Chile have average import duties
of 30–40% while Australia and South Africa have only 8% (*ibid.,* p. 141).

[32] John H. Power, "Import Substitution as an Industrialization
Strategy," *Philippine Economic Journal,* 5 (1966), 167–204; and Albert
O. Hirschman, "The Political Economy of Import-Substituting Industrialization in Latin America," *Quarterly Journal of Economics,* 82 (1968), 1–
32. Much of the relevant literature is to be found in the *Pakistan Development Review.*

If possibilities for any substantial reduction in the import content of investment seem remote for most underdeveloped countries, we must look very closely at the available means for increasing import capacity.[33] One obvious direction, that of exporting manufactured goods, has already been seen not to offer an easy road for progress—for reasons which are in part related to the kinds of import substituting industrialization policies which have been widely followed. (Other reasons are noted in the discussion of the problem in Chapter 4.) The Philippines and the other open economies of Southeast Asia are typical in this regard, with manufacturing contributing little to exports apart from some processing of primary products. The alternative of relying on capital inflows (foreign aid, investment, military expenditures, etc.) is not feasible for more than a few countries over relatively short periods, and we may disregard it except as a marginal factor with little loss of realism. (A study of Thailand, however, would need to take more explicit account of the role of such transfers.) We are left therefore with the export industries described at the beginning of this chapter: traditional, labor-intensive agriculture and modern, capital-intensive plantations, mines, and forestry.

Traditional agriculture in Southeast Asia as elsewhere is characterized by low productivity and slowly changing technology. The rapid expansion in production which followed the large-scale commercial penetration in the latter part of the nineteenth century can be seen as the taking up of a slack in underemployed resources, both of land and labor.[34] In effect,

[33] As noted above, few opportunities remain for changing imports to exclude items which can be produced domestically with relatively little difficulty (albeit possibly at a high cost). We see in the following chapter, however, that the once-over slack represented by substitution for consumer imports may be an important contributing factor to past growth performance, allowing domestic production of manufactures to rise faster than total domestic demand and faster than would be permitted by growth in total import capacity.

[34] The great fall in freight rates (in part as a result of the opening of the Suez Canal) combined with increased demand for tropical

the peasants exchanged leisure for the new consumer goods which were purchased with the agricultural surplus. Once labor was fully utilized, further increments to output were a function of the size of the labor force which could combine with surplus land. This is of course the vent-for-surplus process of growth described by Myint.[35]

As the land surplus disappears, the land/labor ratio must fall and the approximately constant returns to labor become diminishing returns. While in all countries in Southeast Asia (excluding Singapore) there still remain significant amounts of cultivable land for future agricultural expansion, this surplus cannot long bear the main burden of raising output. The degree to which it has done so in the recent past is seen in the data for cereals (which are wholly peasant crops in this region) assembled in Table 2. For the decade 1954–1963, taking five-year averages for the end-points, only West Malaysia shows areal expansion contributing less than half of the increase in output, while for Indonesia and the Philippines the proportion exceeds 80 per cent.[36] (That these area changes are due to ex-

---

products such as rubber, oil seeds, and cocoa led not only to the development of plantations but also to a large increase in production and export of peasant crops. In the Philippines, the export of abaca, tobacco, sugar, and coffee expanded enormously between 1855 and 1895, and the same was true of exports from Indonesia, Malaya, Burma, and Thailand. (Thailand's rice exports, for example, grew from 3.5 million piculs in 1875 to 14.7 million in 1905.) See, *inter alia*, J. S. Furnivall, *Colonial Policy and Practice: A Comparative Study of Burma and Netherlands India* (Cambridge: Cambridge University Press, 1948); *Census of the Philippine Islands, 1903* (Washington: Bureau of the Census, 1905), vol. 4; and J. C. Ingram, *Economic Change in Thailand Since 1850* (Stanford: Stanford University Press, 1955).

[35] Myint, *The Economics of the Developing Countries*, chapter 3. (See also the passage from his 1958 article quoted earlier.) The institutional and other assumptions which would explain a constant land/labor ratio with surplus land without postulating fixed factors are discussed in Chapter 3 below.

[36] Confirmation of this pattern is provided in statistics on rice alone gathered by the International Rice Research Institute. These IRRI data

pansion in cultivated area rather than double cropping is clear
when it is noted that among ECAFE countries, even for rice
land only 30 per cent is presently irrigated and less than 5 per
cent produces a second rice crop.) [37] Similar figures could be
found to illustrate the land surplus conditions in most of Africa
and Latin America—regions, moreover, where the closing of

Table 2. Contribution of change in harvested area and change in yield to
growth in output of cereals, selected countries in Southeast Asia,
1952/1956–1961/1965 (in per cent)

Country	Change in population 1954–1963	Change in cereal production	Contribution to change in production	
			ΔArea	ΔYield
Burma	19	30	67	33
Indonesia	22	19	82	18
Malaysia*	32	52	41	59
Philippines	32	30	87	13
Thailand	31	39	54	46

Sources: United Nations, *Demographic Yearbook*, and *World Economic Survey, 1967*
(New York, 1968), p. 52; *Statistical Pocketbook of Indonesia* (Djakarta: Biro Pusat
Statistik), various issues.
* West Malaysia only.

the land frontier is not as imminent as in Southeast Asia.

Prospects for yield increases in the future to offset or more
than offset diminishing returns to labor are now fairly promising for certain agricultural commodities, notably rice and

---

also permit comparison of Southeast Asia as a whole with the other
regions of Asia: in Southeast Asia, areal changes accounted for 65% of
the 1952–1963 increase in rice production, while the contribution was
30% for South Asia and 14% for Northeast Asia. Department of Agricultural Economics, IRRI; quoted by Vernon W. Ruttan, A. Soothipan,
and E. C. Venegas, "Changes in Rice Production, Area, and Yield in the
Philippines and Thailand," *Economic Research Journal* (Manila), 12
(1965), 185.

[37] Asian Development Bank, *Asian Agricultural Survey* (N.p., University of Tokyo Press, 1969), pp. 183–184.

corn. The implications of the widespread use of new, high-yielding varieties for the traditional sector as a whole, however, are probably much less radical than is often supposed. We examine this controversial issue in Chapter 4.

Some important modern sector exports are faced with a situation analogous to that of traditional agriculture. Plantations compete for land with smallholders (as the perennial squatter problem on estates in Indonesia and elsewhere demonstrates) and increases in exports must depend primarily on rising yields. With tree crops, varietal improvements often take many years to become effective. Forest resources, unlike minerals the known extent of which depends to a large degree on the resources spent in searching, are delimited in a simple geographic sense. The custom of mining rather than farming forests thus threatens them with rapid destruction. As will be seen later in this study, the problem is particularly acute in the Philippines where vast areas of forest have been destroyed and the remainder is being eroded at a rapid rate. Both modern extractive and traditional agricultural exports therefore confront fundamental problems of reducing their natural resource content if total exports and hence import capacity are to be increased or even maintained in the long run.

ANALYTICAL FRAMEWORK

In the preceding pages we have touched on the main issues which form the substance of the present study. The next two chapters proceed to examine these issues with more detail and rigor, firstly through an empirical analysis of the growth experience of the Philippines and secondly by formulating a simple mathematical model of the open dual economy. In both these tasks it is helpful to have explicitly stated the accounting system on which our analysis is based.

The over-all operation of an economy is studied by the reduction of a very large number of flows (of goods, labor and capital, but all translatable into monetary terms) into a relatively small number of aggregates. While the choice of aggregation procedure is necessarily to some extent arbitrary, it is influenced by the object of the study and by explicit or implicit a priori views as to the relevance of specific economic variables. Once chosen, however, the aggregation procedure determines the structural (or accounting) framework within which the economy is analyzed. The addition of behavioral relationships relating the aggregated flows transforms the structure into a model.

Two important problems are immediately apparent in deriving and applying such a structure. First a basic decision must be made as to the general level of aggregation to be adopted and the specific sectors, or junctures between flows, to be identified. Input-output analysis, for example, may identify some hundreds of sectors in an economy, but clearly something is lost in this effort to approach reality. Near the other extreme is the structure underlying the simple Harrod-Domar growth model. For most purposes, some intermediate level would be chosen. The second problem is the fact that a particular structural framework may be initially appropriate as a description of an economy but become progressively less adequate over time. This problem of changing structure may be especially serious in studying a developing economy, because such changes are an essential characteristic of development.

In the open dual economy there are obviously three principal sectors: agriculture, industry, and foreign trade. If we stress only these sectors we are asserting that the important dynamic relationships in such economies involve at most a triangular pattern of flows. The framework developed by the National Planning Association for the study of the development of open economies identifies these three sectors together with two further ones: government and finance; and agriculture, industry, and government are separated into production and income-distribution components.[38]

[38] Details of the NPA accounting framework are given in a number of field work reports. See, for example, Douglas S. Paauw and John C. H. Fei, "The Open Dualistic Economy: Patterns of Development," and

The present study makes use of a variant of this highly aggregated system. We distinguish three sectors (modern, traditional, and foreign) similar to those mentioned above. Industry and government are coalesced to constitute the modern sector (nonagriculture), while agriculture is broadly identified with the traditional sector. The resulting structure can best be seen as a linear graph, in which the directed lines, or edges, represent flows and the vertices are the sectors. Such a graph is drawn for the simplest case in Figure 3a. The arrows show the directions of real flows; the corresponding monetary flows are obtained by reversing them. In this pattern, the basic flows identified are exports from the traditional sector (AF), imports into the modern sector (FM), and the direct exchange between the two domestic sectors: a flow of food into the modern sector (AM), and a reverse flow of manufactures (MA) from the modern to the traditional sector as payment both for the food and for imports. In addition, part of the modern sector output may also be exported, and this is represented by the broken line, MF. We assume, however, that imports are directed only to the modern sector, so there is no flow FA.

This structure, we believe, captures the essence of open economy dualism, albeit in its most basic form. A generally modern and dynamic industrial sector coexists with a traditional agricultural sector. The two sectors are interdependent, interacting both through direct domestic trade and via the foreign sector. The traditional sector provides the food necessary to sustain the industrial labor force and, by exporting its surplus, generates most (if not all) of the foreign exchange necessary to pay for imports of capital goods.

Without changing these postulated intersectoral relation-

"Analysis of the Open, Dualistic Economy: An Application to the Philippines," mimeographed (Washington: National Planning Association, Center for Development Planning, 1966). The major project report is Paauw and Fei, "The Transition in Open Dualistic Economies," mimeographed (Washington: National Planning Association, Center for Development Planning, 1970), 2 vols.

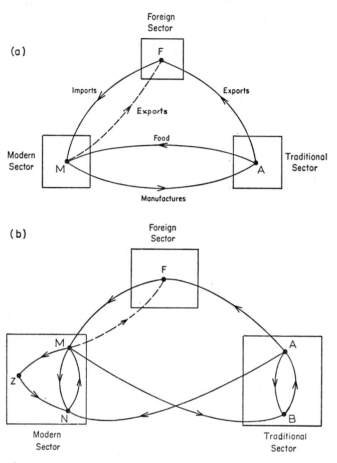

Figure 3. Structural framework for an open dual economy

ships, we may slightly elaborate the structure in order to take into account certain major intrasectoral phenomena. In Figure 3b, *A* and *M* now refer to the production components of the traditional and modern sectors, while *B* and *N* are the respective consumption components. *Z* represents the finance sector. The intersectoral flows between the traditional and modern sectors are directed from the production component of the one to the consumption component of the other (*AN* and *MB*). Within the traditional sector, *AB* represents the flow of food into the households and *BA* the payment (in the form of labor services) for this food. Where the households are both producers and consumers, these flows, of course, may be purely formal. In the modern sector we have analogous flows (*MN* and *NM*) and also the indirect flow through the finance sector (*MZN*). The latter may be thought of as payment (in the form of industrial consumer goods) for modern sector investment funds (savings). Although we do not explicitly examine the case in this study, it would be equally possible to make such funds derive from the traditional sector as well as the modern sector.

The second basic problem mentioned earlier concerned the persistence over time of a postulated structural framework. In Figure 3b, for example, the two flows *FA* and *ZB* have been assumed negligible. But during the process of development it may be that they increase to such an extent that their omission would seriously distort the over-all view of the economy given by the framework. If we are to base an analysis of an economy on this structure, such a possibility must be kept in mind. However, it may well be that observed growth patterns do not substantially change over quite long periods—the "rules of growth" being such that the initial structure remains relevant. This we believe to be the case for most Southeast Asian economies (and specifically, the Philippines), and consequently we are prepared to accept the structural framework given in Figure 3b as the basis of our analysis.

CHAPTER 2

The Philippine Experience

In Chapter 1 we have described some important features of open economy growth, based on a specific sectoral classification of the economy. Although by no means a complete theory (we paid no attention, for example, to domestic intersectoral relationships), the discussion covered several major elements which would enter such a theory and in this and the following chapters we build on these elements.

The present chapter, an analysis of recent economic growth in the Philippines in terms of the structural framework of an open dual economy described above, falls into three parts. First is the pedestrian but essential task of structuring the data into the categories used and examining the validity and relevance of these categories in the Philippine context. Next, we review the performance of the economy in the postwar years at this aggregative level.[1] Finally, we move to the more interesting and demanding area of analyzing the key institutional and behaviorial relationships in some detail. In Chapter 3 the model implied in this analysis is formalized.

CATEGORIZATION PROBLEMS: SECTORAL DIVISIONS

There is little that is original in our sectoring of the Philippine economy. The divisions are the conventional ones, with

[1] The basic period to be considered will be the years 1950–1968. The former year is the earliest to show the economy largely free of the atypical effects of postwar reconstruction, although it could be argued

the partial exception of the category of "extractive exports." Nevertheless, their application in practice involves a number of problems which require attention.

In most dualistic analyses, the traditional production sector is conveniently defined to coincide with the ISIC industry group 1 (agriculture, livestock, hunting, forestry, and fishing) so that no adjustment to existing data is needed. The chief conceptual difficulties concern the treatment of processing industries whose inputs are agricultural goods. If the value added in such industries is a minor part of total output (e.g., as with copra production), there is a good argument for including them with agricultural production. In other cases, for example, coconut oil manufacture, it might be more reasonable to allocate industries to the modern sector.[2] A systematic allocation approach is provided in the classificiation framework developed for the National Planning Association Project in the Philippines.[3] In this framework, which in many respects resembles that used in the national accounts of the Philippine National Economic Council (NEC), the processing, storage, transportation, and marketing services for any product are considered as inputs from industry (i.e., nonagriculture), while in cases where goods are worked on by both sectors they are assigned to the sector contributing the greater share of value, excluding storage, transportation, and marketing services. We follow it here with only slight modifications. As Paauw and Tryon comment,

_____

that an even later year should have been chosen. For a few statistical series, data for 1968 were not published at the time of writing.

[2] In the Philippine case, sugar represents a difficult problem. Its processing is a highly capital-intensive operation, but one which is inseparably linked, geographically and temporally, to cane growing—and unlike the situation in Java, the latter is controlled by independent farmers rather than by the centrals themselves. Largely for this reason, we regard the sugar industry as lying in the traditional sector.

[3] See Douglas S. Paauw, "The Philippines: Estimates of Flows in the Open, Dualistic Economy Framework, 1949–1965," mimeographed (Washington: National Planning Association, Center for Development Planning, 1968).

"classification of the origin of goods for final demand according to [this method] will reflect growing intersectoral flows between agriculture and industry if industrialization, in fact, requires increasing supplies of domestic raw materials. The alternative system of classification, where goods receiving any industrial processing at all would be shown to flow into the industrial sector and, hence, reckoned as industrial goods, greatly obscures this process."[4]

The only important departure we have made from the NEC sectoral division is to exclude forestry and logging from agriculture. Since the productive process in logging bears an important resemblance to mining, especially in the role of capital, we pool these two industries to form the subsector "extractive industries" of the modern sector. A similar analysis applied to Malaysia or Indonesia would have to include the plantation industries (rubber, oil palm, tobacco, etc.) in this category. For the Philippines, however, we have for simplicity left the few large-scale plantations (coconut, pineapple, etc.) in the traditional sector.[5]

---

[4] Douglas S. Paauw and Joseph L. Tryon, "Agriculture-Industry Interrelationships in an Open Dualistic Economy: The Philippines, 1949–1964," in *Growth of Output in the Philippines*, ed. Richard W. Hooley and Randolph Barker (Manila: University of the Philippines, School of Economics, and International Rice Research Institute, 1967), pp. 7–8.

An instance of the serious overstatement of intersectoral flows caused by the latter scheme is the input-output table for 1961 prepared by the Bureau of the Census and Statistics and the University of the Philippines. By valuing agricultural sector product at producers' prices, it excludes the contribution of trade and transport services. More importantly, all food processing industries (such as the large copra industry, to which coconuts contribute some 80% of final production value) are assigned to manufacturing. As a result, the apparent share of agricultural value added in GNP is less than one-half the figure given in the NEC accounts (12% compared to the NEC's 28%). *Inter-industry Relations Study of the Philippine Economy: Partial Report* (Manila: University of the Philippines, School of Economics, and Bureau of the Census and Statistics, 1968).

[5] Technically, a decision on sectoral allocation should depend not only on whether the land has a high opportunity cost but also on

The problems of allocation of agricultural, mining, and manufacturing industries are more easily resolved than those relating to the later ISIC divisions, particularly services. In any dual model, unless one sector is merely defined residually (e.g., nonagriculture), there can be no entirely satisfactory solution. Construction, transportation, communication, utilities, and commerce (together constituting about 24 per cent of net domestic product in the NEC estimates) would seem to have more claim to be regarded as "modern" than "traditional," although the designation is very debatable in the case of commerce which ideally should be split between the two sectors. Services, making up another 24 per cent (of which government services exceed one-third) will arbitrarily be assigned to the modern sector also. However, with all these groups we shall retain sufficient flexibility to exclude them from consideration in instances where they might obscure important relationships.

Once the broad line between sectors has been drawn, there is no great difficulty in classification of exports. In the detailed NPA accounting framework, exports are allocated on the basis of which sector contributes the greater part of export value. Agricultural exports are those with ex-farm value exceeding 50 per cent of the final export value.[6] For our traditional exports we assume a similar though less rigorous definition, an important factor being the accessibility of the data in a form suitable for aggregation. Thus, we assign all food exports to the traditional sector despite the high degree of processing value added in a small part of this large and heterogeneous group.[7] While this allocation may be criticized as overly diminishing manufacturing exports, it is certainly preferable to classifying all exports of processed agricultural goods in the modern sector. Extractive

---

whether other forms of (monetized) capital enter as significant factors of production.

[6] Paauw, "The Philippines: Estimates of Flows," p. 48.

[7] Other traditional sector exports are taken as the following commodity groups: tobacco; oilseeds, oilnuts, and kernels; crude textile fibers; animal and vegetable oils and fats; and miscellaneous crude animal and vegetable products.

industry exports consist of minerals, logs, and lumber. Finally, the few remaining modern sector exports are three groups: chemicals, manufactured goods (including plywood and veneer), and beverages. These are all loosely termed "manufactures." Total exports are taken net of re-exports, while service exports and exports of oil refinery products are excluded from consideration.

The third major problem of classification raised by the analysis is the treatment of imports. One of the more dubious simplifications we shall make is to aggregate commodity imports into only two categories, capital goods and consumer goods. Intermediate goods are allocated to one or the other of these groups. To achieve this end we have used the ECAFE division of intermediate goods into "materials chiefly for capital goods" and "materials chiefly for consumer goods."[8] The breakdown is quite elaborate, allocation being based on the lowest level groups in the revised Standard International Trade Classification (i.e., distinguished by the fourth digit of the SITC code).

Although this obscuring of the usual category of intermediate goods is obviously open to objection, so also is the common practice of treating intermediate goods as a single homogeneous group. In defense of the former procedure (apart from its advantage of simplicity), it may be argued that it avoids the exaggerated apparent reduction of consumer goods imports caused by trivial backward integration into final assembly of these products. In the conventional three-way classification, the imported inputs to this assembling process are regarded as intermediate goods, however small the real value added by assembly. Another relevant consideration is the tendency, with the existence of multiple exchange rates or import licensing, to misclassify consumer goods as intermediate goods in customs declarations. For many analytical purposes, the distinction be-

[8] United Nations, Economic Commission for Asia and the Far East, "Reclassification of Imports and Exports from the SITC," mimeographed (Bangkok, 1967). The resulting series are those published in ECAFE's *Economic Bulletin for Asia and the Far East* (Bangkok, quarterly).

tween, for example, unwrought and worked base metals (the first intermediate goods, the second capital) may be less important than that between unwrought base metals and textile fabrics (most of the latter being also classed as intermediate goods).

STATISTICAL SURVEY OF THE PHILIPPINES[9]

We are now in a position to assemble the relevant data on the Philippine economy in a form suitable for analysis in the open dual economy framework. In a number of areas Philippine statistics are superior to those of many underdeveloped countries, particularly in timeliness and in allowing for independent checks on series and estimates of errors. More than enough limitations remain, however, to preclude their uncritical use.[10] While for some purposes specific adjustments of data for the present study have been necessary, we have preferred where possible to make use of the critical work of other authors more familiar with particular fields. The work of Hooley on savings and long-term growth indices and of Hooley and Sicat on investment are instances of elaborate reworking and analyses of data which are utilized below. Data on direct intersectoral flows of goods are chiefly taken from the series assembled by Douglas S. Paauw for the NPA Philippine Project, on the basis of detailed revisions of official series.[11]

---

[9] The reader less interested in the details of our treatment of data could skim much of this section.

[10] The major critical study of Philippine economic statistics is that of Emanuel Levy, IBRD Statistical Advisor in Manila in 1964–1965. This important work evaluates all the main official series, with particular emphasis given to discussing the National Economic Council's national accounts, and we shall have frequent recourse to it. Emanuel Levy, "Review of Economic Statistics in the Philippines: Interim Report" and "Interim Report-B," mimeographed (Manila: World Bank Resident Mission, 1964–1965). A partial summary is given in Levy, "The Usefulness of Existing National Accounts for the Analysis of the Philippine Economy," *Philippine Economic Journal,* 5 (1966), 134–145.

[11] Paauw, "The Philippines: Estimates of Flows."

Table 3. Sectoral distribution of gross national product,
Philippines, 1950–1968 (million pesos at 1955 prices)

Year	Traditional sector		Modern sector		Total	
	Value	%	Value	%	Value	%
1950	1,809	30.3	4,158	69.7	5,967	100.0
1951	1,954	30.2	4,523	69.8	6,477	100.0
1952	2,037	29.1	4,964	70.9	7,001	100.0
1953	2,207	29.1	5,382	70.9	7,589	100.0
1954	2,449	29.8	5,777	70.2	8,226	100.0
1955	2,465	28.0	6,336	72.0	8,801	100.0
1956	2,467	26.1	6,970	73.9	9,437	100.0
1957	2,562	25.7	7,425	74.3	9,987	100.0
1958	2,712	26.2	7,653	73.8	10,365	100.0
1959	2,797	25.2	8,283	74.8	11,080	100.0
1960	2,708	24.1	8,521	75.9	11,229	100.0
1961	2,856	23.9	9,105	76.1	11,961	100.0
1962	2,887	22.7	9,809	77.3	12,696	100.0
1963	2,964	21.7	10,667	78.3	13,631	100.0
1964	3,102	22.2	10,868	77.8	13,970	100.0
1965	3,282	22.3	11,452	77.7	14,734	100.0
1966	3,449	22.1	12,184	77.9	15,633	100.0
1967	3,580	21.6	13,022	78.4	16,602	100.0
1968	3,800	21.5	13,872	78.5	17,672	100.0

Sources: National Economic Council, Office of Statistical Coordination and
Standards, "The National Income of the Philippines for CY 1946 to 1967," and
"The Philippine Economy in 1968."

Major Aggregates

We consider first the data on sectoral production, foreign
trade, and labor force, which together serve to give an overview
of the main economic trends. The sectoral divisions of gross
national product in constant prices, based on the 1968 revisions
of the NEC national accounts, are presented in Table 3.[12] (The

[12] The official Philippine national accounts for postwar years have
been prepared by the Central Bank for the period up to 1956 and, since
that date, by the Office of Statistical Coordination and Standards of the
National Economic Council. The series have been published annually in
the NEC's journal, *The Statistical Reporter*. In 1968 a new set of accounts was released by the NEC, covering the entire period 1946–1967.
These estimates represent extensive revisions of the old series, which they

only adjustment of the official data which was necessary was to transfer the forestry and logging component from the agricultural sector to industry, forming the aggregate modern sector.) The relative size of the traditional sector is surprisingly small for a country generally thought of as being an agricultural economy, although the distribution of labor force will show that the sectoral difference is largely one of productivity. It is in part explained, of course, by the sectoral classification scheme adopted, which tends to understate the contribution of the traditional sector by excluding most nonagricultural activities irrespective of the actual mode of production. The respective average annual growth rates for the period 1950/1952–1966/1968 computed from Table 3 are 4.0 per cent for the traditional sector, 6.8 per cent for the modern sector, and 6.1 per cent for total GNP.[13]

Turning to the foreign trade sector, we face more complex data adjustment problems. A study of the foreign trade statistics of the major trading partners reveals a considerable degree of understatement on the Philippine side (assuming, as seems reasonable, that the former sources are accurate).[14] Moreover, the errors are erratically distributed: exports were seriously

---

supercede, and "incorporate all improvements in sources and methods so far developed." National Economic Council, Office of Statistical Coordination and Standards, "The National Income of the Philippines for CY 1946 to 1967 and the National Accounts: Overall Revision (as of August 30, 1968)," mimeographed (Manila, 1968). Data for 1968 and minor corrections for 1966 and 1967 are given in "The Philippine Economy in 1968 and the National Accounts, CY 1966 to 1968, with Supporting and Analysis Tables," mimeographed (Manila, 1969).

[13] Unless stated otherwise, all growth rates are computed as the average geometric rate of increase, taking three-year averages for the end points.

[14] See George L. Hicks, "Philippine Foreign Trade, 1950–1965: Basic Data and Major Characteristics," and "Philippine Foreign Trade Statistics: Supplementary Data and Interpretations, 1954–1966," mimeographed (Washington: National Planning Association, Center for Development Planning, 1966 and 1967).

underrecorded in certain years during the period of exchange controls prior to 1962, and imports similarly after the 1960–1962 decontrol measures. In the final years of the period both imports and exports were apparently understated. (The data are given in Table 4.) For this reason the officially recorded

Table 4. Recorded Philippine exports and imports as percentages of totals estimated from statistics of major trading partners*

Year	Exports	Imports	Year	Exports	Imports
1950	102.0	n.a.	1960	93.6	93.8
1951	97.2	n.a.	1961	86.3	89.1
1952	98.1	n.a.	1962	90.2	95.3
1953	98.3	n.a.	1963	101.7	82.9
1954	94.4	99.1	1964	98.7	90.8
1955	92.5	101.7	1965	99.0	87.3
1956	91.3	92.9	1966	94.0	87.6
1957	85.2	92.3	1967	89.7	87.4
1958	102.8	98.2	1968	91.5	89.0
1959	100.1	91.4			

Sources: 1950–1965, George L. Hicks, "Philippine Foreign Trade, 1950–1965 Basic Data and Major Characteristics," and "Philippine Foreign Trade Statistics: Supplementary Data and Interpretations, 1954–1966," mimeographed (Washington: National Planning Association, Center for Development Planning, 1966–1967); 1966–1968, estimates computed from data of Central Bank of the Philippines and major trading partners, using the methodology described in the above reports.

* Computed from f.o.b. values in U.S. dollars.

trade statistics (in U.S. dollars) were adjusted for coverage errors by the factors in Table 4. The series thus obtained were deflated to constant prices by the respective export and import price indices computed by the Central Bank[15] and converted to pesos at the constant rate of ₱3.00 to U.S. $1.00.[16]

We described earlier the way in which the foreign trade data

[15] Central Bank of the Philippines, *Statistical Bulletin* (Manila, quarterly).

[16] This is the estimated equilibrium rate for 1955 and corresponds closely to the average Hong Kong free-market rate for that year. See Paauw, "The Philippines: Estimates of Flows," p. 33.

could be broken down into the broad categories used in our analytical framework. A further point of definition arises here, related to the nature of agricultural exports and the role of food in external trade. Some countries, such as Malaysia, have preferred to specialize in export crops and import a certain proportion of their basic food requirements, while others like Burma and Thailand are self-sufficient in food. A simple means of looking below this surface phenomenon which results from the farmers' alternative of growing either food crops or export crops (where these differ) is to define the *net exportable surplus* of the traditional sector as total sectoral output less the food consumption of the whole population. In effect, then, we measure "net" traditional exports by subtracting from total traditional exports the value of food imports. Correspondingly, the import data must also exclude these food imports. Among the many assumptions here is that the imported food has approximately the same proportion of processing value added as the food obtained directly from the traditional sector.

In the Philippine case, one justification for the lack of statistical finesse in this procedure is that food imports have been largely composed of cereals—mainly, wheat and rice. However, errors are introduced by the tendency for cereal imports to be concentrated in certain years (especially election years), to be stored for unknown periods, and even to be unrecorded in official import statistics.[17] It could be argued that Philippine tobacco imports should be subtracted from traditional exports as being competitive with domestic production, but here the import data are so inaccurate—as a result of smuggling—that the errors introduced would outweigh the theoretical advantages.

Tables 5 and 6 present the main categories of exports and imports with the adjustments described above. For exports, the

[17] The latter point is made strongly in a report to the Director, Office of Statistical Coordination and Standards, National Economic Council, dated April 14, 1965, entitled: "Philippine Milled Rice Imports, 1956 to 1963."

breakdown between traditional and modern sectors reveals very clearly their different growth dynamics. The data from Table 5 are plotted on a semilogarithmic scale in Figure 4. Traditional exports showed only slight growth, averaging between one and

Figure 4. Philippine exports by major category, 1950–1968

two per cent per year. Extractive industry exports, on the other hand, increased by more than 13 per cent annually on average, and even after 1956, when their growth appreciably slowed, a rate of over 9 per cent was maintained. Manufactured goods exports also showed rapid growth (11.5 per cent), although from a very small base. However, as the broken line in Figure 4

| | Traditional sector products | | | Modern sector products | | | | Net exports* | |
| Year | Total value | Net* | | Extractive products | | Manufactured products | | | |
		Value	%	Value	%	Value	%	Value	%
1950	730	589	88.5	58	8.7	19	2.8	666	100.0
1951	897	664	83.4	108	13.6	24	3.0	796	100.0
1952	856	627	76.4	164	20.0	29	3.6	820	100.0
1953	794	606	75.6	162	20.2	34	4.2	802	100.0
1954	912	692	74.9	207	22.5	24	2.6	923	100.0
1955	993	691	70.0	266	26.9	31	3.1	988	100.0
1956	1,091	810	68.3	343	28.9	32	2.7	1,185	100.0
1957	1,093	752	66.6	342	30.3	35	3.1	1,129	100.0
1958	965	629	62.6	334	33.3	41	4.1	1,004	100.0
1959	953	760	64.8	350	29.9	63	5.3	1,173	100.0
1960	1,085	846	63.6	430	32.3	54	4.1	1,330	100.0
1961	1,082	757	57.3	497	37.5	69	5.2	1,323	100.0
1962	1,128	869	59.0	516	35.0	88	6.0	1,473	100.0
1963	1,233	894	56.9	579	36.8	99	6.3	1,572	100.0
1964	1,332	967	58.1	561	33.8	135	8.1	1,663	100.0
1965	1,286	813	51.2	642	40.5	131	8.3	1,586	100.0
1966	1,230	919	48.9	834	44.3	128	6.8	1,881	100.0
1967	1,083	715	42.8	820	49.1	135	8.1	1,670	100.0
1968	1,079	773	44.9	801	46.6	147	8.5	1,721	100.0

Source: Aggregated from data in Central Bank of the Philippines, Statistical Bulletin (December 1968), using correction factors from Table 4.

* Net of food imports (f.o.b.).

Table 6. Philippine imports by major category, 1950–1968*
(f.o.b. values in million pesos at 1955 prices)

Year	Capital goods and materials chiefly for capital goods		Consumer goods and materials chiefly for consumer goods		Total non-food imports	
	Value	%	Value	%	Value	%
1950	n.a.	n.a.	n.a.	n.a.	916	100
1951	373	36.4	652	63.6	1,025	100
1952	361	38.2	583	61.8	944	100
1953	435	39.8	657	60.2	1,092	100
1954	511	41.8	711	58.2	1,222	100
1955	586	44.6	728	55.4	1,314	100
1956	710	53.3	623	46.7	1,333	100
1957	847	53.9	725	46.1	1,572	100
1958	660	52.1	606	47.9	1,266	100
1959	724	54.5	605	45.5	1,329	100
1960	887	63.3	514	36.7	1,401	100
1961	920	60.8	593	39.2	1,513	100
1962	762	56.0	599	44.0	1,361	100
1963	881	58.3	630	41.7	1,511	100
1964	1,051	60.1	698	39.9	1,749	100
1965	1,082	61.1	689	38.9	1,771	100
1966	1,142	58.6	807	41.4	1,949	100
1967†	1,529	63.7	833	35.3	2,362	100
1968†	1,643	62.5	986	37.5	2,629	100

Sources: 1950–1965, United Nations, ECAFE, *Economic Bulletin for Asia and the Far East,* various issues; 1966–1968, Central Bank of the Philippines, *Statistical Bulletin* (December 1968), data aggregated according to ECAFE classification scheme.

* Excluding food imports.
† Preliminary.

illustrates, most of the increase in manufactures was contributed by only two components—plywood and veneer—the exclusion of which reduces the growth rate to an insignificant 3.2 per cent. The significance of this fact will be discussed in detail later. The main trend in imports seen in Table 6 is a substantial rise in the share of capital goods and related intermediate goods. The average annual growth rates of the three series are 9.1 per cent for capital goods, 2.2 per cent for consumer goods, and 5.6 per cent for total nonfood imports.

The third major statistical area after production and foreign trade is that of labor force. Here, the problems are as much conceptual as statistical. The vast literature on both theoretical and measurement issues relating to employment in underdeveloped countries is characterized by relatively little agreement on a definition of underemployment. In a later part of this chapter we shall raise some of these issues as they appear relevant to the Philippine situation. Anticipating our conclusions there, the data to be discussed at present relate only to unemployment and visible underemployment, making use of the conventional benchmarks of hours per week and weeks per year for full employment.

Data on Philippine labor derive from two major sources: the population censuses (the three most recent being taken in 1939, 1948, and 1960), and a semiannual sample survey begun in 1956 known as the Philippine Statistical Survey of Households (PSSH).[18] There are, however, certain problems of comparability between the PSSH and the 1960 census, and more especially between both of these and the 1948 census—which used the gainful worker concept rather than the modern definition of labor force. These raise serious difficulties in estimating the sectoral distribution of labor in the early 1950's.

---

[18] The survey has recently been renamed the Bureau of the Census and Statistics Survey of Households (BCSSH), but because of its familiarity we retain the abbreviation PSSH. It provides highly detailed tabulations on labor force status, hours worked in the survey week, whether additional work was wanted, and whether it was sought, given separately for agriculture and nonagricultural industries. Its major omission (shared, more remarkably, by the published results of the 1960 census) is any breakdown of employment data by region; yet such an analysis is fundamental to an understanding of labor conditions in the Philippines, where regional contrasts are often extreme. (The quality of the PSSH data has undoubtedly improved over time as a result of refinement of sampling techniques and greater experience, and less weight can be placed on the earlier results.)

Table 7. Sectoral distribution of employed labor force,
Philippines, 1950–1968 (numbers in thousands)

Year	Traditional sector		Modern sector		Total	
	No.	%	No.	%	No.	%
1950	3,969	61.7	2,466	38.3	6,435	100.0
1951	4,125	62.2	2,508	37.8	6,633	100.0
1952	4,252	62.2	2,587	37.8	6,839	100.0
1953	4,357	61.8	2,696	38.2	7,053	100.0
1954	4,546	62.5	2,729	37.5	7,275	100.0
1955	4,684	62.4	2,822	37.6	7,506	100.0
1956	4,789	62.2	2,913	37.8	7,702	100.0
1957	4,922	60.0	3,106	40.0	8,198	100.0
1958	5,195	62.4	3,134	37.6	8,329	100.0
1959	5,213	60.8	3,362	39.2	8,575	100.0
1960	5,140	60.2	3,399	39.8	8,539	100.0
1961	5,424	59.6	3,671	40.4	9,095	100.0
1962	5,801	60.4	3,802	39.6	9,603	100.0
1963	5,682	58.2	4,084	41.8	9,766	100.0
1964	5,742	57.1	4,322	42.9	10,064	100.0
1965	5,625	55.7	4,476	44.3	10,101	100.0
1966	6,068	55.6	4,850	44.4	10,918	100.0
1967	6,532	56.6	5,002	43.4	11,534	100.0
1968	6,682	56.5	5,135	43.5	11,817	100.0

Sources: 1950–1956, estimates based on 1948–1960 intercensal growth rates and Central Bank employment indices (see text); 1957–1968, October rounds of Philippine Statistical Survey of Households (except for 1964 and 1967–1968, which are adjusted estimates derived from May PSSH).

The employment estimates given in Table 7 are based on PSSH data for 1957–1968 and on the censuses and the Central Bank's nonagricultural employment index for earlier years.[19]

[19] The detailed procedure underlying Table 7 is as follows. The October PSSH data on employed labor in agriculture and nonagriculture were utilized for the years in which they are available, except for 1956 which internal evidence suggests is less reliable. (The October series was used in preference to the May series or to some average of the two because it is not inflated by the large number of school children recorded in the labor force in May. See Rosario A. Henares, "Some Characteristics of the Economically Active Population," *Statistical Reporter* [Manila], 1,

While we believe the series are the best available, they are not completely satisfactory. The Central Bank's employment index, derived from a sample of reporting establishments, has significantly understated the growth in modern sector employment for the years it overlaps the PSSH, which might indicate that the estimate of 38 per cent for the 1950 share of employed labor in that sector is exaggerated. On the other hand, the proportion in the modern sector in 1950 implied by the 1948 census appears to be as high as 43 per cent, which if correct would mean virtually no net shift in sectoral labor allocation over the entire 19 year period.[20] As can be seen in Table 7, the series adopted do show a slight but persisting shift away from agriculture in the 1960's after the almost constant shares characterizing the previous decade.

For purposes of measuring labor input into a productive process it is of course necessary to take into account variation in hours worked, both over time and in cross-section between the various age and sex components of the labor force. We shall return to this point in the later discussion of labor surplus. At the present stage we assume (as is later argued) that at least in the Philippine case, the simple employment data provide a fairly adequate approximation to an actual index of labor input.

---

no. 4 [1957], 7.) Similar estimates for 1964 and 1967–1968 were based on the May surveys of those years and the average October/May ratio. For the years 1950–1956, the totals were found from the 1948–1960 intercensal growth rate and the sectoral distribution derived from the Central Bank's index of nonagricultural employment. The latter index was spliced to the corresponding PSSH series, permitting the agricultural component to be obtained residually. (This technique was used by Theodore K. Ruprecht in his estimates prepared for the NPA Philippine Project.) Lastly, it was assumed that the small proportion of the labor force engaged in forestry grew at a uniform rate over the period, the absolute numbers being determined by the 1948 population census and the 1961 economic census. These numbers were added to the nonagricultural component.

[20] See the staff report entitled "The Trend of the Labor Force," in *First Conference on Population, 1965* (Quezon City: University of the Philippines Press, 1966), p. 500.

Another opportunity for simplification which is relevant for the analysis in Chapter 3 follows from the fact that the employment/population ratio has remained remarkably constant over the 1950–1968 period. Using the census benchmarks for total population and the employment data from Table 7, the participation rate has varied only between the levels of 31 and 34 per cent with no time trend apparent. (This very low participation rate is a consequence of rapid population growth—implying a high proportion of children below labor force ages—and relatively low female labor force participation.)

In Tables 3 and 7 we have the data to compute sectoral labor productivity. A summary of the resulting estimates of annual gross output per employed person (in 1955 pesos) is as follows:

Period	Modern sector	Traditional sector	Differential (modern ÷ traditional)
1950–1954	1904	491	3.9
1955–1959	2387	524	4.6
1960–1964	2539	520	4.9
1965–1968	2594	567	4.6

Over the whole period the productivity of labor increased at an average annual rate of 2.4 per cent in the modern sector and 1.1 per cent in the traditional sector. As a consequence the apparent intersectoral differential was raised from 3.9 to 1 in the early 1950's to nearly 5 to 1 a decade later.[21] In the late 1960's output per man in agriculture showed indications of improving again after more than ten years of stagnation.

The over-all picture that emerges from this first look at the

---

[21] Although a very substantial differential between sectors undoubtedly exists and the trends indicated in the list are meaningful, the absolute size of the ratio is to some degree exaggerated in this simple computation. Strictly, allowance must be made for the effect of overstatement of modern sector value added resulting from tariff policies (see the discussion of manufacturing indices below).

Philippine economy is one of rapid growth and substantial evidence of economic development. The GNP maintained a fairly high average growth rate of 6 per cent, and more significantly the share of the traditional sector in total output declined by almost a third, indicating a major shift from agriculture to industry. This shift toward the modern sector is shown even more decisively by the changing composition of exports. At the beginning of the period modern sector exports were about 12 per cent of the whole but increased to about 55 per cent over the next two decades. Imports appear to tell the same story with the economy increasingly importing machines to manufacture consumer goods rather than the consumer goods themselves. Only when we turn to employment is the picture less promising. The sectoral distribution of the employed labor force changed relatively little, the share in agriculture apparently falling about four percentage points (from 62 to 56 per cent). In contrast to the rapid change in the sectoral distribution of product there was clearly no similar progress in shifting the "center of gravity" of the economy and moving labor off the land and into industry.[22] The widening differential in labor productivity between the two sectors is also not an indication of healthy development. For the latter we would expect a sustained rise in traditional sector productivity to narrow the intersectoral differential and lay the foundation for an integrated nondual economy. Which of these two perspectives on the postwar performance of the Philippines is the more accurate requires a more detailed analysis of the two sectors.

[22] Cf. the dictum of Fei and Ranis that "[a] basic policy aim of the underdeveloped dualistic economy faced with an initially unfavorable factor endowment and increasing population pressure over time is to reallocate as much labor as possible from its agricultural sector to its industrial sector. This process of labor reallocation must be sufficiently rapid to shift the economy's center of gravity from the agricultural to the industrial sector." John C. H. Fei and Gustav Ranis, *Development of the Labor Surplus Economy: Theory and Policy* (Homewood, Ill.: Richard D. Irwin, 1964), pp. 111–112.

Traditional Sector

The three basic variables appearing in the traditional sector production function are output, labor, and land. The national accounts series given in Table 3 provide an aggregate measure of output, but because of the very real uncertainties in some of the underlying production data we have also computed an index of physical crop production based on a limited number of crops the statistics for which are the least subject to error.[23] This index with the base year of 1955 is shown in the first column of Table 8. A corresponding index for the traditional sector labor input is readily obtained from the data in Table 7. Finally, a series for the land input can be based on the area statistics published by the Department of Agriculture and Natural Resources (DANR). These data refer to harvested areas (since 1954), except for tree crops where the actual area under cultivation is used. Thus, where double and triple cropping is increasing, as in Central Luzon, the data reflect the change. Similarly, double counting of cultivated areas occurs with intercropping (e.g., coconuts and corn), although it may be doubted if the extent of this practice is accurately recorded.[24] (Double cropping, how-

---

[23] The crop and livestock surveys of the Department of Agriculture and Natural Resources are largely oriented toward the chief crops—rice, corn, coconuts, and sugar—and the production statistics for these are probably adequate. (On the large errors in some of the other components of traditional sector output, notably livestock, vegetables, and fish production, see Levy, "Interim Report-B.") Our crop index is based on the following crops: rice, coconuts, corn, root crops, sugar cane, abaca, and fruits and nuts—together representing about 90% of estimated total crop value. The quantity relatives of the various items were weighted by their average production values over the 1958–1962 period.

[24] According to Levy ("Interim Report," p. 35), crop area estimates are based largely on reports by farmers of quantity of seeds or cuttings sown, using fixed conversion factors to arrive at the resulting areas. Although in theory this technique corrects for both multiple cropping and intercropping, the possible errors introduced are considerable. Levy regards DANR area data as weaker than its production data, and biased upwards. (Yield estimates computed from these data may therefore be too low.)

Table 8. Traditional sector indices, Philippines, 1950–1968 (1955 = 100)

Year	Output* (1)	Labor (2)	Land† (3)	Output/ labor (4)	Output/ land (5)	Land/ labor (6)
1950	72.7	84.7	79.6	86	91	94
1951	82.3	88.1	81.8	93	101	93
1952	86.0	90.8	88.1	95	98	97
1953	91.1	93.0	94.2	98	97	101
1954	95.9	97.1	95.4	99	101	98
1955	100.0	100.0	100.0	100	100	100
1956	103.1	102.2	106.0	101	97	104
1957	108.4	105.1	108.9	103	100	104
1958	107.2	110.9	108.8	97	99	98
1959	110.5	111.3	122.9	99	90	110
1960	112.8	109.7	118.1	103	96	108
1961	112.9	115.8	121.8	97	93	105
1962	125.7	123.8	123.1	102	102	99
1963	131.3	121.3	123.3	108	106	102
1964	133.1	122.6	123.7	109	108	101
1965	134.4	120.1	128.3	112	105	107
1966	135.5	129.5	128.9	105	105	100
1967	141.1	139.5	132.2	101	107	95
1968	145.2	142.7	137.0	102	106	96

Sources: Columns 1 and 3: Computed from Department of Agriculture and Natural Resources data (see text); column 2: Table 7.
* Physical output of crops.
† Harvested areas except for tree crops.

ever, has provided relatively little additional output in the Philippines. Golay and Goodstein estimate that on average over 1964–1966 about 650,000 hectares were double-cropped out of a cultivated area of 7.5 million hectares—a proportion of less than 9 per cent.) [25] Apart from the three factor and product indices, Table 8 also computes indices of the three implicit

[25] Frank H. Golay and Marvin E. Goodstein, *Rice and People in 1990* (Manila: U.S. Agency for International Development, 1967), p. 67. The proportion of rice land double-cropped in the mid-1960's was 15% in the Philippines, which can be compared to 7% in Thailand, 13% in West Malaysia and about 25% in Indonesia (Java). Asian Development Bank, *Asian Agricultural Survey* (N.p., University of Tokyo Press, 1969), p. 158.

ratios: output/labor, output/land, and land/labor. These are commented on below.

Traditional sector output is divided in three broad ways by demand use: final consumption in the traditional sector itself, final consumption in the modern sector, and exports. A precise definition of each of these categories, however, is less simple than this statement would imply. Traditional sector consumption consists both of direct consumption by the producers themselves and of output marketed for cash but still consumed by agricultural households. Traditional sector output consumed in the modern sector comprises food sold directly on the intersectoral commodity market and the "indirect" supplies of food obtained via the foreign sector from exports of commercial crops. Finally, exports include both the output exported directly or with only minor processing from the traditional sector and exports of agricultural commodities processed in the modern sector. Given the definition of the second category above, exports must, of course, be taken net of food imports. An added complication which we shall largely ignore is the fact that a small proportion of the output of commercial crops processed in the modern sector is consumed in that sector rather than exported.

In Table 3, we have data on total traditional sector output which, it may be recalled, includes processing, storage, transportation, and marketing costs. The appropriate export series is given in the second column of Table 5—in f.o.b. values, which can be assumed to be priced at the same level as the output data. To estimate the sectoral distribution of domestic consumption two possibilities are open. First, we could use the expenditure data from a family budget survey which provides a breakdown of consumption items (enabling classification by sectoral origin) for urban and rural households—a rough approximation to the modern and traditional sectors. The October 1961 round of the PSSH was such a survey.[26] Alternatively, it would be pos-

[26] *Philippine Statistical Survey of Households Bulletin, Series No. 14: Family Income and Expenditures, 1961* (Manila: Bureau of the Census and Statistics, 1964).

sible to estimate the distribution by end-use for each commodity at the farm level and then make suitable adjustments for processing, transport, and marketing costs for each end-use category. These methods have been used respectively by Paauw and Tryon.[27] The advantage of the former, consumption survey method is that it avoids the necessarily somewhat arbitrary estimates of output allocation and markups and takes into consideration food imports. Despite reservations on relying on a single survey of a type that often contains substantial biases, we have preferred to use this procedure. To obtain the full series from the 1961 data, the sectoral shares are assumed to vary only with sectoral changes in population. This is a conservative assumption from the viewpoint of the modern sector, although studies to be discussed below indicate that demand elasticities for cereals at least are very low in the Philippines and real wages have been fairly constant.

The distribution of output by demand use derived in this way is shown in Table 9. The total agricultural surplus, i.e., output over and above the food consumption of the traditional sector, averages between 55 and 60 per cent of output over these years. This is divided between modern sector consumption and exports, with the former overtaking the latter in magnitude near the middle of the period.

We saw above that the rate of growth of GNP and the trend in the composition of both exports and imports all suggested healthy economic development in the Philippine economy, although the performance was marred by a failure to reduce the labor productivity differential between agriculture and industry. Looking more closely at traditional sector trends, it is clear from Table 8 that the productivity of land as well as labor was relatively stagnant over the two decade period. (The fluctuations reflect the vicissitudes both of the harvest and of Philip-

[27] Paauw, "The Philippines: Estimates of Flows," appendix II–2; and Joseph L. Tryon, "The Behavior of Production, Prices and Productivity in Philippine Agriculture, 1949–1964," mimeographed (Washington: National Planning Association, Center for Development Planning, 1968), appendix A.

Table 9. Distribution of traditional sector output by demand use, Philippines, annual averages, 1950–1968 (values in million pesos at 1955 prices)

Period	Total output		Final consumption in traditional sector		Total agricultural surplus			
					Final consumption in modern sector		Net exports*	
	Value	%	Value	%	Value	%	Value	%
1950–1954	2091	100.0	904	43.2	552	26.4	635	30.4
1955–1959	2601	100.0	1153	44.3	720	27.7	728	28.0
1960–1964	2904	100.0	1203	41.4	834	28.7	867	29.9
1965–1968	3528	100.0	1529	43.3	1194	33.8	805	22.8

Sources: Tables 3 and 5, and Philippine Statistical Survey of Households Bulletin, no. 14 (see text for details of methodology).
* Net of food imports.

pine agricultural statistics.) While total output doubled, so nearly did the land and labor inputs. The situation is reminiscent of the "static expansion" that Boeke observed in rural Java.[28]

Some of the consequences of the coexistence of a static traditional sector and a rapidly growing modern sector can be seen from Table 9. As we would expect there is little change in the "own" consumption of the traditional sector. With productivity and per capita food consumption constant, the total agricultural surplus would be a stable share of output. The more rapid growth in the modern sector is reflected in the share of agricultural output it consumes, which rises from 26 to 34 per cent. (By our definitions of categories, part of this consumption consists of imported food items; the value of these imports is deducted from traditional sector exports to give "net" exports.) With a constant proportion of output remaining in the traditional sector and an increasing share being consumed in the modern sector, it follows that the residual available for export is a declining share of the total. The exported fraction dropped by one-quarter between 1950–1954 and 1965–1968. Moreover, as Table 5 indicates, even the absolute volume of traditional sector exports has shown no secular rise in the 1960's.

Modern Sector

The modern sector, as we have defined it for the Philippines, contains not only manufacturing and the extractive industries (mining and logging) but also the ISIC divisions 4 through 8 —construction, transportation, communication, utilities, commerce, and services. In terms of contribution to net domestic product, manufacturing and extractives make up only one-third of the whole sector. These two components are the most accessible in terms of data, however, and for some purposes the re-

---

[28] J. H. Boeke, *Economics and Economic Policy of Dual Societies* (Haarlem: H. D. Tjeenk Willink, 1953), p. 174.

mainder of the sector can be thought of as complementary to them.[29]

The 1961 *Economic Census of the Philippines* provides a detailed cross-section picture of the modern sector for that year, but unfortunately we have little idea of the stability over time of most of the characteristics revealed. In Table 10 we assemble some important ratios computed from this source: the average factor shares in output, the propensity to invest out of profits, average wages, and three ratios relating output (or margins), labor, and fixed assets. Some caution is necessary in interpreting these data. Returns to labor refer to payrolls only and may therefore be underestimated insofar as noncash payments are not fully recorded. Profits are here taken simply as output (value added) less total payrolls—an admittedly rough procedure which will overestimate them to the extent that other production costs are significant. The census estimates of fixed assets are of dubious use (except, perhaps, for comparison between industry groups) since they are based on original book value. No data on assets are available for establishments with less than ten employees. The final row of Table 10 gives the aggregated estimates for the modern sector. We can expect that the process of aggregation cancels out many of the errors in the individual components.

[29] Structural shifts in the distribution of net product in the modern sector have been relatively minor in the period 1950–1968. Extractive industries have increased their share from 7 to 11%, and construction has fallen from 9 to 5% (but mostly in the early 1950's). The distribution of the other industry groups has remained approximately stable, with the following average percentage shares: manufacturing, 23; transport, communication, and utilities, 7; commerce, 20; and services, 35. National Economic Council, Office of Statistical Coordination and Standards, "The National Income of the Philippines."

Even less change is observed in the distribution of employment among the broad industry groups in the modern sector. The average percentage shares over the period 1956–1967 for which PSSH data are available are: manufacturing, 28; extractives, 3; construction, 7; transport and communication, 7; commerce, 25; and services and utilities, 30.

Table 10. Selected ratios for major industry groups in modern sector, Philippines, 1961

Major industry group	Payrolls/ gross value added (per cent) (1)	Profits/ gross value added (per cent) (2)	Capital expenditures/ profits (per cent) (3)	Payrolls/ paid employees (₱1000) (4)	Gross value added/total employees (₱1000) (5)	Gross value added/fixed assets* (6)	Fixed assets/ total employees* (₱1000) (7)
Manufacturing	25.7	74.3	25.7	1.80	5.90	1.23	6.13
Extractive industries	38.7	61.3	32.1	1.86	4.47	0.83	6.04
Forestry	(37.4)	(62.6)	(40.5)	(1.63)	(3.88)	(0.88)	(5.33)
Mining	(39.8)	(60.2)	(24.8)	(2.08)	(5.13)	(0.79)	(6.72)
Construction	49.1	50.9	19.1	1.45	2.76	2.05	1.41
Transport and communications†	48.0	52.0	33.9	1.59	2.82	n.a.	n.a.
Commerce†	24.0	76.0	3.9	2.06	3.27	2.69	4.26
Utilities†	26.5	73.5	52.3	2.62	9.71	0.21	54.32
Services†,‡	33.4	66.6	10.8	1.32	2.44	1.80	2.65
Total modern sector	28.8	71.2	20.4	1.78	4.17	1.14	6.51

Source: Computed from Bureau of the Census and Statistics, Economic Census of the Philippines, 1961.
* Large establishments (10 or more employees) only.
† For "gross value added," read "gross margins."
‡ Excluding government and domestic services.

As the first two columns of Table 10 indicate, labor appears to receive less than 30 per cent of output in the modern sector as a whole. This very low average return to labor in the Philippines has often been noted. Some evidence that the share has not been rising in recent years is given by household survey data on income distribution: in urban areas, which very roughly coincide with the modern sector, income inequality appears to have increased both absolutely and more rapidly than for rural areas.[30] More direct time-series data on this point are available for manufacturing alone from the *Annual Survey of Manufactures*. The factor shares from this source, defined as above, are shown in Table 11 for the period 1956–1966.[31] The payroll/value added ratio was smaller in 1966 than a decade earlier, indicating that wages have not kept pace with productivity. (A part of the explanation for this, however, may perhaps lie in the changing structure of the manufacturing sector, with its rising median employment per establishment. The well-known inverse association between employment size and labor's share of output is also apparent in the Philippines. Thus, it is possible that returns to labor have been increasing within each specific

[30] Three rounds of the PSSH (1957, 1961, and 1965) have collected data on family income and expenditures. The 1957 and 1961 surveys, analyzed by Reyes and Chan, show that the top 5% of urban households increased their share of total urban income from 19.4% to 28.5% over the period 1956–1961 while the share of the bottom 40% fell from 12.4 to 11.3. Peregrino S. Reyes and Teresita L. Chan, "Family Income Distribution in the Philippines," *Statistical Reporter* (Manila), 9, no. 2 (1965), 31. Early results from the 1965 survey indicate that the trend since 1961 has been an approximately constant share for the high income group and a continued fall for the large bottom group of households. See "Family Income Distribution and Expenditure Patterns in the Philippines: 1965," *Journal of Philippine Statistics*, vol. 19, no. 2 (1968).

[31] The Annual Survey of Manufactures was begun in 1956, but was not held in 1961 (the year of the economic census) or 1964. Data for surveys more recent than 1966 were not available at the time of writing. Note that the Survey covers only "organized" manufacturing—defined as establishments with a minimum employment of five persons.

Table 11. Returns to factors, propensity to invest, and average payrolls in Philippine manufacturing, selected years, 1956–1966*

Year	Payrolls/ value added (per cent)	Profits†/ value added (per cent)	Capital expenditures/ profits (per cent)	Payrolls/ paid employees‡ (₱1000)
1956	32.5	67.5	14.6	1.63
1957	31.3	68.7	19.3	1.59
1958	28.3	71.7	17.9	1.78
1959	28.3	71.7	15.5	1.75
1960	26.7	73.3	20.0	1.71
1962	24.9	75.1	27.6	1.65
1963	22.7	77.3	16.1	1.59
1965	26.5	73.5	21.3	1.72
1966	27.4	72.6	26.8	1.84

Sources: Computed from Bureau of the Census and Statistics, *Annual Survey of Manufactures*, 1959 and 1966. (Ratios based on current price series.)

* Covers establishments with five or more workers.

† Value added less total payrolls.

‡ 1955 prices.

employment-size group, while at the same time the aggregate ratio shows a decline.) [32]

A measure of the propensity to invest in the modern sector is given by the ratio of capital expenditures to profits presented in column 3 of Table 10 and the corresponding time series for manufacturing in Table 11. Capital expenditures here refer to

[32] When data are broken down by industry group, the payroll/value added ratio shows wide interindustry variability both in absolute size and in its trend over time. Labor received only 8% of value added in petroleum products but 40–50% in furniture, leather products, and machinery (which in the Philippines is mostly assembling). Similar, though usually less extreme, size variations occur in other countries. In the United States, for example, the ratio varies from 20–30% for tobacco and chemicals to nearly 60% for wood and leather products. The dominance of a few capital-intensive industries (such as cement production and petroleum refining) in Philippine manufacturing may do much to depress the aggregate ratio.

payments for new buildings, new machinery, and new equipment but exclude expenditures on used fixed assets (including
land) —a minor item—and inventories. They also, of course,
exclude investment achieved without monetary expenditures.
There is wide but not unexpected variation among industry
divisions, with the proportion averaging the low level of 20 per
cent for the whole sector. The time series results do not seem
very stable but they also average about 20 per cent with some
slight indication of a secular increase over the period.

Equivalent data from the national accounts are not directly
obtainable because we have no sectoral breakdown of the factor
returns. The investment estimates, moreover, are among the
weakest areas of the Philippine national accounts, although the
1968 revisions represent substantial improvements over earlier
official series. Despite these limitations, the over-all trends in the
average investment rate in the modern sector are clear from the
following figures (from the same source as Table 3), which
show the three components of gross domestic capital formation
as percentages of sectoral product:[33]

Period	Durable equipment	Construction	Inventories	Total
1950–1954	3.1	11.0	1.2	15.3
1955–1959	4.9	9.6	1.4	15.9
1960–1964	6.5	9.0	1.9	17.4
1965–1968	8.7	9.6	1.6	19.9

The significant increase in the average investment rate is seen
to be almost entirely accounted for by investment in durable
equipment which has nearly trebled as a share of modern sector
product over the period.

We shall defer a discussion of wages in the modern sector
until we come to consider intersectoral wage differentials in a

[33] Sectoral allocation of investment was made according to the following assumptions. Durable equipment investment is all modern sector
except for tractors and agricultural machinery. Construction is taken to
be complementary to durable equipment and therefore divided in the
same proportions. Inventories are proportional to sectoral output.

later part of this chapter. It will suffice here to note that the nearly constant average wage in manufacturing seen in the last column of Table 11 is amply confirmed by independent evidence on real wage levels in the whole sector. Without hypothesizing on the nature of the causal relationships, it is obvious that this constancy is consistent with the two sectoral trends already observed: rising labor productivity and a decline in labor's share of product.

To say that the output/labor ratio has been increasing immediately raises the question of the trend in the output/capital ratio. Unfortunately, we are faced both with a scarcity of data and with the more fundamental problems of nonhomogeneity in the modern sector which effectively preclude any statement on aggregate capital productivity. Our discussion is therefore restricted to the manufacturing component. For this we have available or can compute series of value added and capital stock at constant prices,[34] and also on average annual employment.[35] These data, converted to indices with 1955 as base, are given in the first three columns of Table 12. The table also shows the three ratios derived from the main series.

A note of caution is necessary here concerning these indices

---

[34] Umaña has derived constant price estimates of value added and capital stock up to 1960, using the censuses as benchmark years. Salvador C. Umaña, "Growth of Output of Philippine Manufacturing: 1902–60," in *Growth of Output in the Philippines*, ed. Hooley and Barker. Subsequent years are computed directly from the Annual Survey of Manufactures reports where possible and from the NEC national accounts data for the four remaining years. (The capital series is based on recorded increments to fixed assets using the NEC's depreciation assumptions and price deflators. For value added, the disaggregated survey figures were deflated by the respective wholesale price indices.)

[35] The *Annual Survey of Manufactures* gives data on average employment for 1956–1966. Estimates for 1961, 1964, and 1967–1968 are based on the Central Bank index of manufacturing employment. Prior to 1956, the series was extrapolated assuming the uniform intercensal growth rate of manufacturing employment of 5.3% (see "The Trend of the Labor Force," in *First Conference on Population, 1965*, p. 500).

Table 12. Manufacturing sector indices, Philippines,
1950–1968* (1955 = 100)

Year	Output† (1)	Capital‡ (2)	Labor (3)	Output/ capital (4)	Output/ labor (5)	Capital/ labor (6)
1950	50	47	77	106	65	61
1951	64	62	81	103	78	76
1952	75	75	86	100	88	87
1953	84	86	90	97	92	96
1954	95	94	95	100	99	99
1955	100	100	100	100	100	100
1956	111	102	105	108	105	97
1957	123	105	114	117	108	92
1958	144	120	117	120	123	103
1959	160	129	122	124	131	106
1960	173	151	127	114	136	118
1961	184	163	135	113	137	121
1962	198	169	143	117	139	118
1963	227	190	154	119	147	124
1964	225	201	158	112	142	127
1965	228	209	166	109	138	126
1966	239	222	168	108	142	132
1967	251	237	171	106	147	139
1968	265	248	175	107	151	142

Sources: Columns 1 and 2: 1950–1960, Umaña, "Growth of Output of Philippine Manufacturing"; 1961–1968, Annual Survey of Manufactures and NEC national accounts data (see text for details); column 3: see text.
* Data refer to manufacturing establishments employing five or more persons.
† Value added at constant prices.
‡ Fixed assets and inventory at constant prices.

and the index of capital stock in particular. The underlying data are probably quite weak and the results are inevitably to some extent functions of the deflating procedures used. With these reservations, the following tentative observations may be made. The output/capital ratio has not shown a clear trend over the whole 1950–1968 period, but there is some indication of a slight rise in the 1950's, followed by a decline. On the other hand, the output/labor ratio seems to have risen markedly until about 1960 and then slowed in recent years. Thus, the growth rates of both labor and capital productivities appear to have declined over the period, in the latter case perhaps even becoming negative. A possibly serious statistical bias must be taken into account in evaluating this result: the falling off in productivity increases may be caused by progressive errors in deflating output. However, subsequent trials with other deflators (e.g., the NEC implicit price deflator for income from manufacturing), if anything, tended to suggest some degree of underdeflation. If true, this would accentuate the decline. Again, at a more basic level, the increase in the scale of tariffs on finished consumer goods, with the consequent uncompetitive pricing of domestic manufactures, has led to a progressive overstatement of real value added. If allowance were made for this effect, it may be that much of the recorded increases in productivity would prove illusory.

We noted earlier that "unorganized" manufacturing (establishments employing less than five persons) was not covered by the *Annual Survey of Manufactures,* and it is therefore excluded also from Table 12. An adjustment for its effect on the growth rate of manufacturing can be made on the basis of a comparison of the employment totals estimated by the annual surveys of manufacturing establishments with those given by the PSSH household surveys. If we assume that output per worker in the small industries is comparable to the average level in the traditional sector (since small-scale manufacturing is often an alternative occupation for agricultural workers), then the share of these industries in manufacturing output fell from about 35 per cent to 15 per cent or less in the years under consideration.[36] In constant prices, organized manufacturing

---

[36] Cf. the estimates prepared by the Program Implementation Agency in Manila which show unorganized manufacturing contributing as much as 60% of total manufacturing value added in the early 1950's, falling to 30% a decade later. The absolute size of the unorganized component implied by this result seems implausibly large. Program Implementation Agency, "Trend and Structure of Philippine Manufactures, 1953–1963," mimeographed (Manila, n.d.).

grew at an annual rate of 9 per cent (computed from Table 12),
unorganized at 2 per cent, and the resulting growth of the
whole manufacturing sector was slightly over 7 per cent.

The composition of manufacturing output has shown slight
but persistent changes in the postwar years. The main shift has
been from the lower ISIC divisions such as textiles to the later
industry groups (30–39) —especially chemicals (mainly coconut oil) and certain metal products. It is difficult from data
classified in the conventional broad groupings to make any definite statement on shifts in output by final use—in particular,
on whether investment goods production is becoming more
significant. While there is certainly more rapid growth in the
top ISIC divisions, these include automobile assembly, appliances, and other consumer-oriented industries as well as investment goods. We take up this problem in the later discussion of
import dependence.

One relevant calculation we can make with the data at hand
is to determine approximately the extent to which imports of
consumer manufactures have been supplanted by domestic
production, using the methodology of Maizels.[37] Denoting the
total supply (imports plus domestic production) of these manufactures by S, and the fraction of them imported by m, we have
the simple decomposition of the change in imports between
time 0 and time 1, viz., $S_1 m_1 - S_0 m_0$, into the two components
$S_1 (m_1 - m_0)$ and $m_0 (S_1 - S_0)$. The first of these is defined by
Maizels as the import substitution effect, the second as the effect
of expansion in home demand.

Because of the difficulties of interpretation noted in the preceding paragraph, we shall roughly estimate domestic output
of manufactured consumer goods by taking only the ISIC
groups 21–29.[38] The output series chosen is that from the NEC

[37] Alfred Maizels, *Industrial Growth and World Trade* (Cambridge:
Cambridge University Press, 1963), pp. 151–152.

[38] The category of food manufactures (20) is omitted as not being relevant to the study of import substitution: it contributes a large proportion
of the total value added in manufacturing, but the product is mostly exported and we have assigned such exports to the traditional sector.

national accounts, deflating the current price series by the implicit price index for manufacturing. (The result agrees well with the output series in Table 12 corrected for inclusion of unorganized manufacturing.) Unfortunately, we have no adequate data from this or any other source on consumer goods production prior to 1955. The corresponding import series is that of Table 6, which includes intermediate inputs into the manufacture of consumer goods but excludes food. To convert the f.o.b. data to c.i.f., the figures are marked up by a constant 10 per cent.[39] Total supplies of consumer manufactures are then given by the sum of the two series. Using these data, we find that the import content of supplies apparently fell rapidly in the late 1950's from over 60 per cent to about 50 per cent and thereafter remained approximately constant.

While this downward trend is meaningful, less significance can be attributed to the absolute size of the import content ratio. The data on domestic output of consumer goods in particular are very likely to be underestimated due to the use of the ISIC categories. This would tend to exaggerate the import content. On the other hand, the c.i.f. values for imports should probably be marked up by a substantial amount to cover the importer's margin and tax. Clearly, a more precise statistical analysis would be necessary to obtain an accurate picture of import substitution. Keeping in mind these sources of error, we may nevertheless decompose the observed change in the level of imports of consumer manufactures. Taking three-year averages for the end-points, imports have increased from ₱761 million per year in 1955–1957 to ₱963 in 1966–1968. If the import content of supplies had remained constant at 0.58, its average level for 1955–1957, consumer imports would necessarily have risen by ₱327 million over this period. The difference between the predicted rise of ₱327 million and the observed rise of ₱202

[39] This is the fairly stable difference between the c.i.f. Philippine import data recorded in the International Monetary Fund's *International Financial Statistics* and the f.o.b. figures published by the Central Bank of the Philippines in its *Statistical Bulletin*. See George L. Hicks, "Philippine Foreign Trade, 1950–65," p. 28.

million, i.e., ₱125 million, is the effect of expansion of domestic output "substituting" for imports.

The major shift in the composition of imports that we noted in Table 6 above is closely related to the process of import substitution. With minimal domestic output of capital equipment, the growth of manufacturing is largely a function of the growth of capital goods imports. But success in import substitution implies that domestic manufacturing production is increasing faster than imports of consumer manufactures. Hence the share of capital goods in total imports would be expected to rise.

The final aspect of the modern sector we need discuss in the present survey is the disposition of output among its own uses, traditional sector uses, and exports. The flow of goods from the modern to the traditional sector involves two major commodity categories: agricultural chemicals used as inputs for agricultural production and manufactured consumer goods. Inputs of chemicals (mostly fertilizer) make up only a small part of the total.[40] Instead of becoming enmeshed in the statistically difficult area of estimating the volumes of these commodity flows, we can approach the intersectoral market by evaluating the terms of trade between the sectors. While this calculation also presents problems, the underlying price data are both available and fairly reliable.

Our estimates of the intersectoral terms of trade are given in index form in Table 13. The series is the quotient of an aggregate price series of traditional sector marketed production (identifying foodcrops, copra, and sugar) and a corresponding modern sector series based on manufactures, beverages and tobacco, and chemicals.[41] As Table 13 indicates, the terms of trade

[40] Tryon ("Production, Prices and Productivity in Philippine Agriculture," p. 18) has calculated the value of agricultural chemicals used (in 1955 prices) as about ₱20 million in 1950, rising to ₱70 million in 1964. Paauw's estimates of total agricultural sector consumption of industrial goods for the same two years are ₱1,384 million and ₱2,351 million (Paauw, "The Philippines: Estimates of Flows," p. 118).

[41] The price data are taken from the Central Bank's *Statistical Bulletin* (December 1968), pp. 332, 338. For agriculture, the weights used in com-

show no particular trend in the 1950's, the fluctuations being caused chiefly by instability in the price of copra. In the early 1960's, however, the terms of trade move decisively in favor of agriculture and the trend is maintained in the later years. Over the whole period the average annual increase was 2.1 per cent, but separated into a rate of 0.7 per cent during the first decade

Table 13. Intersectoral terms of trade,*
Philippines, 1950–1968
(index, 1955 = 100)

Year	Terms of trade	Year	Terms of trade
1950	105	1960	107
1951	105	1961	108
1952	98	1962	118
1953	108	1963	133
1954	101	1964	132
1955	100	1965	135
1956	95	1966	134
1957	98	1967	143
1958	110	1968	152
1959	111		

Source: Basic price data from Central Bank of the Philippines, *Statistical Bulletin* (see text for details of weighting procedure).

* Units of industrial goods exchanged per unit of agricultural goods.

and 4.0 per cent subsequently. The discontinuity reflects in part the government's exchange decontrol measures put into effect in the years 1960–1962.

The major component of modern sector output which is not traded intersectorally is the extractive industry products. We saw early in this chapter (in Table 5 and Figure 4) that Philip-

puting the aggregate index were the 1960 production values estimated by the NEC. For industry, the weights were derived from the 1961 PSSH expenditure survey and Tryon's estimates of the value of agricultural chemicals utilized (see Note 40).

pine exports of manufactures apart from the processed forest products of plywood and veneer—which could with some justification be included with extractives—were all but negligible, growing at an average rate of 3.2 per cent. In sharp contrast, the real value of extractive industry output increased fivefold between 1950 and 1968 (based on NEC data), while its performance in the export sector was even more impressive with an average growth rate of 13 per cent. Among the factors stimulating this growth were the 1960–1962 exchange decontrol and favorable world price movements. Extractive industries are capital intensive, with a ratio of fixed assets to employment similar to organized manufacturing (see Table 10). The propensity to invest derived from the 1961 economic census is higher than for the modern sector as a whole and probably as a result the productivity of labor, already high, increased rapidly over the postwar decades. A fairly constant 3 per cent of the modern sector labor force raised its share of sectoral production from 7 to 11 per cent of the total.[42]

It is more than a truth by definition to state that there is a dramatic contrast between the modern sector excluding extractives, which exports a completely negligible share of its output, and the extractive industries which export a high and rising share.[43] Although the extractive subsector is modern with respect to capital, productivity, and growth through reinvestment, it also shares with the traditional sector the essential character-

[42] See Note 29 above. The high rate of gross investment in forestry shown in Table 10 is due in part to the rapid capital depreciation experienced in this industry: much of the equipment used (such as logging trucks, yarders, and loaders) has a life of less than ten years. A major reason for the high level of labor productivity in extractive industries as a whole is the exceptionally low proportion of unskilled labor they employ.

[43] The overall export ratio for extractives has risen from below 40% in the early 1950's to over 60% in the mid-1960's. Most mineral production is for export, but an important domestic demand exists for lumber. The latter will increase with population growth and therefore has implications for the future level of log exports.

istic of vent-for-surplus growth. Based far more on forests than minerals, its postwar growth has involved the continuous using up of forest land in the same way that the traditional sector has consumed agricultural land. The combination of modern sector, capital-intensive growth dynamics with vent-for-surplus land consumption has proved a highly effective resource-using machine. As with land, however, forest resources are limited and because in the Philippines the bulk of the forest is not permitted to regenerate (see Chapter 4) the growth of extractives is largely a once-over process. Indeed, as a given area can usually be logged only once, the maintenance of output depends on the continued growth of the exploited area. In this respect the nature and performance of extractive exports is quite distinct from that of the rest of the modern sector.

It is clear from this brief overview of modern sector performance contrasted with the earlier description of the traditional sector that the differences are both sharp and multifaceted. Not only did the modern sector grow rapidly throughout the period, but labor productivity in contrast to the situation in agriculture also increased substantially. An annual increase of 2.4 per cent in real output per worker over nearly two decades is an impressive performance, even if apparently not associated with any similar improvement in the productivity of capital (inferring from our data for the manufacturing subsector).

The trends we have described, however, perhaps raise more questions than they answer. How, for example, do we explain the rapid modern sector growth? What were the constraints on this growth? What part did import substitution play? What was the role of technical change? Why did the domestic terms of trade move so markedly in agriculture's favor? What progress has the economy made in developing an investment goods industry? Where do extractive exports fit in? In attempting to answer these and related questions we need to look more closely at a few specific features of the Philippine economy and explore some of the major technical and behavioral relationships involved.

LAND SURPLUS OR LABOR SURPLUS?

In Chapter 1 we discussed a number of issues of importance in studying the development of the open dual economies of Southeast Asia. These included the contribution of land and other natural resources to aggregate growth, the degree of dependence on imports for industrial development, and the sectoral production functions. The analytical framework introduced at the end of the chapter indicates other significant points which should enter any comprehensive treatment of such economies: notably, the size and disposition of the agricultural surplus, and the modern sector investment function. While some of these aspects have been touched on in the above descriptive survey of the Philippine economy, they each deserve more intensive study. In the present section we examine the facts and implications of a land surplus in relation to issues of sectoral employment and labor transfers.

Land/Labor Ratio

The data presented in Table 2 showed that areal expansion could explain a substantial part of recent increases in cereal production in Southeast Asia. For the Philippines at least, the same is true of the whole of traditional agricultural production (see below). This suggests that, abstracting from problems of factor mobility, these countries might more properly be called "land surplus" than "labor surplus." Although it is only in the perfect world of economic theory that the two are mutually exclusive (in the absence of demand constraints or extreme factor immobility), the distinction is by no means a quibble. It affects, for example, the interpretation given to the level of unemployment in the economy.

We will assume that the agricultural production function has only two factor inputs, land and labor (defined as in Table 8). Capital can be subsumed in part by the land input (since it permits a higher proportion of the land to be double-cropped and therefore raises the measured harvested area), and in part by a time-dependent improvement in factor productivity—

technical progress. Moreover, with surplus land, the constraining factor on sectoral growth is taken to be labor. This is approximately true at the extensive frontier in the Philippines: in Mindanao, for example, migrant families have been able to take up an area of land limited only by their willingness to clear and cultivate it.[44] In such an instance, while a money cost could of course be imputed, there is an obvious sense in which the land is free. Institutional factors and, more simply, the farmers' physical inability to cultivate more than a small area with a given technology, would allow the existence of a surplus of free land where substitution is clearly possible.

To relate land and labor where only the latter is regarded as an independent variable, we define the elasticity of land with respect to labor, γ, by the equation:

$$R = cL_a{}^\gamma,$$

where R is harvested area; L_a, employment in agriculture; and c, a constant. Equivalently, γ is the ratio of the geometric rate of increase of R to that of L_a. With this simple formulation, the transition from a land surplus to a land shortage could be observed as a decline in γ from an initial value equal to (or greater than) one. The limiting case when no further expansion of the land input is possible is represented by $\gamma = 0$.[45]

The data on land and labor for Philippine agriculture over the years 1950–1968 were given in Table 8. To estimate the average value of γ in this period, we can regress the logarithm of harvested area on the logarithm of employed labor. The data are plotted in Figure 5. The regression line, accounting for some 90 per cent of the variation in R, gives an estimate for γ of 1.04.[46] Visual inspection of the data indicates clearly that γ

[44] The rapid expansion of cultivation in Mindanao in postwar years is described by Frederick L. Wernstedt and J. E. Spencer, *The Philippine Island World: A Physical, Cultural, and Regional Geography* (Berkeley: University of California Press, 1967), pp. 504, 548–553.

[45] See Chapter 3 for a formal statement of this argument.

[46] Inclusion of the extrapolated 1950–1955 labor force data adds to an already serious problem of serial correlation (although the 1950 figure

has decreased since the early 1950's. The high proportion of variation in area "explained" by labor suggests that, even without attributing causality to the relationship, labor can act as a proxy for land in the sectoral production function. While the

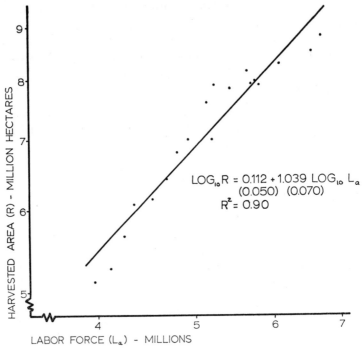

$$LOG_{10} R = 0.112 + 1.039 \, LOG_{10} \, L_a$$
$$(0.050) \quad (0.070)$$
$$R^2 = 0.90$$

Figure 5. Regression of harvested area on labor force employed in agriculture, Philippines, 1950–1968

data are inadequate to permit the formal testing of any specific functional form, it has been possible at least to demonstrate that exclusion of the factor R from a Cobb-Douglas function

can be regarded as representing the 1948 census result) but does not materially change the estimated coefficients. The constant in the regression equation can be interpreted as a scale factor, depending upon the units of measurement. It is not significant at the 5% level. The estimate of γ is highly significant.

(using the data of Table 8) does not appreciably increase the unexplained residual variation in output. No more positive result than this should be expected, as the conceptual and statistical difficulties of aggregation largely preclude analysis on this level.

To place the postwar trends in historical perspective, we can make use of the data on cultivated areas and labor from the various censuses beginning with the first census taken in 1903. Despite the many problems of comparability, it is possible to obtain indices of these quantities with a fair degree of consistency. The following table presents the indices constructed by Hooley from the censuses up to and including 1948,[47] to which have been spliced the data from Table 7 for labor and estimates of cultivated areas for three more recent years (the base year is 1902) :[48]

Year	Land	Labor	Land/labor
1902	100	100	100
1918	227	161	141
1938	340	256	133
1948	359	243	148
1955	496	331	150
1960	561	363	154
1968	678	472	144

Over nearly the entire period, land appears to have expanded at a considerably faster rate than the agricultural labor force. A rough calculation puts the average elasticity of cultivated area with respect to labor at about 1.4.[49] (For harvested area, it

[47] Richard W. Hooley, "Long Term Economic Growth in the Philippines, 1902–1961," in *Growth of Output in the Philippines,* ed. Hooley and Barker, p. 25.

[48] The postwar series for cultivated area is derived from Department of Agriculture and Natural Resources data (assembled by the International Rice Research Institute) on total crop area and second rice crop area, by assuming that the ratio of rice to other crops among second crops has remained approximately constant.

[49] A value for the elasticity of land with respect to labor greater than one can be explained by the necessity to cultivate larger areas of non-

Table 14. Philippine land/labor ratios by major region,
1954–1968 (harvested area per person in the
agricultural labor force [in hectares])

Year	Luzon (1)	Visayas (2)	Mindanao (3)	Philippines (4)
1954	n.a.	n.a.	n.a.	1.35
1955	n.a.	n.a.	n.a.	1.37
1956	1.30	1.41	1.77	1.42
1957	1.31	1.38	1.73	1.42
1958	1.23	1.14	1.93	1.35
1959	1.40	1.32	1.98	1.52
1960	1.27	1.37	2.16	1.48
1961	1.27	1.16	2.27	1.44
1962	1.56	1.13	2.21	1.36
1963	0.93	1.09	2.30	1.40
1964	1.09	1.07	2.13	1.39
1965	1.08	1.10	2.08	1.46
1966	1.10	1.09	1.92	1.37
1967	1.06	1.06	2.01	1.30
1968	1.08	1.08	1.92	1.32

Sources: Columns 1, 2, 3: 1956–1964, Raymundo E. Fonollera, "Labor and Land Resources in Philippine Agriculture: Trends and Projections" (paper presented to an International Rice Research Institute seminar, Los Baños, May 28, 1966); 1965–1968, unpublished Department of Agriculture and Natural Resources data on crop areas, and projected estimates of labor force. Column 4: Table 7 and Department of Agriculture and Natural Resources data on crop areas.

would be slightly higher.) At some time in the late 1950's or early 1960's the rate of expansion of cultivated area fell behind the growth rate of agricultural labor.

Labor intensification due to double cropping can account for some of this recent decline in the cultivated land/labor ratio, though not for the decline seen in Table 8 where the area data refer to harvested areas. Rising population densities have no necessary effect on the harvested area/labor ratio,

irrigated land on the extensive margin (less labor-intensive techniques are required for crops such as corn and upland rice than for wetland paddy), and by the changing composition of crops in established areas in favor of land-extensive commercial crops like sugar and coconuts. Only if crops were effectively homogeneous would its maximum be unity.

since investment in irrigation facilities on a sufficiently large scale could temporarily offset a declining trend. (As mentioned earlier, the Philippines is notable among countries of the region for the small proportion of its land presently devoted to multiple cropping.) Closer analysis of postwar changes suggests that the aggregate land/labor ratio obscures several underlying but mutually offsetting trends. If the data are broken down into the three broad geographical regions, Luzon, the Visayas, and Mindanao, it is seen that the regions exhibit similar but temporally displaced patterns, in each case a steady increase to a peak, followed by a decline. But in Luzon and the Visayas, harvested area per person in the agricultural labor force has been declining since at least the mid-1950's, while in Mindanao the peak was probably reached around 1963 (see Table 14 and Figure 6).

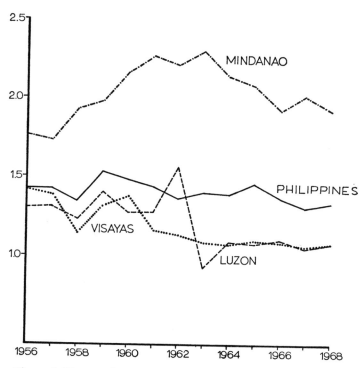

Figure 6. Harvested area per person in the agricultural labor force (in hectares)

Fonollera has further analyzed these changes, showing, for example, that the decline in area per person in Central Luzon
since 1959 has been partially offset by expansion in the Cagayan
Valley, and in Mindanao a decline had begun in the northern
and eastern region after 1960, although obscured in the aggregate ratio by a continued increase in the southwest.[50]

Unemployment and Underemployment

Before we may conclude that the Philippines has shown (at
least until the present decade) the characteristics of a land surplus economy, it is necessary to examine the situation from the
perspective of employment. It is possible that imperfections in
the labor market are such that a large degree of unemployment
in industry could exist side by side with virtually free land.
Ruprecht in particular has argued, and other writers have more
or less explicitly assumed, that the Philippines is a labor surplus
economy in the sense of Lewis or Fei and Ranis.[51] However,
while accepting the same basic data, we shall attempt to argue
that for certain purposes a different interpretation is both possible and useful.

The 1960 census indicated that the totally unemployed made
up 6.9 per cent of the (civilian) labor force. The rate for males
was 5.7 per cent, and for females 10.5 per cent.[52] The corre-

[50] Raymundo E. Fonollera, "Labor and Land Resources in Philippine
Agriculture: Trends and Projections" (paper presented to an International Rice Research Institute seminar, Los Baños, May 28, 1966).

[51] Theodore K. Ruprecht, "Labor Absorption Problems and Economic
Development in the Philippines," *Philippine Economic Journal*, 5 (1966),
289–312.

[52] The reference period is one week, and the minimum age ten years.
The same definition is used in the PSSH.

We shall not discuss the appropriateness of the actual concept of labor
force as applied to underdeveloped countries except for noting that it
would seem to us desirable to have a theory of labor utilization which is
not coextensive with one's theory of economic development; we believe
there is some point in identifying a "labor force" by the conventional
survey question technique even though the different attitudes to employ-

sponding rates obtained from the PSSH held in October 1960 (eight months after the census) were 6.3, 5.1, and 8.8 respectively. The differences are not serious enough to preclude using the detailed breakdowns from the PSSH, and are in fact within the range of seasonal variation. Rates derived from the May surveys are one or two percentage points higher than for October.

According to the PSSH, about half the unemployed were "experienced," meaning that they had previously held a full-time job for at least two consecutive weeks. Classifying these persons by the industry group in which they were most recently employed allows the calculation of industry unemployment rates. The results for one typical year (there is little appreciable trend over time), are given in Table 15. The construction industry, as could be expected, has a high level of unemployment, but on the basis of these data none of the other major industrial groups can be regarded as having a very serious unemployment problem—given the gross imperfections that must exist in the labor market. (The median time spent looking for work in the years covered by the PSSH ranged between seven and nine weeks, a surprisingly short period.) The argument for the Philippines being a labor surplus economy must therefore depend to a large extent on the numbers of persons who have never held a job and the magnitude of visible underemployment.

Despite the many objections to the procedure, it is usual to take forty hours per week as a norm for full employment, and treat as visibly underemployed those who both worked fewer hours and were seeking or would accept additional work in the

---

ment, seeking work, etc., vitiate the comparison with similar findings in advanced economies. Two approaches to the problem are represented by Myrdal and Dovring; our attitude is closer to Dovring's. Gunnar Myrdal, *Asian Drama: An Inquiry into the Poverty of Nations* (New York: Twentieth Century Fund, 1968), appendix 6; and Folke Dovring, "Underemployment in Traditional Agriculture," *Economic Development and Cultural Change*, 15 (1967), 163–173.

Table 15. Unemployment rates in the experienced labor force by sex and major industry group, Philippines, 1960 (in per cent)

Sector and industry group	Distribution of experienced labor force	Unemployment rates		
		Males	Females	Both sexes
Traditional sector	60.2	1.6	7.1	2.9
Modern sector	39.8	4.4	3.2	4.1
Manufacturing and extractive industries	(13.5)	3.2	2.9	3.0
Construction	(3.0)	12.6	*	12.5
Commerce	(8.9)	2.1	5.2	4.0
Transport and communications	(3.2)	4.3	*	4.2
Services and utilities	(11.2)	4.7	2.0	3.3
Total	100.0	2.7	4.9	3.4

Source: Philippine Statistical Survey of Households Bulletin, no. 8 (October 1960).
* Total too small for estimation.

survey reference period. With this definition, we can readily compute the number of fully unemployed workers which would be equivalent in terms of labor time to the visibly underemployed population. Combining these estimates with those of the totally unemployed obtained directly from the PSSH, gives what might be termed the "surplus labor pool." In the Philippines this pool varied between 9 and 12 per cent of the total employed labor force and between 20 and 27 per cent of modern sector employment in the period 1958–1967. No time trend was apparent in either case.[53]

Table 16. Characteristics of surplus labor in the Philippines, selected years, 1958–1967 (percentage distribution computed from data in fully unemployed equivalents)

Characteristic	1958	1960	1963	1965	1967
Male					
Unemployed	35	34	30	32	29
Experienced	(20)	(17)	(16)	(13)	(14)
Never worked	(15)	(17)	(14)	(19)	(15)
Underemployed in agriculture	16	16	18	12	11
Underemployed in nonagriculture	4	4	7	8	4
Female					
Unemployed	36	30	26	29	39
Experienced	(22)	(16)	(13)	(8)	(15)
Never worked	(14)	(14)	(13)	(21)	(24)
Underemployed in agriculture	5	10	9	8	13
Underemployed in nonagriculture	4	6	10	11	4
Total surplus	100	100	100	100	100

Source: Computed from Philippine Statistical Survey of Households, October rounds.

[53] Our procedure here is closely parallel to that of Ruprecht, who calculates a surplus labor index defined as the ratio of the number of equivalent fully unemployed nonagricultural workers plus the actual number of fully unemployed in agriculture, to the nonagricultural labor force. (Underemployed agricultural workers are excluded from the numerator on the

At a first glance an estimated proportion of surplus labor as high as these figures indicate would seem clearly to demonstrate the existence of an effectively unlimited supply. We saw, however, that the levels of full unemployment in the experienced labor force were not abnormally high and it is therefore worth analyzing the characteristics of the surplus labor pool with some care. Table 16 shows the breakdown between unemployed as against underemployed equivalents and experienced unemployed as against those who had never held a permanent job. The separation by sex is also given. The distributions are of interest for several reasons. First, the totally unemployed constitute about two thirds of the pool, so that visible underemployment is relatively of minor importance. The problem of "work expanding to fill the time available" of course arises here, but the proportions of the labor force in the occupations where such disguised unemployment is most likely—commerce and personal services—are not unduly large.[54] (The recorded level of underemployment may also to some extent reflect the consequences of administrative inefficiency, poor organization, and lack of information—resulting in an inability to make full use of presently employed labor—as well as being a surplus labor phenomenon.) Secondly, we see that women contribute about one-half of the total pool. It seems doubtful if these women could be drawn upon as fully as the male unemployed and it would be surprising if they were as active in seeking employment. This, however, cannot be demonstrated. More important is the distinction between experienced and inexperienced unemployed. A substantial (and for females apparently rising) proportion of the unemployed have never held a job for more

---

grounds that they are mostly seasonal workers who would not in fact be available for full employment in industry.) For the four years 1959–1962 this ratio is almost constant at 20%. Ruprecht, "Labor Absorption Problems."

[54] PSSH data for October 1960 estimate that the labor force shares in commerce and personal services (other than domestic) were respectively 8.9 and 2.2%. Domestic services accounted for 3.7%.

than two weeks. These are mainly young persons (35 per cent of the total unemployment recorded in the 1960 census was in the age group 10–19, a further 16 per cent in 20–24), and given the liberal attitude toward popular education in the Philippines, many are probably seeking white collar jobs. Where there is a lack of opportunities at such levels, they may prefer temporary unemployment to positions of lower status.

It is, of course, a relatively easy exercise to explain away each component of unemployment in this manner, and also a little unconvincing. The separate parts cannot be obliterated entirely, and the total remains significant. Hopefully we have demonstrated, however, that when factors such as the absence of a well-organized labor market, poor diffusion of information on job opportunities, and the comparative immobility of a traditional society are taken into account, even an apparent labor pool as large as we observe in the Philippines cannot be regarded as overwhelming evidence of unlimited labor. As it turns out, the question may be academic.[55]

Labor Absorption and Migration

From the labor force series assembled in Table 7 it was seen that the sectoral distribution of employment has changed only slightly in the postwar years. Since there is no reason to suppose a much lower natural increase in urban than in rural areas in presently underdeveloped countries, we may infer that intersectoral migration has also been relatively small. Thus the Philippines, in common with most of the underdeveloped world, has been absorbing the bulk of its population increase in rural

[55] For a clear statement of the view, to which we subscribe, that surplus labor is often better regarded as a phenomenon associated with modernization and industrialization (and a creation of these processes) than as a pre-existing situation which is to be remedied by development (even as it supports it, à la Nurkse), see W. Arthur Lewis, "Unemployment in Developing Areas," in *A Reappraisal of Economic Development: Perspectives for Cooperative Research,* ed. Andrew H. Whiteford (Chicago: Aldine, 1967), pp. 1–17.

areas.[56] Why should this have been so? The main factors which enter the explanation are on the one hand the determinants of the level of modern sector employment and on the other, the existence of surplus land.

The slow rate at which the modern sector has generated employment is a consequence of both technological and institutional features of the economy. We have seen, on the persuasive if less than conclusive evidence from manufacturing (Table 12), that the capital/labor ratio has apparently increased steadily by as much as 3 per cent annually over the 1950–1968 period. The census-based estimates prepared by Hooley allow us to see this recent trend in historical perspective. Hooley finds that the capital/labor ratio for manufacturing grew on average by 1 per cent per year between the first census of 1902 and 1961.[57] In the prewar decades this trend was evidently a result of factor substitution rather than technical progress, since total productivity in manufacturing showed a slight decline.[58] More recently, the indications are that labor-saving technical progress has had a more important if not a dominant effect; our data in Table 12 can be interpreted as showing a rise in total productivity since 1950, while the increase in the capital/labor

[56] To say this is not to ignore the existence of large numbers (relative to the *urban* population) of rural migrants in the major cities. The squatter settlements on the outskirts of Manila pose especially serious social and economic problems for that city and obviously have a high incidence of unemployment. Nevertheless, the rapid increase in urban population observed in the Philippines as in virtually all the under-developed countries is in a large part accounted for by urban natural increase rather than by rural-urban migration. See Kingsley Davis, *World Urbanization, 1950–1970* (Berkeley: University of California, Institute of International Studies, 1969–70), vol. 1, table C, and vol. 2.

[57] Hooley, "Long Term Economic Growth in the Philippines," p. 32. (An exception to this long-run upward trend was the sharp decline in the 1940's. Part of the rise observed after 1950 reflects the reconstruction of industrial plant to its prewar level.)

[58] *Ibid.* Hooley's index of total productivity was obtained by combining the values of the capital and labor inputs. There is admittedly much room for error in these estimates.

ratio took place despite an over-all fall in the price of labor relative to capital.[59] However, further substitution of capital for labor has also occurred. Sicat, in a study of the effects of the 1960–1962 devaluation on manufacturing, has computed the changes in labor productivity and changes in employment over 1962–1966 for each two-digit ISIC division (using the Central Bank indices of employment and physical production). He finds a highly significant negative correlation between gain in labor productivity and gain in employment. The largest productivity gain, for example, was 157 per cent, recorded for the category of electrical machinery—in which employment fell by 53 per cent.[60]

Many reasons have been adduced to explain the continuing substitution of capital for labor and/or the capital-using bias in technical progress in a relatively labor-abundant economy. Undoubtedly there are a number of contributing factors, some less real than others. Among the former may be mentioned the declining role of unorganized manufacturing establishments (those with less than five employees), which are presumably highly labor-intensive, other structural changes in the composition of the sector (for example, the rapid growth of petroleum refinery plant in the 1960's), and statistical errors in the valuation of capital. A largely unknown influence on the recorded capital/labor ratio are variations in the degree of capacity utilization. But probably more important than these effects are

[59] Using the series published in the Central Bank's *Statistical Bulletin* (December 1968), we can accept the wholesale price of imported machinery and transport equipment (p. 334, column 9) as a proxy for the price of capital goods and the index of money wages for unskilled workers in industry (p. 395) for wages. The price of capital relative to labor showed an initial decline in the early 1950's and approximate constancy for the rest of the decade. A sharp rise of some 40% accompanying the 1960–1962 decontrol was followed by a renewed slow decline. The average trend over 1950–1968 was a rise of 0.6% per year.

[60] Gerardo P. Sicat, "The Manufacturing Sector after Decontrol," mimeographed (Quezon City: University of the Philippines, School of Economics, 1967), p. 41.

the very real consequences of disequilibrium in factor prices. A complex of regulations involving exchange controls, import licensing, interest rates, and capital taxes has kept the price of capital well below its true scarcity value, at least until 1960, while minimum wage laws may have raised the market price of labor above its opportunity cost. Sicat has summarized these development policies:

Firstly, the belief was that in order to attract new industries, incentives for investment had to be given. An examination of the economic incentives in the Philippines which were adopted to assist the establishment of new industries shows that they have been tied largely towards cheapening the price of capital while . . . the legislature was busy enacting laws which raised the price of labor. The law on tax exemption of new and necessary industries, the basic industries act, the investment incentives act, interest rate policy, and foreign exchange rate policy (in the days of controls) had all added to the bias against labor-use in the Philippines.[61]

In a dualistic economy the opportunity cost of labor to the modern sector is governed in theory by the level of wages in traditional agriculture. In practice, the competitive assumptions underlying this statement are all but absent, and the situation is much less simple. We should first examine the wage data themselves.

Comparable data on wage rates in the two sectors are not directly available. The Central Bank compiles data on real wages of various skilled and unskilled workers in industrial establishments in Manila and suburbs, based on information for some 800 selected private firms. The lowest of these, wages of "common laborers," are given in the first column of Table 17. For agriculture, we have statistics on money wages for four categories of farm workers (plowmen, planters, harvesters, and common laborers) in nine geographical regions. As each of

[61] Gerardo P. Sicat, "Labor Policies and Philippine Economic Development," mimeographed (Quezon City: University of the Philippines, School of Economics, 1969), p. 26.

Table 17. Real daily wage rates in agriculture and industry,
Philippines, 1950–1968 (pesos, at 1955 prices)

Year	Industry* (1)	Agriculture† (2)	Year	Industry (1)	Agriculture (2)
1950	4.10	2.05	1960	4.74	2.28
1951	4.08	1.95	1961	4.78	2.24
1952	4.67	2.28	1962	4.65	2.19
1953	4.97	2.59	1963	4.64	2.23
1954	4.98	2.73	1964	4.33	n.a.
1955	5.18	2.75	1965	4.52	n.a.
1956	5.12	2.38	1966	4.57	n.a.
1957	4.98	2.39	1967	4.52	n.a.
1958	4.84	2.37	1968	5.02	n.a.
1959	4.93	2.33			

Sources: Column 1, Central Bank of the Philippines, Statistical Bulletin (December 1968), pp. 359, 364; column 2, DANR data from Central Bank Annual Reports (see text for method of adjustment).
* Common laborers in industrial establishments.
† Agricultural laborers (weighted average of farm wage rates adjusted for payments in kind).

these occupations is relatively unskilled and susceptible to unemployment, the average wage weighted by the numbers in each category is used. The series presented in column 2 of Table 17 comprises these data adjusted to allow for payment in kind—usually taken as two meals per day for each worker—and deflated to constant prices.[62]

The two most obvious features of Table 17 are the virtual constancy of the wages in both sectors over time and the large

[62] The adjustment for payment in kind is made by reference to the 1961 PSSH survey of family incomes (see Note 25 above). From table 16 of the survey report we can compute the ratio of wages in cash to wages not in cash paid to workers in the agricultural sector. It indicates that some 78% of total wages are in cash and 22% in kind. Thus, the cash wage can be inflated by the factor 100/78 = 1.28. To convert the money wage series to 1955 prices, a composite index was formed consisting of the consumer price index for regions outside Manila (available since 1957) spliced to the Manila price index for domestic consumer goods for the period 1950–1957.

intersectoral differential. The constancy of the modern sector wage has sometimes been adduced as evidence of a perfectly elastic supply of labor.[63] The existence of a minimum wage law in the Philippines, however, somewhat blunts this interpretation. Nevertheless, we would argue that the wage levels in the least organized parts of the modern sector are determined by corresponding agricultural wages. (The latter are constant as a result of stable labor productivity—itself a consequence of the land surplus combined with negligible technical progress.)

The gradation of wage levels within manufacturing is seen clearly in the wage data derived from the 1961 economic census.[64] Average payrolls per paid employee can be computed from this source for both large establishments (ten or more workers) and small establishments (fewer than ten), and making the rough assumption of 300 working days per year we can find the equivalent average daily wage, as follows:

	Large establishments	Small establishments	Total
Total payrolls (₱1000)	507,258	36,094	543,352
Number of paid employees	258,088	43,328	301,416
Average income per employee(₱)	1,965	833	1,803
Equivalent average daily wage (₱)	6.55	2.78	6.01
Real average daily wage (₱ at 1955 prices)	5.79	2.46	5.31

Differences between large and small establishments are very substantial.[65] Moreover, the 1961 average wage in small establish-

[63] See, for example, Gerardo P. Sicat, "Analytical Aspects of Two Current Economic Policies," *Philippine Economic Journal*, 4 (1965), 113.

[64] Bureau of the Census and Statistics, *Economic Census of the Philippines, 1961*, vol. 3.

[65] This finding is confirmed by the wage data implicit in the Annual Survey of Manufactures payroll figures. Establishments employing more than twenty persons showed average daily wages, in 1955 prices, of ₱6.0–6.5 over the period 1956–1966; those employing 5–19 workers, ₱3.1–4.0.

There is evidence that the 1961 economic census seriously undercovered small establishments, so that the weighted average wage in the above table

ments (at 1955 prices), ₱2.46, is remarkably close to the corresponding agricultural wage which we estimated in Table 17 to be ₱2.24.

Part of the wage differentials we have observed can be explained by differences in the cost of living between urban and rural areas. Little information is available on this point as most price statistics are gathered in urban areas. Retail food prices are generally higher in Manila than in provincial cities, although it is notable that the price of rice is often lower.[66] Probably of more significance is the effect on industrial wage levels of the minimum wage law and other modern labor legislation. The legal minimum wage for nonagricultural workers was ₱4 from 1951 to 1965, and increased to ₱6 in April of that year. It may be supposed that compliance with the law was more complete for large establishments from among which the Central Bank draws its wage data.[67] Other legislation embodying welfare policies which may have effectively raised the price of labor include the recognition of collective bargaining between unions and management (1953), the establishment of a social security

---

is overstated. The October 1961 PSSH household survey shows a total of 487,700 wage and salary workers in manufacturing (excluding self-employed and unpaid family workers), compared to the 301,416 recorded in the census of manufacturing establishments. It is reasonable to suppose that most of the disparity is due to underrecording of small establishments (in particular, household industries) in the census. If this is the case, and payrolls per worker in the unrecorded industries are similar to those in small establishments (a "high" assumption), then the average daily wage in 1955 prices would be reduced from ₱5.31 to ₱4.22.

[66] See the data published in the early issues of the Bureau of the Census and Statistics' *Journal of Philippine Statistics*.

[67] The law strictly applies also to agricultural workers on farms of over 12 hectares, although with lower set minimums. (This size restriction justifies our ignoring the effect of the law on the traditional sector.) Sicat cites a 1965 labor force survey in Manila which indicates that over 40% of employed workers were receiving incomes below the legal minimum. Evidence from the PSSH income surveys supports this finding. Sicat, "Labor Policies and Philippine Economic Development," pp. 8–11.

system (1954) , and the creation of a forty-hour week (1957) .[68]

The picture of the labor market which emerges from this brief discussion is one in which there is no sharp distinction between the traditional and modern sectors. Rather, the former agricultural laborer who turns his hand to small-scale manufacturing can initially expect only marginally increased wages. It is only in the more organized parts of the sector that wages are appreciably higher, and even here higher living costs may partly vitiate the increase. Manufacturing, of course, is not the whole modern sector, but in most other parts of it median wages are approximately the same.[69] The extent to which industrial labor absorption has been slowed because of specific policies distorting factor prices is impossible to quantify with the data available. We noted above, however, that the level of agricultural wages has remained constant in the virtual absence of technical change mainly through expansion of cultivated area. It is possible to say, therefore, that the effect of the failure of the modern sector to generate very much employment has been mitigated to a large degree by the availability of surplus land.

We can illustrate this latter proposition by looking at the postwar redistribution of population, separating rural-urban migration from migration to frontier areas. Since the frontier can only be delimited geographically, this migratory flow will underestimate the numbers of people absorbed by expansion in *harvested* area. The major regions of outmigration in the Philippines are the Central Plain of Luzon (the most important rice growing area) , the Ilocos coast in northwestern Luzon,

[68] *Ibid.,* pp. 4–5.

[69] This is true, for example, of construction, transportation, commerce, and services other than government and domestic services. Government services have a higher median wage, and for domestic services no meaningful estimate is possible. See PSSH *Bulletin,* no. 3, October 1956 to October 1957. (Note that such comparisons can be made only from sex-specific data, due to the wide differences in wage levels for males and females. The average wage recorded in column 4 of Table 10 shows somewhat more variability.)

and parts of the Visayan islands—notably the small and severely eroded island of Cebu. To obtain a rough estimate of the extent of outmigration in recent years we can apply the average 1948–1960 rate of increase of the whole population to these regions in 1948 and compare the resulting "expected" populations in 1960 with those actually enumerated in the census.[70] The results are seen in the second row of Table 18. The Central Plain seems to have absorbed three-quarters of its intercensal natural increase, while the Ilocos provinces and the Visayas have absorbed less than half. (This is consistent with what is known of the labor absorption possibilities in wet-rice agriculture, since Central Luzon has the highest proportion of irrigated land.)

The destination of the outmigrants can be estimated from the 1960 census data on birthplace. It can be shown, with the same assumption of uniform natural increase used above, that most of the outborn enumerated in 1960 are postwar migrants.[71] Making a simple and somewhat crude division between industrial and frontier areas we obtain the distributions given in the lower half of Table 18. Metropolitan Manila and its important contiguous provinces are not the only areas of significant nonagricultural employment, but together they include about 60 per cent of total modern sector employment and produce over 65 per cent of its value added.[72] On the other hand, almost all the extensive regions of arable land brought under cultivation since the war have been in the Cagayan Valley (northern Luzon) and Mindanao.

The resulting distributions are of some interest, if not unexpected. Of the relatively small proportion of migrants from Central Luzon, nearly twice as many persons have been drawn

---

[70] The many refinements possible in this technique are not essential for our present purpose. In particular, we disregard the small number of inmigrants to these regions.

[71] See Frederick L. Wernstedt and P. D. Simkins, "Migrations and the Settlement of Mindanao," *Journal of Asian Studies,* 25 (1965), 95.

[72] Calculated from the 1961 economic census.

Table 18. Characteristics of postwar interregional
migration in the Philippines

Population and number and destination of outmigrants	Major regions of outmigration			
	Central Plain of Luzon*	Ilocos coast†	Central Visayas‡	Other Visayas§
Population in 1960 (thousands)	3,332	919	2,523	5,587
Number of outmigrants, 1948–1960 (thousands)	249	159	463	950
Outmigrants as percentage of 1948–1960 natural increase	24.0	50.8	53.5	52.9
Distribution of outmigrants by residence in 1960 (%)				
In industrial areas‖	54.4	37.5	6.6	29.3
In frontier areas	28.1	33.4	79.6	54.4
Cagayan Valley#	(16.9)	(20.7)	(0.1)	(0.2)
Mindanao	(11.2)	(12.7)	(79.5)	(54.2)
Elsewhere	17.5	29.1	13.8	16.3
Total	100.0	100.0	100.0	100.0

Source: Basic data from Census of the Philippines, 1960: Population and Housing, vol. 2 and appendix.
* Bulacan, Nueva Ecija, Pampanga, Pangasinan, Tarlac.
† Ilocos Norte, Ilocos Sur, La Union.
‡ Bohol, Cebu, Negros Oriental.
§ Excluding Masbate province.
‖ Manila, Cavite, Laguna, Rizal.
Cagayan, Isabela, Nueva Vizcaya.

to the nonagricultural opportunities of the industrial areas as have moved to the extensive margin of agriculture. In contrast, Visayan migrants have shown an opposite proclivity with the majority moving to the land frontier of Mindanao. Migrants from Ilocos are found about equally in industrial and frontier areas. Without invoking any elaborate sociological or historical reasons for these large differences, the immediate explanation that suggests itself is the classic notion of the "friction of space." Central Luzon is much closer to Manila and Rizal than is Cebu. The migrants who move to the cities in search of jobs are to this extent taking fewer risks, and often may have received prior information on the opportunities available. Similar reasoning can explain the observed difference between the Central Visayas and other islands in that region, although here the institutionalization of the migratory flow to Mindanao must also be taken into account.

It is worth our summarizing the main points of the present section, in which we have looked at the facts of Philippine land and labor supplies and their utilization. We began by showing that the over-all land/labor ratio has remained approximately constant in the postwar period, while closer analysis reveals the start of a declining trend in several major regions of the country. The conventional measures of unemployment and underemployment do not seem to indicate an exceptionally serious problem, despite the fact that modern sector employment has increased at a rate of only 1.2 percentage points above the natural increase of the population itself. The explanation for the poor performance of the modern sector in generating employment we saw in terms of a combination of protective policies to encourage (and cheapen) investment in capital equipment and welfare-oriented labor policies. Together, these have served to encourage substitution of capital for labor and the use of capital-intensive technologies.[73] Finally, an examination of population movements in the 1948–1960 intercensal period shows the largest migrations being directed toward the frontier lands of Mindanao and the Cagayan Valley. While the factor of distance (or some more sophisticated measure of difficulty of access) is apparently an important determinant of the destination of migrants, it seems clear that the existence of an open land frontier has acted to alleviate the pressures which tend to stimulate rural-urban migration. An alternative,

---

[73] The elasticity of substitution between capital and labor is obviously of critical importance in distinguishing between movements in and movements along the production isoquant. We discuss the difficult estimation problems involved in the following section.

perhaps more secure than the vagaries of city life, is offered the potential migrant. Less certainly, it may also explain the constancy of real wages in agriculture and, by implication, in the small-scale industries at the sectoral interface.

One conclusion that we may draw from this discussion concerns the dependence of any description of an economy in terms of its land or labor surplus upon the particular perspective adopted. If our emphasis is on modern sector growth by means of a labor transfer, without postulating a low rate of transformation between consumer manufactures and investment goods as a basic constraint on the system, then an economy such as that of the Philippines can be usefully described according to the labor surplus models. The industries of Manila can draw on labor pools in Central Luzon which are surely surplus in any but a strict, *ceteris paribus* sense. If, however, we accept capital specificity and see the capital-using bias in technical change as a perhaps unfortunate but strongly entrenched mode of development in industry, then agriculture comes to be viewed as a quasi-capital goods sector and the significance of export growth directs attention to the factor of land. With this emphasis, which characterizes the present study, the Philippines is, and for a limited time will remain, a land surplus economy.

TRADITIONAL SECTOR RESPONSES

In the dualistic framework we have been using in this study there are three important output variables in the traditional sector. These are the sectoral output, the total agricultural surplus (i.e., the surplus over local sectoral food consumption), and the net exportable surplus (over total domestic food consumption). Among the many questions which arise in moving from a conceptual to an operational analysis of agriculture, perhaps the most crucial concern the levels of the various supply and demand elasticities associated with these quantities. Although we shall often not be able to reach firm conclusions on the significance of price and income effects in the Philippine case, the available evidence does indicate the likely patterns.

Changes in product prices can influence agricultural production through their effect on crop areas or on yields. Various studies have demonstrated that changes in the relative hectarage devoted to different crops can be explained as responses to changes in the price of one crop relative to its major competitor or to all alternative crops. Mangahas, Recto, and Ruttan have estimated price elasticities with respect to hectarage for rice and corn by regression of harvested area on various lagged relative price indices.[74] Their results for the decade 1953–1954 to 1963–1964, although not significant at the conventional levels, indicate that elasticities are greater in areas with strong commercial markets or (for rice) a high proportion of irrigated land.[75] The overall shift from food crops to export crops which has taken place since 1960 appears to be a direct consequence of the increased export crop profitability caused by the exchange decontrol measures of 1960–1962. Treadgold and Hooley show a strong linear relationship between the proportion of crop area devoted to commercial crops and a lagged moving average of the relative wholesale price of export products compared to domestic consumption products. Almost 82 per cent of the variability in the relative share of commerical crops can be accounted for by the price changes.[76]

While there is thus fairly conclusive evidence of the effect of price on hectarage allocation between crops, any similar price effect on total agricultural output has yet to be demonstrated. Mangahas could find no measurable yield response to price for rice or corn,[77] and similar negative results have been obtained in

[74] Mahar Mangahas, Aida E. Recto, and Vernon W. Ruttan, "Market Relationships for Rice and Corn in the Philippines," *Philippine Economic Journal*, 5 (1966), 1–27.

[75] *Ibid.*, p. 18.

[76] Malcolm Treadgold and Richard W. Hooley, "Decontrol and the Redirection of Income Flows: A Second Look," *Philippine Economic Journal*, 6 (1967), 109–128.

[77] Mangahas, Recto, and Ruttan, "Market Relationships for Rice and Corn," p. 26. Note, however, that price may have an indirect adverse in-

other countries of Southeast Asia.[78] Of the important Philippine commercial crops, only sugar cane can possibly be adduced as an example of price-responsive yield increases. We can therefore find little support for the type of "technology adjustment mechanism" postulated by Fei and Ranis, by which agricultural innovation intensity can be made a function of the relative price of output.[79] Total harvested area, as we have seen, has apparently expanded more or less regularly in response to population growth rather than to any price changes. This limited evidence would thus suggest that, although the composition of agricultural output may vary considerably, aggregate output is relatively price inelastic.

Turning next to the total and exportable agricultural surpluses, we find a much more complex situation. Relevant behavioral factors determining the size of these surpluses include the price and income elasticities of demand for food both by the producers and by the modern sector. If we look simply at the past trends in food consumption in the Philippines there is little doubt that per capita consumption has remained fairly constant over a long period in the face of significant changes in real income and in the relative price of foodstuffs. Two studies may be cited, both based on the disappearance method.[80] Golay and Goodstein have computed the apparent per capita absorption of cereals (milled rice, milled corn, and wheat flour, combined by weight) over the entire period since 1910.[81] Their

---

fluence on yield because of the negative association between hectarage and yield. We discuss this further in Chapter 4.

[78] Randolph Barker, "The Response of Production to a Change in Rice Price," *Philippine Economic Journal*, 5 (1966), 265.

[79] John C. H. Fei and Gustav Ranis, "Agrarianism, Dualism, and Economic Development," in *The Theory and Design of Economic Development*, ed. Irma Adelman and Eric Thorbecke (Baltimore: The Johns Hopkins Press, 1966), p. 34.

[80] I.e., estimation of consumption as production plus imports less exports less net additions to inventories less allowances for losses and alternative uses.

[81] Golay and Goodstein, *Rice and People in 1990*, pp. 24–32. Weight-for-weight, the caloric content of these three cereals is almost identical.

results are summarized in Table 19. In the postwar period particularly, the annual data show remarkable stability with the single exception of 1965, an election year, in which there was a large importation of rice.[82] This picture is reinforced by data for 1955–1964 from the Program Implementation Agency's

Table 19. Apparent per capita direct absorption of
cereals,* Philippines, 1910–1965
(five-year averages; index 1951–1955 = 100)

Period	Index	Period	Index
1910–1914	88.8	1935–1939	97.5
1915–1919	102.1	1947–1950	92.0
1920–1924	118.3	1951–1955	100.0
1925–1929	121.4	1956–1960	102.1
1930–1934	105.3	1961–1965	104.4

Source: Based on data in Golay and Goodstein, *Rice and People in 1990*, p. 55.
* Milled rice, milled corn equivalent, and wheat flour equivalent.

series of national accounts, quoted in an unpublished paper by Williamson. When expressed in constant prices, apparent per capita expenditures on food show almost no change over this decade although total per capita consumption expenditures rose by an average of 1 per cent per year.[83]

[82] A rather surprising finding in the Golay and Goodstein study is that per capita consumption of cereals is some 5–10% below the recommended annual nutritional requirement of 120 kg. per year. This observation perhaps raises some doubt as to the accuracy of the absolute levels of consumption estimated from the supply side, although not necessarily affecting year-to-year comparisons. An independent estimate of rice and corn absorption from the consumption side in 1960 gave a result of 148 kg. for per capita consumption of these two cereals alone. (Computed from PSSH October 1960 data for direct consumption in one week in October.)

[83] Jeffrey G. Williamson, "Consumption Patterns in the Philippines, 1955–1964," mimeographed (Quezon City: University of the Philippines, School of Economics, 1967). The national accounts prepared by the Program Implementation Agency in Manila diverge in many respects from

A comparison of the three PSSH family income and expenditure surveys, taken in 1957, 1961, and 1965, tends to give a contrary impression on this important issue. In real terms, these data indicate that mean family income increased at an average annual rate of 2.8 per cent over 1957–1965 while family expenditure on food grew at twice this rate.[84] A possible explanation for this anomalous result is increased consumption of higher priced, processed food items, for which the income elasticity of demand may be supposed to be quite high. Rises in median expenditures on food are probably much lower than average expenditures. It is more likely, however, that faults in the surveys themselves either in coverage or in respondent errors—especially in the earliest survey—effectively preclude their use to show changes over time.[85]

Constancy of food consumption in itself says little about the price or income elasticity of demand for food nor of the price elasticity of home consumption of food producers. On the last mentioned, nothing is known in the Philippines. Mangahas, Recto, and Ruttan suppose it to be negative but small enough to be ignored, and hence conclude that it is possible to estimate the elasticity of the marketed surplus by simply raising the output elasticity by a constant factor, the inverse of the average proportion of output which is marketed.[86] As we discussed

the NEC series, but give useful critiques of a number of statistical series. They remain unpublished.

[84] Computed from PSSH *Bulletins,* nos. 4 and 14, and *Journal of Philippine Statistics,* 19, no. 2 (1968), xx–xxii. Within each survey, the data show the expected inverse relation between family expenditure and the proportion of it spent on food items.

[85] A household survey of metropolitan Manila held by the Central Bank in 1954 is consistent with the 1961 PSSH but strongly in conflict with the 1957 results. Food expenditures in Manila averaged 43.7% of total expenditures in 1954 and 42.3% in 1961; for cereals the proportions were 13.1% and 10.8%. Central Bank of the Philippines, *Annual Report, 1954* (Manila, 1955), p. 23.

[86] Mangahas, Recto, and Ruttan, "Market Relationships for Rice and Corn," p. 20.

previously, there is no evidence to suggest that yield elasticities are of much significance. If it could be assumed that they are both small and non-negative, then the elasticity of cultivated area might be used as a proxy (and a lower bound) for the elasticity of output. Following this reasoning, Mangahas has derived the surplus elasticities for rice and corn with respect to expected price. The results suggest high elasticities for corn in the Visayas and Southern Tagalog. For rice, these regions stand out less clearly and are joined by Central Luzon and Bicol. However, the legitimacy of this method is open to question. Barker has criticized the relationship assumed between output elasticity and hectarage elasticity on the valid grounds that yields and hectarage are inversely correlated.[87] Changes in hectarage for any established crop usually take place on the margins of the crop land where yields tend to be lower than average. The results are therefore inconclusive. Mears and Barker comment, for the case of rice: "The empirical evidence either for or against a positively sloping [supply] function for marketed surplus is not convincing. It may well be that the slope changes, being positive over some price levels and negative over others."[88]

We might argue from the above discussion that an assumption of zero price elasticity of supply for the total agricultural surplus would not be unreasonable. It is another question, however, when we consider the exported surplus. In the latter case, the price and income elasticities of demand for food are of crucial importance. Various estimates of these elasticities exist. An FAO estimate of income elasticity based on the period 1950–1960 is 0.75. Williamson, using the Program Implementation Agency data for 1955–1964 mentioned above, obtains an income elasticity of demand for food of 0.95 and price elasticity

[87] Barker, "Response of Production," p. 268. (See also the discussion of agricultural productivity in Chapter 4.)
[88] Leon Mears and Randolph Barker, "Effects of Rice Price Policy on Growth of the Philippine Economy: An Analytical Framework" in *Growth of Output in the Philippines,* ed. Hooley and Barker, p. 28.

of -0.6137.[89] The former estimate may be inflated in terms of quantity changes insofar as increased expenditure on foodstuffs is directed towards higher quality items. Two studies of the income elasticity of demand for cereals concluded that it was very low or negative for rice and negative for corn. Only for wheat flour was a positive elasticity found.[90] Unfortunately, these results are based on absorption data similar to those quoted above and so are not independent estimates. We would nevertheless expect that, at least in quantity terms, the income effect on demand for traditional sector output of food crops would be quite small. Moreover, if the intersectoral terms of trade are moving against the modern sector (as they have been), a negative price elasticity would further retard the growth of modern sector demand for this output.[91]

INVESTMENT AND IMPORT DEPENDENCE

We have previously looked at the domestic intersectoral relationships in the Philippines, particularly those which involve labor flows and employment levels. Implicit in much of that discussion was the assumption that, from the viewpoint of the modern sector, labor could be regarded as a dependent variable. Our emphasis was on how industrial growth generated employ-

---

[89] These, and the FAO estimate, are given in Williamson, "Consumption Patterns in the Philippines," pp. 16, 18–19.

[90] U.S. Department of Agriculture, Economic Research Service, *The Philippines: Long-Term Projection of Supply and Demand for Selected Agricultural Products* (Jerusalem: Israel Program for Scientific Translations, 1962?) p. 96; and H. L. Cook *et al., Long Range Requirements for Selected Foods in the Philippines* (Manila: International Cooperation Administration, 1957), p. 18; cited by Golay and Goodstein, *Rice and People in 1990*, p. 30.

[91] It is likely, however, that the demand for cereals is relatively price inelastic (as well as income inelastic) and hence that a reduction in demand for traditional sector cereal output could take place only if cereal imports (such as wheat flour) were available at lower prices. On demand elasticities for rice, see Mears and Barker, "Effects of Rice Price Policy," pp. 30–32.

ment rather than the converse. To complete our analysis according to the structure identified in Figure 3, therefore, it remains to examine the foreign sector flows and their impact on the modern sector. Our focus now will be the extent to which growth in the modern sector is constrained by its import capacity—and thus in part by the level of traditional exports and by the sectoral allocation of the labor force which largely determines the size of the agricultural surplus.

Export Dependence of Imports

As a first, intermediate step we should examine the degree of dependence of imports upon exports. It is a simple identity that imports in any given period are equal to exports plus net invisible earnings minus the net increase in reserves. Philippine international reserves have not shown any very significant long-run changes. The major shift was from 1950 to 1957 when reserves fell almost continuously from U.S. $356 million to $140 million.[92] The average annual decline in reserves over this period was about 7 per cent of the average value of exports. Since 1957, reserves have fluctuated from year to year about a mean of approximately $140 million. Changes in net invisible earnings have generally been much larger than changes in reserves, but also with no marked secular trend. Both invisible earnings and invisible payments have tended to grow with the volume of trade while showing substantial short-run fluctuations. Over the three-year period 1950–1952, net invisible earnings averaged 27 per cent of exports; during 1966–1968, 25 per cent.[93]

The invisibles account has in most years shown a positive balance, with the striking exception of 1963 when net invisible

[92] Central Bank of the Philippines, *Twentieth Annual Report, 1968* (Manila, 1969), p. 68.
[93] Central Bank of the Philippines, *Statistical Bulletin* (December 1968), pp. 155–156. Invisible earnings include gold, U.S. government expenditures (such as military spending and payments to Filipino war veterans), and war reparations from Japan.

106   Trade and Growth in the Philippines

payments of $114 million were recorded. This apparent deficit is almost entirely illusory, however, as it is accounted for by the massive underrecording of merchandise imports for that year.[94] Because changes in international reserves have been relatively small compared to the volume of trade, we would expect that after adjusting for recording errors in the data there would be a close correlation between merchandise exports and merchandise imports. The series presented in the last columns of Tables 5

Table 20. The financing of Philippine imports, 1951–1967 *

Year	Exports as percentage of imports	Year	Exports as percentage of imports
1951	79.0	1960	90.2
1952	79.1	1961	96.7
1953	78.1	1962	99.6
1954	74.8	1963	101.9
1955	80.0	1964	95.8
1956	78.3	1965	93.8
1957	79.5	1966	84.5
1958	79.3	1967	76.0
1959	87.8		

Source: Tables 5 and 6.
* Computed from constant price export and import series expressed as three-year moving averages.

and 6 above incorporate these error adjustments, and the results for exports as a percentage of imports are given in Table 20.

From this table it is seen that through most of the 1950's, exports financed about 80 per cent of imports. Most of the balance reflects net invisible earnings, especially the large United States

[94] Invisibles are estimated as a residual and therefore include all errors and omissions. As can be seen from Table 4 above, we estimated recorded imports in 1963 to be only 82.9% of actual imports. This discrepancy is equal to $127.7 million, which more than offsets the apparent loss on invisibles.

government expenditures in the early postwar years. In the early 1960's, merchandise trade was approximately in balance, with a large deficit appearing again in 1967 and 1968. There is little to suggest that the Philippines is likely to be able to increase her invisible earnings relative to merchandise trade on any sustained basis in the near future. The major receipts that have in the past provided the favorable balance of invisibles are U.S. payments to war veterans, foreign loans and private foreign investment, war reparations, and short term capital movements. All of these, together with U.S. military procurements, helped to finance the exceptionally high level of imports in 1967–1968. However, with the likely decline in U.S. military expenditures, a general trend unfavorable to foreign aid, and a phasing out of war reparations and veterans payments, it may become increasingly difficult for the Philippines to maintain a favorable invisibles balance and thus a very high share of imports will probably have to be financed by exports.

A balance of payments problem would of course be aggravated by any significant deterioration in the foreign terms of trade. So far in the postwar years, the Philippines has not suffered very greatly in this respect, although the practice of using price indices based on the untypically high levels of the Korean War years sometimes makes it appear so. This, indeed, has been the experience of most other countries of the region: a secular decline in the prices of certain agricultural exports has been more or less offset by improved extractive industry prices. (The possibility of large rice surpluses in the future, however, gives cause for worry to the major rice exporting countries.) The result for the Philippines has been a slow deterioration in the terms of trade, averaging 1.2 per cent annually over 1950–1968 or 0.7 per cent over 1955–1968.

We have earlier observed, from the data given in Table 6 above, the rapid postwar shift in the composition of imports from predominantly consumer goods to predominantly capital goods and related raw materials. This substitution enabled capital goods imports to rise at an average annual rate of 9.1

per cent, while total imports increased at 5.6 per cent. The rate of decline in the proportion of consumer goods in total imports has been diminishing, however, and was close to zero in the 1960's. This fact could be interpreted to suggest either that the process of import substitution for consumer goods is slowing or that fewer capital goods imports are required—for example, because of the growth of a domestic capital goods industry. The evidence we review in the discussion of import dependence below, although not conclusive, suggests that the latter is not the case in the Philippines.

It is not possible on the basis of the available data to make any definite statement on the potential for further import substitution in the future. The import data in Table 6 disguise an important shift from finished consumer goods to intermediate inputs for domestic manufacture: in the mid-1960's, finished goods (excluding food) made up only a quarter of the total, compared with two-thirds in the early fifties. But it is quite likely that further reduction in this proportion would be difficult. Sicat has computed the 1953–1963 income elasticities of import demand for detailed commodity divisions and shows very clearly the wide variability between different consumer items.[95] The considerable inequality in income distribution, which as we noted above even seems to be increasing, may do much to maintain a demand for luxury finished imports. Continued import substitution by backward integration of existing industries, while undoubtedly possible, may prove to be extremely inefficient. This question, however, is more one of industrialization policy, the course of which it would be hazardous to predict.

Import Dependence of Investment

From the arguments of the preceding paragraphs we may reasonably conclude that, at least in the decade of the 1960's

[95] Gerardo P. Sicat, "Notes on Import Demand in the Philippines," mimeographed (Quezon City: University of the Philippines, School of Economics, 1967).

and very likely in the future, there is a high degree of dependence of capital goods imports on the level of total exports. Foreign exchange reserves and invisibles serve to cushion this relationship on a year-to-year basis without affecting its operation in the longer run. The next and crucial stage in our analysis concerns the connection between capital goods imports and total domestic capital formation. Unfortunately this is statistically a very muddy area.

Data on total imports of durable equipment can be assumed to be quite reliable but less so in the case of domestic production.[96] The NEC estimates of gross capital formation in durable equipment are derived from c.i.f. import values marked up 50 per cent, and Central Bank data on domestic output marked up 25 per cent. Of the total supplies of durable equipment at purchasers' prices thus obtained, a fixed proportion is assumed to be investment goods.[97] This procedure does not permit us to disaggregate the investment data into its imported and locally produced components. However, it is possible to use these NEC mark-ups to estimate the import content of output for complete industry groups. For 1961, taking the value added data from the economic census, we obtain the following results for industry groups with large components of capital goods in their output: basic metal products, 75 per cent; machinery other than electric, 91 per cent; electric machinery, apparatus, and appliances, 73 per cent; transport equipment, 84 per cent.[98]

These estimates are of course subject to a high margin of error, but the pattern they indicate is clear. Support for the high value of the import content of investment in durable equipment is provided by Levy, who on the basis of a much more detailed acquaintance with the data, puts the value of investment in locally produced equipment (mostly transporta-

[96] Levy, "Interim Report," p. 26.   [97] *Ibid.*
[98] The 1961 Central Bank import data (in U.S. dollars) were converted o pesos at the rate ₱4.00 = $1.00.

tion equipment and agricultural machinery) at about 10 per cent of the total in the early 1960's.[99]

As a rough means of observing the time trend in the import content proportion we can compute indices of imports and

Table 21. Indices of imports and domestic production of durable equipment, Philippines, 1955–1967 (three-year moving averages, 1954/1956 = 100)

Year	Domestic production* (1)	Imports[†] (2)	Domestic production/ imports (1) ÷ (2)
1955	100	100	100
1956	116	119	97
1957	129	123	105
1958	137	123	111
1959	140	126	111
1960	152	140	108
1961	165	142	116
1962	185	142	130
1963	203	149	136
1964	219	167	131
1965	233	181	129
1966	244	208	117
1967	260	239	108

Sources: Column 1, Central Bank of the Philippines, *Statistical Bulletin* (December 1968), pp. 293–294; column 2, from the sources given for Table 6 above.
* Physical production.
† Valued at 1955 prices.

domestic production of durable equipment. Table 21 assembles these series: domestic production is based on the Central Bank's indices of physical production of durable equipment (available only since 1955), while the import series is obtained directly from the ECAFE data underlying Table 6. It is ap-

[99] Levy, "Interim Report," p. 25.

parent that there is little evidence here of an over-all decline in the import content over the period 1955–1967.[100]

Investment in durable equipment is of course only a part of total gross investment. If we make use of the NEC estimates of gross domestic capital formation and extend our definition of investment goods imports to cover not only durable equipment but also related intermediate goods (i.e., the classification used in Table 6), it is possible to compute an aggregate import content of investment. This ratio, although not very stable, has averaged about 65 per cent over the period 1950–1968 and shows no systematic trend. On average, investment goods imports have increased at 9.1 per cent per year, gross investment in 1955 prices at 8.5 per cent. We would stress, however, our reservations on using this technique to evaluate the degree of import dependence in an economy. A cursory acquaintance with the usual methods of deriving national accounts estimates of investment would argue for the greatest caution in drawing conclusions from these data, while the complex problems of lags, markups, inventories and vagaries of pricing all help to obscure whatever direct linkage exists between imports and capital formation. The more satisfactory approach to the question is to actually look at what investment goods are produced domestically in the most significant categories. For this reason we put more store in the observation by Levy, noted above, than in findings based on aggregate import and investment series.[101]

---

[100] An interesting distinction obscured in the data presented in Table 21 is that between investment in fixed assets and additions to inventory. There is some suggestion that imported inputs into the manufacturing sector have been growing faster than manufacturing value added. The proportion of gross output contributed by value added has shown a steady decline from 44% in 1956 to 38% in 1966 (computed from *Annual Survey of Manufactures* data), although this may at least partly be due to rising relative prices of inputs. The decline is more marked for heavy industry, i.e., the later ISIC divisions.

[101] Following this line of reasoning, the arguments and evidence (international cross-section correlations) offered by David Wall, "Import Ca-

Investment Function

Thus far we have not considered the determinants of capital goods imports from the side of demand. While realized (*ex post*) investment may be constrained by the level of exports, the propensity to invest is largely a behavioral characteristic of the individual entrepreneur. Such individual *ex ante* investment decisions are reconciled with the availability of foreign exchange by changes in the price of capital goods. Further flexibility (and complexity) is introduced by the possibilities for varying the composition of imports between capital goods and consumer goods.

The only substantial study of investment functions in the Philippines is that by Hooley and Sicat for the manufacturing sector.[102] Using 1961–1962 data, derived from a stratified sample of some 200 firms, they attempt to fit a number of linear, logarithmic, and ratio-type investment models. The explanatory variables considered are net profits, sales (current and past), retained earnings, capital stock, and depreciation. Regressions were carried out for firms classified by size of assets and by industry group as well as for the pooled data. The results of most interest for the purposes of the present study pertain to the linear model. In fitting the function:

$$I(t) = a_0 + a_1 P(t) + a_2 K(t-1)$$

---

pacity, Imports and Economic Growth," *Economica*, 35 (1968), 157–168, for the absence of an import constraint on growth in underdeveloped countries are not convincing when applied to the Philippines—and perhaps for other countries also when the data are examined critically and on a less aggregated level. Regression of domestic fixed capital formation on imports of capital goods (and thence on import capacity) should at least be based on one-country time series data, and here the results of Alfred Maizels, *Exports and Economic Growth of Developing Countries* (Cambridge: Cambridge University Press, 1968), chapter 3, clearly conflict with Wall's cross-section findings.

[102] Richard W. Hooley and Gerardo P. Sicat, "Investment Demand in Philippine Manufacturing," mimeographed (Quezon City: University of the Philippines, School of Economics, 1967).

(where I is gross investment—i.e., accumulation of fixed capital; P, net profits; and K, end-year capital stock, all measured in million pesos) to the pooled data, the coefficients were estimated as follows (standard errors in parentheses):

$$a_0 = -3.0 \ (125.5)$$
$$a_1 = 0.7833 \ (0.1205)$$
$$a_2 = -0.0369 \ (0.0270).$$

The estimate of a_1 is highly significant, that of a_2, not significant. The correlation coefficient was 0.54.[103] When other variables were introduced, the coefficient of P was little changed and remained highly significant. Not unexpectedly, therefore, profits are clearly the major determinant of investment, at least in the linear model. On the basis of all the regressions on the pooled data, Hooley and Sicat conclude, *inter alia*, that "manufacturing investment displays a strong profits-push type of behavior. In all the fits, at least half—and generally much more than half—of explained variance is traceable to profits or retained earnings rather than to sales pull."[104]

When the firms were grouped into five classes by size of assets, some further interesting results emerged. For the smallest class, profits were dominant in the linear-type function, the coefficient rising to 1.4 and the correlation coefficient to 0.7.[105] However, in progressing to larger firms other variables, particularly depreciation, became important and the role of profits diminished. At the same time the linear model fit became poorer and that of the ratio model improved. A similar grouping by industry allowed a more detailed analysis of investment behavior by reducing within-group variation. Industries with positive and significant profit coefficients (using the linear model) were: tobacco and beverages; textiles, wood products, furniture, and fixtures; paper, paper products, and printing; rubber, chemicals, and petroleum products; and metal products. Of the other groups, food is dominated by the sugar mills, which because of the quota arrangements have had little rein-

---

[103] *Ibid.*, p. 108.   [104] *Ibid.*, pp. 47–49.   [105] *Ibid.*, p. 111.

vestment over a long period; heavy industry (ISIC groups 36–38), on the other hand, consists largely of assembly plants in which investment in fixed assets is outweighed by investment in inventory (excluded from the analysis). With the industry group of footwear, wearing apparel, and leather products, profits were also not significant in determining investment, but here the authors suggest that the small optimum size of firms in this group results in low investment requirements which usually can be financed out of depreciation.[106] Analysis of investment behavior by firm is therefore inappropriate.

A rough calculation suggests that in the whole manufacturing sector about one-half of total output is contributed by firms with assets (in 1961) of less than ₱3 million (corresponding to the two smallest size classes in the above study). Hence, the Hooley-Sicat finding of profit-pushed investment behavior in small firms lends some degree of support to the use of a classical reinvestment-type model $(I = sP)$ if any one function must be chosen to cover the whole sector. Estimates of the values of the propensity to invest out of profits (s) were obtained earlier in Tables 10 and 11. It was seen that, in manufacturing at least, s had shown a slight rising trend and in the 1960's was in the neighborhood of 20 per cent.

Modern Sector Growth

Whether or not a high and increasing rate of investment in the modern sector leads to more rapid growth of output depends on factors such as the level of the capital/output ratio and the difference between its average and marginal values, the relative prices of capital and labor, and the degree of substitutability between them.

Determination of the average capital/output ratio is made difficult by the absence of a satisfactory estimate of total capital stock. We do know, however, that the share of services in modern sector output has been declining in postwar years and that

[106] *Ibid.*, pp. 73–74.

the capital/output ratio in this subsector is considerably less than the sectoral average (see Table 10). Hence, the effect of this structural shift within the sector would tend to lower the aggregate ratio. If we can assume that within each subsector the capital/output ratio has not significantly altered (a generalization based on the manufacturing component), then the sectoral ratio must have shown a slight decline. Some corroboration of the approximate constancy of the average ratio is provided by estimates of the incremental capital/output ratio which despite substantial unpredictable fluctuations does not evince any clear trend.[107] For the whole economy, the incremental ratio in the postwar years appears to have ranged from 1.25 to nearly 3.0 with a mean of about 2.0. For manufacturing alone, Umaña's constant price estimates put the average ratio in the range 1.3–1.6.[108] Since it is intuitively reasonable that the ratio for the modern sector should lie between that for manufacturing and that for the whole economy, we can accept the range 1.5–2.0 for the modern sector capital/output ratio.

These observations, together with the better documented upward trend in the output/labor and capital/labor ratios that we commented on earlier in this chapter, raise the issue of the role of pure technical progress in explaining output growth. Not wishing to enter this complex field, however, we shall simply summarize the modern sector performance in terms of the partial productivity indices, without postulating any an-

[107] See, for example, Pierre R. Crosson, "Capital-Output Ratios and Development Planning," mimeographed (Washington: National Planning Association, Center for Development Planning, 1964), p. 29; Richard W. Hooley, *Saving in the Philippines, 1951–1960* (Quezon City: University of the Philippines, Institute of Economic Development and Research, 1963); and Gerardo P. Sicat, "Some Aspects of Capital Formation in the Philippines," Ph.D. dissertation, Massachusetts Institute of Technology, 1963.

[108] Salvador C. Umaña, "Growth of Output in Philippine Manufacturing: 1902–60," table IV. His estimates of value added/fixed assets ranged from 0.76 to 1.20, rather lower than the 1961 census figure of 1.23. The latter, however, is in current prices, whereas Umaña's results are based on 1938 prices.

alytical form for the production function. On the important question of the elasticity of substitution between capital and labor we can only record our intuitively based expectation that it is very low in the Philippines. Ideally, of course, this should be tested against the data—for example, by fitting a CES production function and obtaining a direct estimate of the elasticity. In fact, this estimation has not been possible with any precision in the Philippine case; the necessary time series data are not available over a sufficient period. Attempts to fit a CES function to cross-section data from the *Annual Survey of Manufactures* founder on the fact that the wage rates (apart from the problem of whether or not they reflect marginal productivity) show little interindustry variation. Moreover, the use of cross-section data rests on very dubious theoretical grounds in assuming an identical elasticity of substitution in each industry division.[109] (The absence of any satisfactory estimate of factor substitutability in Philippine industry is hardly surprising when we consider the same problem in statistically advanced countries. In U.S. manufacturing, for example, while most estimates of the elasticity of substitution are significantly less than one and greater than zero, different methods of fitting give rise to a wide range of results.) [110]

Even if we had sectoral data on inputs adequate to distin-

[109] Sicat has computed the logarithmic regressions of labor productivity on wages, using two-digit ISIC cross-section data for each year 1956–1959. Although he obtained statistically significant estimates for the elasticity of substitution, on average, only 40% of the variation in productivity was explained. The elasticities lay in the range 1–1.5. Gerardo P. Sicat, "Production Functions in Philippine Manufacturing: Cross-Section Estimates, 1956–59," *Philippine Economic Journal*, 2 (1963), 107–131.

[110] See, for example, the summarized results given by Bodkin and Klein. Of their own findings (for the U.S. private, nonfarm sector, 1909–1949), they write: "The estimates of the elasticity of substitution from our CES model vary from approximately zero to approximately unity." Ronald G. Bodkin and Lawrence R. Klein, "Nonlinear Estimation of Aggregate Production Functions," *Review of Economics and Statistics*, 49 (1967), 35.

guish between alternative forms of production function and to give good estimates of their parameters, the attempt to impose a single function over the whole modern sector would nevertheless be misconceived. This is because of the fundamental difference between extractive industries and the remainder of the sector. In the markets they face, and in their ownership and management, extractives differ in important respects from most manufacturing and other modern sector industries. We consider these characteristics in more detail in Chapter 4.

SUMMARY OF THE PHILIPPINE EXPERIENCE

The present chapter has explored in some depth various issues which seem to us of great importance in describing the postwar pattern of development in the Philippines, while at the same time skimming the surface of other topics which from another perspective might appear equally significant. We shall briefly summarize the main features of the Philippine experience that have emerged from this analysis.

Gross national product has increased at an average rate of 6.1 per cent over 1950–1968, or, in per capita terms, at 2.9 per cent. This over-all growth disguises the more rapid modern sector development (6.8 per cent in total output) and very slow growth in the traditional sector (a 4.0 per cent aggregate growth rate or 1.1 per cent per capita). Growth in agriculture can be largely accounted for by increases in land and labor inputs,[111] although there have been apparent offsetting trends of improving technology in established areas and diminishing

[111] More precise computations than we have attempted are given by Lawas, who estimates the following percentage contributions to growth in farm output over the intercensal period 1948–1960: nonirrigated land, 41.2; irrigated land, 9.4; labor, 14.4; farm equipment and building services, 8.5; current expenses, 15.3. Total resource inputs are therefore 88.8%, leaving a residual of 11.2% to be attributed to technology. José M. Lawas, "Output Growth, Technical Change, and Employment of Resources in Philippine Agriculture: 1948–1975," Ph.D. dissertation, Purdue University, 1960.

returns in some marginal frontier land.[112] Traditional sector exports have increased less fast than output, a trend consistent with static productivity, surplus land, a small change in sectoral labor allocation, and approximately constant per capita cereal consumption.

In sharp contrast with traditional exports which grew at 1.6 per cent (net of food imports), exports from the modern sector had an average annual increase of 13.0 per cent. This growth was overwhelmingly accounted for by extractive industry products (minerals and logs) and their derivatives (lumber, plywood, ore concentrates, etc.). Manufactured exports not associated with agriculture or the extractive sector contributed less than 3 per cent to exports and increased at a rate of only 3.2 per cent. Over the two decades since 1950, there has been a trend for exports to finance an increasing share of merchandise imports, with trade in invisibles moving into approximate balance. The reversal of this trend observed in the late 1960's did not appear to be sustainable.

The composition of imports changed radically in the 1950's in response to a vigorously implemented policy of import substitution. Capital goods imports were enabled to rise at 9.1 per cent, whereas total imports increased at 5.6 per cent. If the share of consumer goods in total imports had remained at its value for 1950–1952 (63 per cent), then by 1966–1968 capital goods imports would have increased by only 46 per cent of the rise actually observed. In this sense we may say that 54 per cent of the growth of capital goods imports was due to the falling share of consumer goods in the total. As this fall slowed in the 1960's, so also did the growth rate of capital goods imports.

The importance of capital goods imports for modern sector growth became apparent on examining the over-all import content of capital formation and, more directly, the import content

[112] In our discussion of land/labor ratios we have not taken account of fisheries, mainly for reasons of data. Clearly developments in this industry can affect the significance of changes in the land/labor ratio although we have no evidence that such developments did occur.

of the output of strategic heavy industries such as machinery and transport equipment. To the extent that total capital formation is linked fairly closely to investment in durable equipment, the economy clearly exhibits a high and apparently nondecreasing level of import dependence.

It would be possible in theory for the modern sector to respond to an import constraint on investment by a continual substitution of labor for capital in industry, or by a deliberate attempt to foster labor-intensive techniques of production. That this has not been the Philippine response in part reflects political realities and a perhaps short-sighted concern with welfare-oriented labor policies. The postwar years have seen a steady deepening of capital, with labor productivity in the modern sector rising at a rate of 2.4 per cent in the face of more or less constant capital productivity. The modern sector's share of the labor force has changed relatively little (from 38 per cent in 1950–1952 to 43 per cent in 1966–1968—if we can trust the somewhat dubious data underlying these estimates).

Real wages for unskilled or semiskilled labor in both sectors have been virtually unchanged for most of the 1950–1968 period. While unravelling the causality is necessarily a speculative exercise, we argued that agricultural wages reflected the nearly stationary average and marginal productivity of labor in that sector (a consequence of expansion in land inputs) and that these wages determined the base wage levels in the unorganized sector of industry. In large-scale industry the effect of minimum wage laws and premiums for skill probably swamp this mechanism of determination. Nevertheless, we viewed the lowest level of wages as neoclassically rather than institutionally determined and the unemployment rates as being to a substantial degree accounted for in terms of market inefficiencies.

If we distinguish between average and base level wages it is likely that the growth of a skilled labor force has raised average real wages. This is suggested in the data on average payrolls per worker in manufacturing given in Table 11. Despite this, we argued on the basis of income distribution and other manufacturing data that labor's share of output in the modern sector was not increasing over the postwar years and may even have been declining. Profit levels have remained substantial despite the squeeze which followed the 1960–1962 devaluation.[113] If the propensity to invest out of profits has not been falling (and our data for the manufacturing sector suggest it has been stable or rising), then we may probably conclude that modern sector growth is not constrained by insufficient entrepreneurial savings. Rather, we may attribute the decline in the growth of output in the 1960's to the corresponding decline in the growth of capital goods imports—the latter being a result of the slowing of the process of import substitution. We would therefore expect that future modern sector growth will be at a level close to the growth rate of capital goods imports and that the latter will approach the growth rate of total exports. This is of course assuming that modern sector productivity changes remain of the labor-saving type and that there is no substantial and sustained net capital inflow. Both assumptions would seem to be realistic.

With the modern sector output of consumer manufactures, for which there is no export market, growing much more rapidly than traditional sector output, we would expect a tendency for the intersectoral terms of trade to move in favor of the traditional sector. Government policies regarding exchange rates and tariffs can intervene to prevent an actual movement, as we observed prior to the freeing of the exchange rate in 1962. Subsequently, there was a marked shift in agriculture's favor.

This, then, is our picture of the Philippines—an economy undergoing rapid and dynamic change in many respects but very clearly facing or soon to face intractable problems of resource utilization, labor absorption, and export growth. An analysis of some of these problems is the subject of Chapter 4.

[113] Hooley's sample data of manufacturing corporations, referred to earlier, showed profits (as a percentage of sales after tax) of 10% in 1959, declining to 6% in 1965. Even a 6% profit on sales corresponds to about 20% on net worth. Treadgold and Hooley, "Decontrol and the Redirection of Income Flows," pp. 6–7.

CHAPTER 3

A Theory of Open
Economy Growth

From a descriptive and statistical account of Philippine development we now turn to a more abstract but parallel approach. Despite the very broad categories used in the preceding analysis and the various problems of data quality, we believe that the pattern of development revealed is meaningful and that the trends are indicative of certain unfavorable aspects of growth which can be expected to lead to serious obstacles in the near future. Further investigation of the consequences of the economic course so far pursued requires a study of the sources of export growth and the inherent difficulties in changing the patterns evolved in the postwar years. This will be taken up in Chapters 4 and 5. That discussion will be facilitated, however, by pausing here to draw out in explicit and formal terms the model described verbally in Chapter 1 and used in the Philippine analysis.

We would hope that such an exercise is also of some interest in itself, both in presenting an abstract growth model for a specific type of economy aimed at highlighting a few relationships of immediate relevance for development, and by locating it in relation to the extensive theoretical literature on growth models.

It might be argued that this model should have been specified in such a manner before proceeding to an empirical study, so that the Philippine data could have been used to test its validity. This approach would certainly have been followed if we were concerned with an elaborate and disaggregated model of the sort which would be essential for planning purposes. Our present purpose is rather different: it is to distill from the processes of economic change observed in the Philippines and, in variant forms, in some other Southeast Asian countries, a set of simple equations in a small number of strategic variables. Obviously in such a reduction we can hope to capture only a small part of the totality of interrelationships relevant to economic development. It is scarcely realistic, therefore, to expect that the data from a single country over two decades arranged in this mold can do more than roughly indicate the magnitudes of the parameters specified. The usefulness of the model itself as a tool of analysis must be judged by different criteria.

We do not intend to discuss at any length the role of formal aggregative models in empirical studies of development. Two comments, however, should perhaps be made. Firstly, we believe that the model approach is helpful in conceptualizing economic relationships and often in giving new insights into them, and that it is all but essential for general equilibrium studies beyond an elementary level of complexity. A formal model is generally to be preferred to its implicit or informally stated analog, because of its clarity in revealing underlying assumptions and the ease with which comparisons with alternative formulations can be made. These considerations amply justify resort to algebra.[1] Secondly, as has often been pointed out, the very nature of aggregative models militates against the possibility of their being tested against empirical data by the conventional techniques of statistics. We are concerned with general func-

---

[1] For a sharply critical view of aggregative models in development economics, see the appendix by Paul P. Streeten, "Economic Models and Their Usefulness for Planning in South Asia," in Gunnar Myrdal, *Asian Drama: An Inquiry into the Poverty of Nations* (New York: Twentieth Century Fund, 1968), pp. 1941–2004. His strictures are usually well taken, but serve to underline the danger of reliance on such models for planning purposes rather than their disutility as explanatory tools.

tional relationships rather than the linear or log-linear forms of most regression analyses, and with aggregates of at best dubious homogeneity. Explicit solutions of a model obviously require all functions to be specified, but the degree of arbitrariness in these specifications (which as often as not are chosen for algebraic simplicity) should be recognized.

Our procedure in this chapter will be to consider first the structure of the two major sectors, giving a formal treatment of the land surplus situation in agriculture and of growth under capital specificity in industry. The intersectoral relationships are then introduced: the direct and indirect (via the foreign sector) transfers of goods and the sectoral reallocation of labor. At this stage we are able to state the complete model, and by giving analytical expressions for some of the functions, to solve it in some simple cases for the growth paths of the main variables. Realistic values of the various parameters are available from the Philippine data of Chapter 2, and the time scale of the growth process can then be studied in numerical terms. The final section of the chapter attempts to draw out the major economic implications of the open dual economy model, and to discuss the similarities and contrasts between it and certain other formal growth models.

TRADITIONAL SECTOR OUTPUT

The structural framework underlying our analysis (presented in Figure 3b above) differs from that of the well-known treatments of dualistic growth by Fei and Ranis and Jorgenson only in its recognition of foreign sector flows.[2] Within this general similarity, however, our assumptions will often diverge in im-

[2] See John C. H. Fei and Gustav Ranis, *Development of the Labor Surplus Economy: Theory and Policy* (Homewood, Ill.: Richard D. Irwin, 1964), and Dale W. Jorgenson, "The Development of a Dual Economy," *Economic Journal*, 71 (1961), 309–334. (It will be one task in the present chapter to demonstrate that identifying such flows results in significantly different economic implications, before the present model can be regarded as offering any additional insights into the growth process.)

portant ways from those made by the writers mentioned, reflecting our focus on a restricted class of economies. The role we assign to capital-intensive extractive industries and our assumption of an initial land surplus in agriculture are cases in point. The latter is of interest in this section.

By definition, in the traditional sector of the dual economy capital (in the sense in which the term is used of the modern sector) is negligible as a factor of production. The inputs to be considered are only land (R) and labor (L_a). In general terms, the production function can be stated:

$$Y_a = f(L_a, R, t) \tag{1}$$

where Y_a is output in suitable physical units, and t expresses the simplifying assumption that the level of technology is a function only of time.

The labor input L_a is measured as the number of full-time equivalent workers at time t or, since we are elsewhere assuming an invariant population structure, by an unweighted total of "persons engaged in agriculture." While it is argued that strictly L_a should take account of long-term variations in total man-hours input per worker—in particular, of a secular rise in man-hours per worker expected with spreading commercialization of agriculture—we have preferred to attribute such changes to the technology factor in the production function.[3]

The factor R, loosely referred to above as the land input, could have a number of interpretations. The two major ones relevant in the Asian context are the actual land area cultivated and the crop area planted or harvested. The difference between them is of course important: cultivable area is limited in a simple geographic sense, while harvested crop area can continue to expand through multiple cropping with no clearly definable end point. The latter measure was used in the Philippine analysis on the grounds that it improved the homogeneity of the sec-

---

[3] The appropriate form of labor input depends closely on the concepts of labor force and underemployment being used. (A brief discussion of our attitudes was given in Chapter 2.)

tor; we retain it here also because it makes less unrealistic our assumption of zero capital in agriculture.

Equation (1) is of little interest unless the function is further specified. It is simplest and in many ways convenient to assume the Cobb-Douglas form with neutral technical change represented by the shift factor $b(t)$:

$$Y_a = b(t)L_a{}^\alpha R^\beta, \quad 0 < \alpha < 1, \quad 0 < \beta < 1. \quad (2)$$

This function has the disadvantage, however, that if land is taken to be an essentially costless factor—as we shall want to assume in the early stages of settlement—no equilibrium is possible. We would have the absurdity that all available free land must be brought under cultivation irrespective of the size of the labor force. The actual constraints to expansion are as likely to be institutional or physical as economic.[4] Incorporating them into the production function itself would mean postulating an uneconomic region in the input space, at any point of which output could be raised by reducing the land input alone. The land-labor isoquant might resemble that pictured in Figure 7a, where optimal combination of inputs, determined by technological rather than price considerations, is that for which the marginal physical productivity of land (MPP_R) is zero (see Figure 7c).

Figure 7 illustrates a highly artificial case in which land and

---

[4] Social norms governing the appropriate size of an individual holding and the simple factor of distance (given the existing transport facilities and village settlement patterns) are important limitations on expansion. A classic instance of their operation is found in the case of Javanese migrants (other than those settled under government programs) moving to the Indonesian frontier areas, especially in Sumatra. Confronted with virtually unlimited land, the average size of holding is nevertheless little greater than in Java. The case of Visayan migrants in Mindanao, mentioned earlier, is analogous if less extreme. See Karl J. Pelzer, *Pioneer Settlement in the Asiatic Tropics* (New York: American Geographical Society, 1945), pp. 230–231; and W. F. Wertheim, "Inter-Island Migration in Indonesia," in his *East-West Parallels: Sociological Approaches to Modern Asia* (The Hague: W. van Hoeve, 1964), pp. 183–209.

crops are homogeneous. The effect of each farmer taking his optimum area is thus to raise output proportionately to total land input: the maxima of the total physical productivity (TPP_R) curves lie on the same ray through the origin (Figure 7b). More realistic situations can of course be envisioned. If the frontier land is of lower quality than that under cultivation

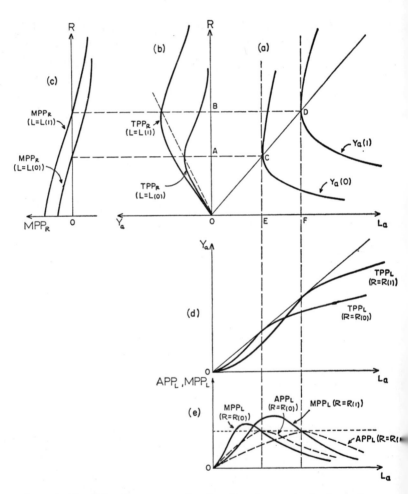

Figure 7. Traditional sector production function: pure land surplus

(which would normally be true where settlement begins in the fertile river valleys) the migrant farmer may claim a larger than average holding merely to ensure the same return. Well before the extensive frontier has finally closed, moreover, increases in crop area will probably be found mainly at the intensive margin where the assumption of free land cannot reasonably be sustained.

Considerations of this sort suggest that a useful simplification of the model of the traditional sector can be made by regarding the rate of land expansion as a variable dependent on the growth of agricultural employment:[5]

$$G(R) = f[G(L_a)], \qquad (3)$$

where f has the property $f'[G(L_a)] > 0$ for $G(L_a) > 0$. We need not cover the case when L_a is decreasing, since this typically is a phenomenon only of the later stages of economic growth. More importantly, as development proceeds and modern inputs and technological improvements are increasingly employed, the assumption that labor is the only independent factor in the sector would have to be dropped.

To elicit the consequences of equation (3) we may suppose that the function is of the elementary form:

$$G(R) = \gamma G(L_a), \quad 0 \leqslant \gamma \leqslant 1 \qquad (4)$$

where γ is a constant. This is now integrable, and gives the relationship:

$$R = cL_a{}^\gamma, \qquad (5)$$

where c is a constant of integration. The parameter γ can be interpreted as the elasticity of the land input with respect to

[5] The fortuitous development of the notation of calculus has provided no recognized symbol to represent the proportional rate of change of a variable x with respect to time: $(dx/dt)/x$. The symbol η_x used by some writers is awkward when x happens to be an algebraic expression or involves subscripts. In this chapter we shall use the notation $G(x) = (dx/dt)/x$, where G is therefore to be understood as an operator and not as a function.

labor. This form of the equation we used to estimate γ in Chapter 2.

If we retain the assumption of homogeneity of land and crops, or alternatively weight the factor R to take account of differing intensities of land use, then γ will have a maximum value of one. The situation when $\gamma = 1$ we shall call a pure land surplus. Over time, it is clear that the observed elasticity of land with respect to labor will not be constant, although that may be an adequate approximation over short periods—say, one or two decades. Even in the early stages of land expansion the rate at which the land/labor ratio changes will depend not only on the growth rate of labor, but also on the level of technology and on the fertility gradient (measured crudely, for example, by $\partial V/\partial R$, where $V = Y_a/R$ at the point where Y_a reaches its maximum). As the extensive land frontier closes and costs of intensification rise, γ will decline and (if labor continues to increase) may become zero or even negative.

If the initial production function in the traditional sector were of the form (2), then the effect of constraining land expansion by equation (4) would be to give the realized expansion path:

$$Y_a = b(t)L_a^{\alpha+\beta\gamma}, \tag{6}$$

where $b(t)$ incorporates the necessary scale factors. The consequence of permitting some land expansion is formally equivalent to raising the output elasticity with respect to labor above its value for fixed land (α). A similar result is obtained from a production function represented by backward bending isoquants along the R axis as illustrated in Figure 7a: the form of the isoquants below the line OCD can be assumed identical with the Cobb-Douglas form (in this case with constant returns to scale).

Although no further theoretical points are brought out by an analytical example, we include one for completeness. A possible specification of the function drawn in Figure 7a is:

$$Y_a = bL_a^{\alpha}R^{\beta}[1-c(R/L_a)^{\delta}], \quad \delta > 0,$$

where b and c are functions of time and δ can be arbitrarily small. For large values of L_a relative to R this approaches the usual Cobb-Douglas form, while as R increases with Y_a constant, L_a passes through a minimum (given by $\partial L_a / \partial R = 0$) and then increases.[6] Applying the land expansion constraint of equation (5) gives the realized expansion path:

$$Y_a = b^* L_a{}^{\alpha + \beta \gamma} [1 - c^* L_a{}^{(\gamma - 1)\delta}],$$

which is asymptotically identical to (6). (Under our homogeneity assumption, $\gamma \leqslant 1$; hence $(\gamma - 1)\,\delta \leqslant 0$ and the term in brackets rapidly approaches 1.)

It would be reasonable to ask what are the economic implications of the assumption of surplus land in agriculture, if it gives rise to an *ex post* production function formally the same as the assumption of fixed land $(Y_a = b(t) L_a{}^\alpha)$. Part of the answer lies in the formal treatment of the movement under population pressure from a situation of pure land surplus to fixed land (seen as a decrease in γ, which induces a corresponding decline in the composite elasticity $\alpha + \beta\bar{\gamma}$ in equation (6)). This Ricardian process is illustrated in Figure 8. OP is the expansion path of the factors under a pure land surplus regime (corresponding to OCD in Figure 7a). When L_a exceeds OD, we enter the stage of diminishing returns: thereafter, any given labor force is associated with an area of land less than the optimum size in the previous stage. For example, the level of employment represented by OE would maximize output with a pure land surplus by working an area equal to EK. But the constraints on expansion are such that the actual area worked to give maximum output is only EB. The equation to the line PB is given by (6), for γ positive but less than 1 and the variables measured from the new origin P. The realized growth of output as a function of labor is shown in Figure 8b as the curve QHH'. It lies between the straight line QGG', representing the growth of output had the pure land surplus continued, and the curve QJ,

[6] The characteristics of the function are readily seen by expressing it in the polar coordinates r, θ, where $L_a = r \cos \theta$ and $R = r \sin \theta$.

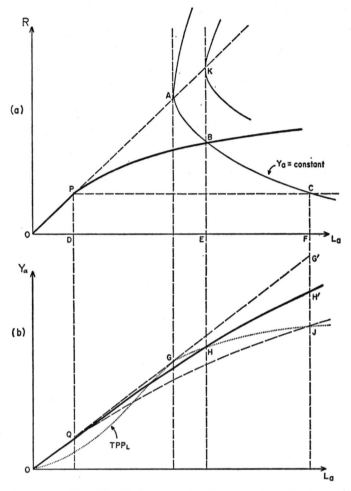

Figure 8. Traditional sector production function: slowing of land expansion

which would be the path followed if *DP* had been the maximum land input attainable.

Another reason for our lengthy discussion of surplus land is less obvious but follows from the treatment of the question in Chapter 2. The recognition of the existence of additional land affects the interpretation to be given to unemployment and underemployment in the traditional sector. The conventional view of these as constituting pools of labor to be tapped in the course of industrial growth is de-emphasized, and stress is put instead on the roles of market frictions and other social and institutional impediments to labor mobility. To the extent that such pools can be drawn upon, their use in extending or intensifying agriculture is an obvious alternative (as realistic or as unrealistic) to their absorption into an employment generating industrial sector.

Both Figures 7 and 8 are of course temporal cross-sections, and very different expansion paths could result from allowing for technical progress over time. (Neutral) technology appears in equation (6) in the time-dependent coefficient b. The simplest explicit form of b is that for which its growth rate $G(b) = \epsilon$ is constant:

$$b(t) = b(0)e^{\epsilon t}. \tag{7}$$

As was pointed out in Chapter 1, agricultural productivity has been relatively stagnant over long periods in most of the countries of interest here. For these cases $\epsilon = 0$ has been a valid description, though it is now perhaps an unreasonably pessimistic forecast. A more general form of $b(t)$ for the case where ϵ is a changing function of time can be written:

$$b(t) = b(0)\exp\int_0^t \epsilon \, dt. \tag{8}$$

AGRICULTURAL SURPLUS

In the preceding section we have been concerned with the growth of traditional sector output Y_a, and with the form of the sectoral production function. We now introduce some specific assumptions relating to the disposition of this output.

In the open dual economy, Y_a is divided three ways: food consumption in the traditional sector, F_a; food consumption in the modern sector, F_m; and exports, X_a.[7] We assume that this ex-

[7] "Food" is here used to describe basic nutritional requirements. Imports of luxury food items can be considered as belonging to the category of nonfood consumer goods imports.

hausts the product, so that we have the accounting identity:

$$Y_a = X_a + F_a + F_m. \tag{9}$$

Implied in this equation is the important assumption that all traditional sector output, less (at most) domestic food consumption, is exportable. Provided that Y_a (measured in physical units) is sufficiently large and relative prices remain stable, it makes little difference whether the product consists of food crops or nonfood crops or any combination of the two. If domestically produced food is inadequate, imports can be financed by other traditional exports. (The problem of homogeneity, however, is of importance here, and the difficulties it raises were seen in Chapter 2.) Indeed, it is entirely possible for Y_a to be less in magnitude than the total food consumption, in which case "traditional sector exports" are negative. Where changing relative prices of food and nonfood crops induce reallocation of land to the more profitable crop—as observed in the Philippine case—equation (9) provides a highly simplified but nonetheless powerful means of distinguishing the meaningful underlying trend. The interesting policy alternatives connected with interactions between tariffs and food price policies, however, are not of direct concern to us at present.

The three-way division of output represented by equation (9) immediately suggests two types of traditional sector surplus. First, there is the so-called total agricultural surplus, common to all dual economy models, defined as output less intrasectoral food consumption: $Y_a - F_a$. Second, and of more importance in the present model, there is the exported surplus, X_a, defined as output less total food consumption:

$$X_a = Y_a - F_a - F_m.$$

This expression may be written in the equivalent form:

$$X_a = Y_a - g_a L_a - g_m L_m, \tag{10}$$

where g_a and g_m denote average food consumption per worker in the traditional and modern sectors and L_a and L_m are the respective sectoral employment totals, which, under our labor market assumptions (to be discussed below), can be taken as proxies for sectoral populations. Although we shall loosely refer to X_a as traditional sector exports, strictly X_a is exports net of imports of foodstuffs. (It will be recalled that the foreign trade data presented in Chapter 2 subtracted from total exports an amount equal to the value of food imports for this reason.) The conventional concept of marketed surplus, covering also agricultural goods marketed within the traditional sector, does not appear in the dual economy model.

Food consumption increases directly with population size and is usually supposed to have a positive (though small) income elasticity. This could be expressed in the present model by writing:

$$g_a = f(Y_a/L_a), \quad f'(Y_a/L_a) \geqslant 0, \tag{11}$$

$$g_m = f(w^*), \quad f'(w^*) \geqslant 0. \tag{12}$$

The arguments on the right hand sides of equations (11) and (12) are respectively, average product in agriculture (Y_a/L_a) and the modern sector average wage measured in units of agricultural goods (w^*). The sectoral income elasticities of demand need not of course be identical.

In an underdeveloped economy, where food consists to a large extent of cereals, vegetables, and relatively small amounts of animal protein in the form of meat or fish, the income elasticity of demand for food (measured, as here, in simple quantity terms) is likely to be small—unless incomes are barely above subsistence. In the case of the Philippines, the physical absorption data for all cereals (rice, corn, and wheat) showed quite remarkable constancy over 50 years, notwithstanding a very substantial rise in real per capita income over the same period (Table 19). We perhaps may sacrifice little realism, therefore, by regarding g_a and g_m as constants—and no more by making them equal. Writing L for total employment, we would then have the simple relationship:

$$X_a = Y_a - gL. \tag{13}$$

The total and exportable surpluses are shown in Figure 9 for the case where $g_a = g_m = g$. As with the earlier diagrams, it represents the situation at a single point in time and therefore makes no assumptions about technical progress in agriculture—

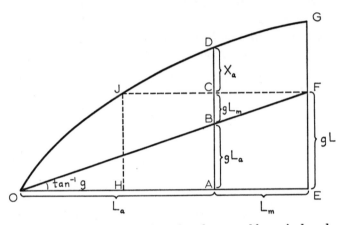

Figure 9. Determination of total and exportable agricultural surpluses

or about changes in the value of g over time. $OJDG$ is the production possibility curve corresponding to $OQHH'$ in Figure 8b. If we consider a given sectoral allocation of labor specified by the point A in Figure 9, so that OA represents agricultural employment L_a, then AD is the total output of agricultural goods (Y_a) when this labor force cultivates the optimum land area. The gradient of the line OBF is the average food consumption, and hence AB is the total consumption in the traditional sector. The total agriculture surplus is therefore measured by BD. Subtracting the food consumed in the modern sector, gL_m (given by BC), leaves the surplus available for export, CD.

The diagram serves to show that the exportable surplus at any time is largely a function of the relative share of the labor force in agriculture rather than of the absolute size of L_a. (Shifting both the lines AD and EG an equal distance to the right or left, equivalent to changing the absolute size of L_a, has little effect on the residual X_a.) Closely related to this, and of more significance here, is the interdependence revealed between L_m and X_a: for a given total labor force OE, an increase in L_m is achieved only at the cost of a decrease in X_a. Since in the model we are proposing, exports play an essential role in industrial growth by permitting capital goods imports, a balance may have to be struck in which the traditional sector serves both as a source of labor and, indirectly, as a producer of the capital goods which will enable that labor to be employed. To study the nature of this balance we now turn to the modern sector of the economy.

MODERN SECTOR

The practical problems encountered in the previous chapter in making a dualistic division of an economy fortunately need not concern the aggregative model builder. While retaining the reservations stated there on the lack of homogeneity of the modern sector, we can nevertheless write a single general production function for sectoral output (Y_m) :

$$Y_m = f(K_m,\ L_m,\ t), \tag{14}$$

where K_m and L_m are the capital stock and labor input (measured respectively in appropriate physical units and as number of persons employed at time t) and technology is again (as in the traditional sector) assumed to be disembodied and time-dependent.

On the controversial issue of the degree of factor substitutability to be permitted, we need make no firm commitment. Growth models have mostly assumed either the zero elasticity of substitution of the Harrod-Domar tradition or the unit elasticity of Cobb-Douglas. Intermediate levels can also be treated with the well-known CES production function or a variety of more exotic forms recently developed. However, given the dubious nature of the empirical data on factor inputs and the inherent difficulties of aggregation which plague production theory, there seems little justification for selecting any but the simplest analytic forms for equation (14). Hence the present discussion will make reference only to fixed factors on the one hand and Cobb-Douglas on the other. In our view, the actual possibilities for factor substitution in an underdeveloped country are more closely approximated by the former than by the latter.[8] It should be recognized also that even the assumption of zero substitutability at the aggregate level does not preclude factor substitution at the enterprise level. As was true of the production function in agriculture, decisions regarding factor combinations are made on the basis of a production function confronting the firm, which may bear little resemblance to the realized relation between inputs and output applicable to the sector as a whole.[9] The disregarding of the possible effects of aggregation in translating the behavior of the firm on to a sectoral level has been a frequent cause of misunderstanding.

Arguments on the rate of substitution are rendered to some degree academic when growth is considered over a period longer than a few years. Short-run changes in the capital/labor ratio are then of less interest, while secular trends are more likely to be accounted for by productivity changes associated with structural shifts within the sector or with technological progress.

Technical change, as noted earlier, is regarded as disembodied, dropping, in the familiar simile, "like manna from heaven

---

[8] In support of this view see, *inter alia*, Benjamin Higgins' review of Fei and Ranis, *Development of the Labor Surplus Economy*, in *Economic Development and Cultural Change*, 14 (1966), 239.

[9] This point is made by Frankel. By a simple, though *ad hoc*, argument he shows how enterprises governed by Cobb-Douglas or CES functions can lead, on aggregation, to an economy-wide production function with fixed coefficients. The necessary assumption is that the enterprise's production for given factor inputs is dependent on the "level of development" of the whole economy as measured by the total capital intensity. Marvin Frankel, "The Production Function in Allocation and Growth: A Synthesis," *American Economic Review*, 52 (1962), 995–1022.

on all men and machines.''[10] It is observed as an exogenous and autonomous increase in one or both of the partial factor productivities. If the production function has fixed coefficients, u and v:

$$Y_m = \text{Min}(uK_m, vL_m), \qquad (15)$$

technical progress is simply incorporated by making u and v nondecreasing functions of time. For simplicity, we might assume their respective growth rates, $G(u) = \theta$ and $G(v) = \phi$, to be constant, so that:[11]

$$u(t) = u(0)e^{\theta t}, \quad \theta \geqslant 0 \qquad (16)$$
$$v(t) = v(0)e^{\phi t}, \quad \phi \geqslant 0.$$

By adjusting the units of measurement of K and L, the initial values $u(0)$ and $v(0)$ can be chosen as unity. (However, for the sectoral employment totals to remain additive the corresponding parameter $b(0)$ in equations (7) and (8) cannot also be made unity.)

One advantage of fixed coefficients is the ease with which bias in technical progress can be treated. Neutral progress, in the Hicksian sense, occurs when $G(u) = G(v)$. When $G(u) = 0$ and $G(v) > 0$, we have purely labor-saving (or labor-augmenting) technical progress, and when $G(v) = 0$ and $G(u) > 0$, purely capital-saving progress. These last two cases correspond to Harrod-neutrality and Solow-neutrality, respectively. In the general case, when both $G(u)$ and $G(v)$ are positive but not equal, we shall say that the technical change has a labor-saving or capital-saving bias depending on whether $G(v)$ is greater or less than $G(u)$. Two instances are illustrated in Figure 10, for

[10] R. G. D. Allen, *Macro-Economic Theory* (New York: St. Martin's Press, 1967), p. 254.
[11] This assumption will provide a convenient mathematical formulation for the growth path of output; we would not defend it as a valid economic observation in the long run. As a purely descriptive device, however, it was seen in Chapter 2 that θ and ϕ can be regarded as the average values of $G(u)$ and $G(v)$ when the latter do not vary substantially over a period.

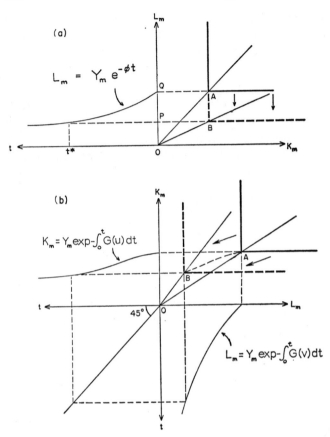

Figure 10. Modern sector production function with fixed coefficients: (a) pure labor-saving technical progress, (b) labor-saving bias

the case in which the labor force is allocated between the two sectors to maintain the equality $uK_m = vL_m$ (which corresponds, in the terminology of Harrod, to equating the warranted and natural growth rates of the modern sector). Figure 10a shows pure labor-saving technical progress at a constant rate ϕ; its effect is to raise the efficiency of each unit of labor so that the same output can be obtained from fewer workers. This is seen as a parallel shift of the capital/labor isoquant defined by the point A towards the K axis, following a time dimension given by the negative exponential curve in the left-hand quadrant. After a period t^*, the labor required to produce a constant output Y_m has diminished from OQ to OP. Figure 10b is an analogous picture for the case when both G (u) and G (v) are positive and variable over time. Here the isoquant is moved diagonally closer to both axes along the line AB, the gradient of which at any time is a function of the current bias in technical change (represented by the quotient of, or difference between, G (u) and G (v)) and the initial conditions (the coordinates of A). In the special case of (Hicks-) neutral technical change, B would lie on the ray $OA;$ as drawn, the labor-saving bias reduces the labor force by a more than proportional amount so that the capital/labor ratio at B is greater than at A.

While the above discussion has referred only to a production function with fixed coefficients, the concept of bias is of course general. Thus equation (15) may be replaced by the Cobb-Douglas form with constant returns to scale:

$$Y_m = c(t)K^\lambda L^{1-\lambda}, \quad 0 < \lambda < 1. \qquad (17)$$

Neutral technical progress is now defined by making G $(c) > 0$; the effect on the capital-labor isoquant is to move it proportionately closer to the origin. The distinction between Hicks-, Harrod- and Solow-neutrality does not arise. A labor-saving bias is represented by a twist in the isoquant so that equilibrium with the same factor price ratio is attained at a higher level of the capital/labor ratio.[12]

It is arguable that the assumption of disembodied technical

[12] For a treatment of bias in technical progress for the class of production functions with constant returns to scale and a positive elasticity of substitution between factors, see Fei and Ranis, *Development of the Labor Surplus Economy*, Chapter 3. A recent attempt at generalization and systematization of the various concepts of neutrality and bias has been made by Sato and Beckman. See, for example, Ryuzo Sato and Martin J. Beckman, "Neutral Inventions and Production Functions," *Review of Economic Studies*, 35 (1968), 57–66.

change is particularly unrealistic, since many improvements are demonstrably embodied in new additions to capital stock. The analytical complications of treating embodied technology, however, are considerable—requiring, for example, the decomposition of capital stock by vintage and assumptions regarding obsolescence.[13] Moreover, provided fluctuations in the level of investment are not great, it is by no means obvious that a purely time-dependent rise in the productivity of successive vintages of capital adds very much in realism compared to the simpler disembodied case. A more significant limitation which applies to both formulations, is just this assumption that the technical progress is wholly a function of time, rather than being determined at least in part by other forces in the economy. As yet, the empirical observations necessary to indicate the likely mechanisms involved in such an endogenous determination are lacking.

In writing a single production function for modern sector output Y_m, we are obscuring two distinctions made in Chapters 1 and 2 which are highly important for the countries of chief interest here. Firstly, we observed that a substantial fraction of modern sector activity was typically related to the extractive industries (defined to comprise mining, logging, and in certain cases large-scale plantation enterprise), the output of which in contrast to manufactured goods was readily exportable. Sec-

---

[13] The one-sector model analyzed by Solow, Tobin, von Weizsäcker, and Yaari is of this kind. Technical progress results in the progressive increase of the output/investment ratio or the output/labor ratio (or both) for the gross investment in each successive year. The capital of any single vintage is combined with labor in fixed proportions; but if labor is limited, it will work with newer capital in preference to the older. The latter is then obsolete. R. M. Solow, J. Tobin, C. C. von Weizsäcker, and M. Yaari, "Neoclassical Growth with Fixed Factor Proportions," *Review of Economic Studies*, 33 (1966), 79–116. One of the first incursions of embodied technical change in an open model, using a similar form of analysis and retaining the clay-clay assumptions of the above authors, is due to Bardhan. P. K. Bardhan, "International Trade Theory in a Vintage Capital Model," *Econometrica*, 34 (1966), 756–767.

ondly, it was argued that the commonly-made assumption that industrial output can be arbitrarily allocated between investment and consumption, depending only on the average propensity to invest, is quite inadequate—overlooking both the differences in level of complexity and in economics of production between consumer goods and capital goods (taken as broad industry groupings) and the fact that with few exceptions developing countries import a large part of their total capital formation in durable equipment. Hence, we should attempt to take account of this phenomenon of capital specificity. Both these points, the role of extractive exports and the existence of capital specificity, are basic to the model we are proposing and together account for its chief difference from closed dual economy models.

The extractive industry subsector of the modern sector is distinguished from the remainder by its dependence on a stock of natural resources in addition to the factors of capital and labor.[14] The concept of natural resources is notoriously difficult to treat quantitatively. Timber resources may be thought definable with some precision, but their extent depends on the degree to which the forest areas are replenishable.[15] Mineral reserves can be specified only with respect to current geophysical knowledge (a function of prior investment in exploration),

[14] Clearly, we are here describing the usual post-colonial situation, at least in Asia. If the capital involved in extractives were largely foreign-owned, the technology highly capital-intensive with a small skilled labor force itself perhaps foreign, and linkages with the rest of the economy (for geographical or other reasons) relatively weak, then their role is, in effect, an exogenous injection of foreign exchange into the country's reserves, enabling a higher level of imports to be maintained. This pattern of "enclave dualism" was described briefly in Chapter 1. In the countries of major interest for the present study, the colonial enclave has been at least partially integrated with the national economy.

[15] A sharp distinction cannot always be drawn between replenishable and nonreplenishable resources, as the case of timber illustrates. However, plantations would normally be in the first category, and minerals in the second.

the level of technology in exploitation, and the known marketing possibilities. Abstracting from these intractable questions
of definition and homogeneity, we might postulate the existence of a number Z, denoting total exploitable reserves at some
initial time, so that, if all output is exported, $\int_0^\infty X_e(t)\,dt = Z$.
X_e is the rate of flow of extractive exports valued at world
prices.[16] Both the time span until X_e finally declines below some
given low level (say, the current flow from replenishable resources) and the shape of the growth path of X_e particularly in
the early stages are undetermined.

On purely a priori grounds, it is possible to argue for various
different growth paths for X_e. The corporate institutional structure in the sector and the resource policy of the government are
major influencing factors. Thus, where reserves are under the
control of the government or large corporations, decisions regarding investment would take into account the depletion of
reserves and hence some policy of conservation may be adopted.
On the other hand, where investment takes the form of a pro-
liferation of competing enterprises, X_e may grow very rapidly
in the early stages and fall off equally rapidly as exhaustion
approaches. Other factors, such as available skills, technology,
interest rates, and world prices, would also be expected to influence the growth path. It was with reference to this thicket
that Hotelling noted, in his classic work on the subject, that
"problems of exhaustible assets are peculiarly liable to become
entangled with the infinite."[17]

In incorporating extractive industries into the present model,
we can ignore many of these determinants of the level of production by concentrating instead on the growth rate of X_e. If

[16] Since the greater part of extractive output is typically exported, and
it is only as a generator of exports that we identify extractives as a distinct
subsector of the modern sector, we lose little realism in equating output
with exports.

[17] Harold Hotelling, "The Economics of Exhaustible Resources," *Journal of Political Economy*, 39 (1931), 139.

Y_m in equation (14) is defined to exclude extractive exports, we may formally write:

$$G(X_e) = f(Z, I_e^*),\qquad(18)$$

where I_e^* is the rate of real investment. Because of the dominance of Z in explaining the level of X_e, we need not explicitly introduce a stock of capital or labor in the extractive subsector.[18]

Investment in extractives can be related to total real investment I^* by an allocation coefficient μ:

$$I_e^* = \mu I^*,\quad 0 \leqslant \mu \leqslant 1,\qquad(19)$$

with the corresponding rate of investment in the remainder of the modern sector, I_m^*, therefore given by:

$$I_m^* = (1 - \mu)I^*.\qquad(20)$$

The asterisks on I^* and its components are to denote that they are measured in "units of capital goods." The equivalent domestic investment fund, I (measured in units of industrial consumer goods), is determined by the entrepreneurial investment function, which can be taken as being of the classical form:

$$I = s(Y_m - wL_m),\qquad(21)$$

where s is the propensity to invest out of profits—using the latter term loosely to refer to output (Y_m) less total payrolls (wL_m). The precise relationship between I^* and I depends on the intersectoral terms of trade, various world prices, and the savings behavior of farmers and owners of extractive industries. This will be discussed in the following section.

The growth of modern sector nonextractive output is determined by I_m^* through the production function (14) and capital accumulation:

---

[18] Often the extractive industries employ only a small fraction of the modern sector labor force (about 3% in the Philippines). However, for a country with a significant modern plantation sector it may be of use to identify a separate component, L_e, for extractive employment.

$$\dot{K}_m = I_m{}^* - \delta K_m, \quad \delta \geqslant 0, \tag{22}$$

(where the dot signifies a time derivative) allowing for depreciation at a constant rate, δ.[19] This equation can of course be written in the equivalent form:

$$G(K_m) = I_m{}^*/K_m - \delta. \tag{23}$$

By separately identifying investment in the two main divisions of the modern sector, we raise the issue of how it should be allocated. In the discussion of Figure 1 in the first chapter this point arose in comparing the investment priorities of colonial and independent economies. Both market forces and development strategy are involved in determining μ in equation (19), although we shall defer consideration of the latter at present. Where a country has substantial exploitable reserves and a high rate of investment can be maintained in the modern sector as a whole, it would be reasonable to expect it to be allocated so that $G(Y_m)$ and $G(X_e)$ were of the same order of magnitude after allowing for changes in relative prices. External factors could induce a shift in the composition of modern sector output without affecting these growth rates in the long run. For example, a rise in export prices for extractives would raise profits and the profit rate for these industries significantly above the modern sector average. This would induce a higher level of investment, continuing until the profit rate was reduced to its initial level. (The fall in the profit rate could be caused by rising costs or, if world demand were less than perfectly elastic, by lower prices.) The effect of the export price increase would therefore be to raise the share of exports in output to a new equilibrium level. Obviously, government intervention through fiscal or tariff policy could also effect changes of this sort.

The necessity for distinguishing between I^* and I is one consequence of the existence in the present model of capital specificity—in its simplest form, the recognition that manu-

[19] There are various ways of treating depreciation of capital stock in aggregative models, but as this is not an important point of focus here we choose probably the simplest—exponential decay.

factured goods are not substitutable in use between investment and consumption. A slight extension of the concept of specificity covers also our assumption that the various categories of domestic output differ radically in the degree to which they are easily exportable, thus narrowing the opportunity for using the foreign sector to overcome these rigidities. Output of the modern sector is comprised of extractive industry products, consumer manufactures and services, and capital goods. The first of these can almost all be exported, and we assume that the domestic market for them can be ignored. The remainder, for reasons to be described in the following chapter, are not readily exportable. The poor performance of the Philippines in exporting manufactures was seen earlier and it is entirely typical of other countries of the region. Introducing this constraint limits the possibility of converting domestic savings, in the form of foregone consumption of manufactures, into realized investment by means of the foreign market. Moreover, the obvious alternative—the domestic production of capital goods —has also been seen to be beset with difficulties, notably the problems of realizing the large economies of scale often involved. We need not, however, explicitly consider the case of a domestic capital goods industry since, formally at least, it is similar to exporting consumer manufactures and importing machinery. (It is recognized, of course, that underdeveloped countries may have a substantial construction industry which is in part a capital goods producer—it would in fact be characterized by fairly low specificity—some final assembly of capital goods, and some production of intermediate inputs for capital goods. The output of these industries is likely to be closely complementary to capital formation in durable equipment, and hence does not have to be considered separately.)

Denoting the (small) fraction of Y_m which can be exported by ζ, we have the equation:

$$X_m = \zeta Y_m, \quad 0 \leqslant \zeta < 1, \tag{24}$$

where X_m is the volume of manufactured exports.

The assumption that capital formation is dependent on imported equipment can be expressed:

$$I^* = f(M_K), \quad f'(M_K) > 0, \tag{25}$$

where M_K is the volume of imports of capital goods. If we do not identify a domestic capital goods industry, this simplifies to:

$$I^* = M_K. \tag{26}$$

Clearly, the proportion of capital goods in total imports (or in total import capacity) will be a major instrumental variable in the model.

INTERSECTORAL RELATIONSHIPS

The intersectoral commodity flows identified in the accounting system underlying the present model are the flow of agricultural product to feed the industrial labor force, the reverse flow of manufactures exchanged both for this food and for the claim to the exportable agricultural surplus, and the various trade flows through the foreign sector. (The corresponding financial flows need not be mentioned separately, except where they involve transfers of savings.) In addition, there is the highly important transfer of labor out of agriculture which has always accompanied economic development. We shall consider the external relationships first, and then the more complex internal relationships.

Total commodity exports have already been encountered in the form of traditional sector exports X_a, manufactures X_m, and extractives X_e. Denoting commodity imports by M, we may write the accounting equation defining M as:

$$p_M M = p_a X_a + p_m X_m + p_e X_e + N - p_s M_s, \tag{27}$$

where M_s is net invisible imports, N is net capital inflow, and the p's are the respective prices (unit values). The relative sizes of $p_s M_s$ and N determine the extent to which commodity imports are directly dependent upon commodity exports. Only in exceptional cases can a country expect capital inflows to permit a trade deficit over any significant period. As common, perhaps, would be a negative value of N reflecting capital flight. We shall suppose that we can ignore N in this equation although recognizing its importance in the short run. Invisibles will also be omitted from most of the following discussion because, although by no means negligible, they raise few points of especial interest. Our assumption will be that (as was found in the Philippine case) the flow of invisibles rises *pari passu* with volume of merchandise trade but the net total remains small apart from short-run fluctuations. Finally, we suppose that all the export prices (p_X) move together (a convenient but patently unrealistic assumption in many instances) so that the trade balance equation may be written:

$$M = (X_a + X_m + X_e)\pi, \tag{28}$$

where $\pi = p_X/p_M$, the foreign terms of trade.

The two components of commodity imports are those specified in the earlier chapters and broadly described as consumer goods and capital goods. Only the latter need be identified:

$$M_K = \nu M, \quad 0 < \nu < 1. \tag{29}$$

The coefficient ν is an instrumental variable in the sense that even though it may not be directly determined by government policy, its level is a consequence of the extent of import substitution, which in turn is closely dependent on a complex of policies. Consumer goods imports are assumed not to enter intersectoral trade in the domestic economy.

The intersectoral labor transfer accompanying industrialization involves a number of complex phenomena which can only be reflected crudely in an aggregative model. Of particular importance among these are the nature of the stimuli which induce rural-urban migration, the determination of the base wage level in industry, the institutional structure of the traditional sector, and the intricate relationships between total population, labor force, and level of employment. Further complications result from demographic facts such as rural-urban differentials in rate of natural increase and the age and sex selectivity of urban migration. The basic labor market assumptions we make are familiar. Firstly, the modern sector of the economy is not constrained by labor supply, being always able to draw on the agricultural sector—although in general at some cost in foregone output. Secondly, labor is employed in industry to the point where its marginal product, when converted into equivalent units of agricultural goods at the prevailing price, is equal to the current agricultural wage plus whatever premium is required to maintain the incentive to migrate. (The implicit assumption here is that labor can allocate itself between sectors in a time period which is short compared to changes in industrial capacity. The opposite situation, of course, is also arguable: that it is precisely the relative immobility of labor that determines the structure of output.) If w is the modern sector wage determined in this manner (and measured in units of industrial goods), then the modern sector employment would be given by the value of L_m satisfying:

$$\partial Y_m/\partial L_m = w. \tag{30}$$

Alternatively, in the fixed coefficients case, employment rises sufficiently fast for the sector to grow at its warranted rate; i.e., so that, in the notation of equation (15),

$$L_m = (u/v)K_m. \tag{31}$$

The first of these assumptions will probably not be questioned. It is observed in the history of the developed countries, for example, that industrial employment grew at an approximately constant rate for long periods, while in agriculture it showed a corresponding decelerated increase and accelerated decrease—strongly suggesting its residual character.[20] The tra-

---

[20] See Folke Dovring, "The Share of Agriculture in a Growing Population," in *Agriculture in Economic Development,* ed. C. K. Eicher and L. W. Witt (New York: McGraw-Hill, 1964), pp. 78–98.

The relationship between $G(L_a)$ and $G(L_m)$ is given by:
$$G(L_a) = [r - z\,G(L_m)]/(1-z),$$

ditional sector still bids for labor, but more and more it is forced
to adapt socially and institutionally to routinized outmigration.
Employment in the traditional sector, in other words, is determined according to the equation:

$$L_a = L - L_m. \qquad (32)$$

The determination of the industrial wage by agricultural
productivity is less clear-cut. As we saw in the Philippine analysis, the modern-traditional dichotomy in fact disguises a gradation of labor productivity and wage rates with no sharp
interface. At the base levels, for unskilled labor, however, it is
not unreasonable to suppose that such a mechanism at least
plays a significant role. The assumption that the *average* wage
(w) is similarly determined is somewhat more gross.

A simple but noteworthy corollary of the above is that in a
pure land-surplus situation with no productivity gains in agriculture the industrial wage in units of agricultural goods remains constant, just as in the labor-surplus stage of development in the Fei and Ranis model.

Two further problems arise in respect of these labor transfer
assumptions. The wage in a commercialized agricultural sector
would be given by $\partial Y_a/\partial L_a$, but where peasant proprietorship
was dominant the average product Y_a/L_a would be the closest
analog. If, as is usually the case, the sector includes both institutional forms, the pool of potential migrants might be found
in either part.[21] For convenience we shall use the single relationship to determine w^*, the industrial wage in terms of agricultural goods:

---

where r is the (constant) rate of increase of total employment, and z is
the current share of labor in the modern sector. If $G(L_m)$ is a constant
greater than r, say $2r$, then $G(L_a) = r(1 - 2z)/(1 - z)$. The derivative
with respect to z is always negative and L_a would decline absolutely after
z exceeded 50%.

[21] For an interesting model of agriculture, taking account of institutional
differences within the sector, see Ashok Mathur, "The Anatomy of Disguised Unemployment," *Oxford Economic Papers*, 16 (1964), 161–193.

$$w^* = f(\partial Y_a/\partial L_a), \quad f'(\partial Y_a/\partial L_a) > 0. \tag{33}$$

The wage in terms of industrial goods would then be given by:

$$w = \tau w^*, \tag{34}$$

where τ is the intersectoral terms of trade.

Another difficulty is how to account for the unemployment in the modern sector which characterizes all underdeveloped countries. With limited substitutability between capital and labor and a sticky wage, one answer would be that the wage differential between sectors is not a sensitive means of regulating migration, and there are obvious frictions inhibiting the back-migration of unsuccessful job-seekers. The unwillingness of urban unemployed to move to the agricultural frontier would also perpetuate the situation if the generation of employment in industry were below the natural increase of the labor force, even with no rural-urban migration.

It was seen in Chapter 2 that imperfections in the labor market could well account for a substantial proportion of the observed "surplus labor pool" in the Philippines. With this slight justification, and so as not to add greatly to the complexity of an already involved model, we shall assume simply that in a land surplus economy the unemployment rate remains constant over time. We can then ignore it for practical purposes and equate the growth rates of employment and labor force. (It was earlier noted that the labor force participation rate is taken to be constant.)

The labor force accounting equation (32) is made dynamic by the conventional assumption, common to most aggregative models, that:

$$G(L) = r, \tag{35}$$

where r is constant. Following from the argument of the previous paragraph, r is also the average rate of natural increase of the population (in the absence of international migration). Although a simplification entirely lacking in demographic sophistication, an exogenous and constant rate of population growth has some claim to realism in countries not seriously overpopulated. At the least it is preferable to incorporating quasi-malthusian flourishes which happen to have convenient equilibrium properties. Neither the birth rate nor the death rate is now a simple function of income per capita, the relationship usually invoked when an endogenous explanation of $G(L)$ is wanted. The death rate has declined precipitously in most countries in response to relatively small investments in public health and sanitation, even when per capita income has been stagnant or dropping. The economic determinants of the birth rate are not well known, but to the extent that fertility is related to income the relationship is frequently an inverse one.

The third major set of intersectoral relationships in the open dual economy (after foreign trade flows and contacts through the labor market) is the direct domestic interchange of goods. In simple terms, we might visualize this intersectoral commodity market by supposing that the modern sector entrepreneurs bargain directly with the farmers for the latters' total surplus, offering manufactured goods in return. The entrepreneurs then divide the purchased agricultural goods into the portion required to feed the industrial labor force and the remainder—which is to be exported to finance imports. Assuming perfect competition, the exchange rate between food and manufactures (the domestic terms of trade, τ) is determined by the usual market-clearing condition.

While this description is useful as a starting point, we cannot avoid complicating it in a number of ways to achieve even minimal realism. One problem, for example, is that the industrial workers' wage w, defined by equations (33) and (34), is itself a function of the terms of trade. Thus, the returns to labor and capital cannot be determined without knowledge of τ. If w were assumed to be paid in kind, we have in fact two bargaining agents from the modern sector: entrepreneurs desiring to obtain exportable goods, and workers requiring to get food. Since no distinction is drawn between food and export crops, however, we still would have a unique exchange rate.

This sort of difficulty is, of course, one that disappears in a model permitting simultaneous determination of the variables, as is seen by some simple algebra. Supposing for the present that farmers do not save, then the agricultural surplus offered for trade is $Y_a - gL_a$, i.e., output less sectoral food consumption.[22] Supposing also that modern sector entrepreneurs do not consume domestically produced manufactures, then the volume of manufactures given in exchange is total output Y_m, less exports ζY_m, less the quantity consumed by the workers $(w - g\tau) L_m$, in units of industrial goods. (An amount of manufactures $g\tau L_m$ must be given in exchange for the food needs of the labor force.) The terms of trade are therefore determined uniquely, although implicitly, by the equation:

$$\tau = \frac{(1 - \zeta)Y_m - (w - g\tau)L_m}{Y_a - gL_a}.$$

On rearranging, τ is given explicitly by:

$$\begin{aligned} \tau &= (1 - \zeta)Y_m/[Y_a - gL_a + (w^* - g)L_m] \\ &= (1 - \zeta)Y_m/(X_a + w^*L_m), \end{aligned} \qquad (36)$$

(by equations (15) and (34)). This last expression may also be obtained directly.

From the viewpoint of the entrepreneurs, the determination of τ might be seen as the problem of dividing $(1 - \zeta) Y_m$ into two components such that one will satisfy the farmers so that they will give up a surplus $Y_a - gL_a$, and the other, the modern sector workers so that they receive a total real wage (including food) of w^*. Figure 11 illustrates this procedure. The vertical axes are in units of agricultural goods, the horizontal axis in industrial goods. BE represents the total agricultural surplus; AD, the nonfood component of modern sector payrolls; and AB, the total output of manufactured goods which has to be marketed domestically. Each of these three quantities is de-

[22] A highly important assumption underlying this argument is that agricultural production is price inelastic so that the surplus itself is not a function of τ.

terminate in its respective units. The problem devolves into the simple geometric exercise of choosing a point C on the line AB such that the terms of trade given by the ratio AC/AD equal those given by CB/BE. The correct point, shown on the diagram, is that which makes the angle ACD equal the angle BCE.

The consequences of permitting savings in the traditional

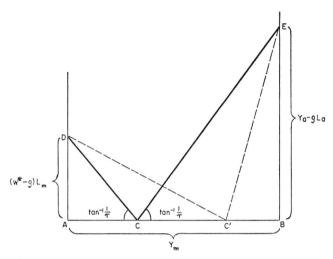

Figure 11. Formal determination of intersectoral terms of trade

sector can now be observed. If savings take the (admittedly unlikely) form of a reduction in food consumption, then the farmers can gain assets in industry and in doing so raise the over-all growth rate of the economy. In this case there may be no short-run effect on the terms of trade. If savings take the form of foregone consumption of manufactures, however, there is no change in the total volume of traditional sector exports and therefore in the growth rate of the economy. Instead, the effect would be to transfer ownership of some industrial assets to the traditional sector, while moving the domestic terms of trade in favor of agriculture. The same volume of manufactures is traded for a smaller available surplus.

One complication in the model as we have so far formulated it lies in the role of the modern sector investment function (21). We earlier assumed for simplicity that the industrial entrepreneurs did not consume food or domestic manufactures. Hence, their consumption, given by $(1 - s) (Y_m - wL_m)$ in units of industrial goods, is the volume of manufactures exchanged for export crops to be used to finance consumer goods imports. It is for this reason that the average propensity to invest (s) does not enter into the determination of the intersectoral terms of trade. It is clear, therefore, that there must be some relationship between s and the share of capital goods in total imports. The precise nature of this relationship unfortunately depends also on the investment behavior in extractive industries.

An approach which avoids the elaborations which would otherwise have to be introduced at this point is to consider the investment decision as being made in terms of the composition of imports rather than in terms of undifferentiated domestic manufactures as in equation (21). One could imagine both extractive and manufacturing industries owned by a group of entrepreneurs whose income is directly (in the former case) or indirectly (in the latter) obtained as foreign exchange available to finance imports. Seen in these terms, the investment function (21), while still meaningful, need no longer enter explicitly. Instead, we have a composite of equations (26) and (29):

$$I^* = \nu M, \tag{37}$$

where the allocation coefficient, ν, applying to the whole of the modern sector, takes the place of the propensity to invest. Where savings were transferred from the traditional sector, this equation would still hold, but ν would then be an economy-wide average rather than a modern sector average.

GENERAL MODEL

In the previous sections we have described at some length the various elements that enter an open dual economy model.

Often we have presented only general formulations and, in other instances, two distinct alternatives without choosing definitely between them. The reason for this approach was mentioned at the beginning of the chapter: it was an attempt to avoid introducing gratuitous assumptions in the form of unduly specific analytical forms which can only be chosen arbitrarily. Now, however, in order to regain some cohesion in the discussion, we shall state a "general" version of the model, retaining generality where this appears to be necessary, but using simple specific forms where the issues involved are either not significant in their implications or not at the center of present interest. This formulation will still not be explicitly solvable, and later we shall introduce a further simplification.

The model can be expressed in some 20 equations, which are reproduced below using their original numbers and with a brief note on each. It will be recalled that the operator G denotes the geometric growth rate.

Production behavior, traditional sector.	$Y_a = f(L_a, R, t)$	(1)
Constraint on land (R) expansion in agriculture.	$G(R) = \gamma G(L_a), \quad 0 \leqslant \gamma \leqslant 1$	(4)
Production behavior, modern sector (excluding extractives).	$Y_m = f(K_m, L_m, t)$	(14)
Determination of modern sector wage in units of agricultural goods (w^*).	$w^* = f(\partial Y_a/\partial L_a), \quad f'(\partial Y_a/\partial L_a) > 0$	(33)
Modern sector wage in units of industrial goods (w).	$w = \tau w^*$	(34)
Determination of modern sector employment (L_m).	$\partial Y_m/\partial L_m = w$	(30)
Labor allocation accounting equation.	$L_a = L - L_m$	(32)
Export surplus, traditional sector (X_a).	$X_a = Y_a - g_a L_a - g_m L_m$	(10)
Per capita food consumption in traditional sector (g_a).	$g_a = f(Y_a/L_a), \quad f'(Y_a/L_a) \geqslant 0$	(11)
Per capita food consumption in modern sector (g_m).	$g_m = f(w^*), \quad f'(w^*) \geqslant 0$	(12)

Export of manufactures (X_m).	$X_m = \varsigma Y_m, \quad 0 \leqslant \varsigma < 1$	(24)
Trade balance accounting equation.	$M = (X_a + X_m + X_e)\pi$	(28)
Composition of commodity imports, M (behavioral relationship).	$M_K = \nu M, \quad 0 < \nu < 1$	(29)
Import dependency constraint.	$I^* = M_K$	(26)
Allocation of investment within modern sector (behavioral relationship).	$I_e{}^* = \mu I^*, \quad 0 \leqslant \mu \leqslant 1$	(19)
Investment allocation accounting equation.	$I_m{}^* = I^* - I_e{}^*$	(19–20)
Growth rate of extractive exports (X_e).	$G(X_e) = f(\mathcal{Z}, I_e{}^*)$	(18)
Capital accumulation accounting equation.	$G(K_m) = I_m{}^*/K_m - \delta, \quad \delta \geqslant 0$	(23)
Determination of intersectoral terms of trade (τ).	$\tau = (1 - \varsigma)Y_m/(X_a + w^*L_m)$	(36)
Growth of population and employment (L).	$G(L) = r$	(35)

While there is no unilinear causal order of determination, the ordering of equations here has some logical basis. $Y_a(0)$ and $Y_m(0)$ are the initial levels of output in the two sectors (except for extractives), determined by the initial capital stock $K_m(0)$ and the sectoral allocation of labor. $Y_a(0)$ determines the modern sector real wage w^* by equation (33), and thence the wage in terms of industrial goods w, provided the domestic terms of trade are given. The wage w defines the size of modern sector employment, $L_m(0)$, by the marginal productivity condition, and the residual employment in the traditional sector, $L_a(0)$ (equations 30 and 32). Exports from the traditional sector, X_a, are determinate once food consumption is known, the latter varying with employment levels and average income (equations 10–12). Modern sector exports derive simply from $Y_m(0)$. Given an initial level of extractive exports $X_e(0)$ and assuming zero net invisible imports and net capital inflow, the volume of merchandise imports, $M(0)$, is found by equation

(28) —equaling total exports adjusted by the international terms of trade π. The share of capital goods in imports—a consequence, knowing $M(0)$, of domestic investment decisions—in turn determines the level of real investment achieved (equations 29 and 26) and this is allocated between the extractive and nonextractive subsectors (equations 19 and 20). Finally, this investment gives the stock of capital $K_m(1)$ and level of extractive exports $X_e(1)$ in the next period (if time were discrete) or the growth rate of capital and extractives (for continuous time). Equation (36) shows the endogenously determined domestic terms of trade, depending on the volumes of commodities available for intersectoral exchange.

Altogether 28 symbols appear in this set of equations. We identify as constants the stock of natural resources Z, the population growth rate r, the rate of captial depreciation δ, and (except in the long run) the elasticity of land expansion with respect to agricultural employment γ. In equation (28), the variable π, the foreign terms of trade, is assumed to be given exogenously. We are left, then, with 23 variables satisfying 20 equations. The instrumental variables we shall choose to stress from among these are the following three:

ν, the share of capital goods in merchandise imports;
μ, the proportion of real investment allocated to extractive industries; and
ζ, the proportion of modern sector manufactures exported.

It is arguable that in many countries there is little scope for further reduction in ν, while the determinants of ζ may be largely outside the control of some governments. Even μ may not be fully determined by national resource policies—especially where, as in the Philippines, a vigorous and poorly disciplined private sector exists. It would therefore not be entirely unrealistic to regard these variables as being given exogenously and the model as fully determined.

The operation of the model can be described very simply. For the modern sector to expand it must draw on the resources of the traditional sector for capital goods (via the foreign sector) and for labor. The two requirements conflict, since migration out of agriculture lowers the growth rate of traditional exports. Referring to Figure 9, a movement of the point A (representing the sectoral division of the labor force) towards E simultaneously raises the exported surplus (CD), and thus the potential increment to capital stock, and lowers the labor force (AE) available to work with that capital. The converse occurs with a shift of A towards H. In the absence of alternative sources of foreign exchange the relative increments to the modern sector factors would be balanced by movement along the modern sector production function or (especially if factor substitutability were low) by variation in the behavioral parameter v. Factor prices are determined by the respective sectoral outputs and by the level of marginal productivity of labor in agriculture. Over time, an important determinant of sectoral labor allocation is the nature of the bias in modern sector technical change. (Although the causes are not well understood at least some of this bias is influenced by government wage and tariff policies.)

Other sources of foreign exchange would generally exist, however. Part (and in some cases most) of imported capital equipment is intended to develop extractive industries which can make an immediate contribution to exports. In addition a small proportion of domestically produced manufactures can probably be exported. To the extent that these industries can raise import capacity, the role of the traditional sector as a source of labor can be stressed over its role as a generator of exports. This, however, is an unreal situation in the modern world where growth is virtually never constrained by labor shortages. The more realistic outcome of a large modern sector contribution to exports is an accentuation of dualism with the traditional sector stagnating.

As an aid in considering the fairly broad issues raised by this formulation we will analyze a highly simplified and thoroughly mechanistic special case which nevertheless incorporates some of the main features of import-dependent growth. Let us sup-

pose that: (a) the modern sector production function has fixed
coefficients and infinitely durable capital; (b) no manufactures
are exported while extractive exports grow at a constant rate
over some initial period (and investment in extractives can be
ignored); (c) food consumption per capita is constant; (d)
foreign terms of trade do not alter; (e) only capital goods are
imported; and (f) technical progress proceeds at a constant rate
in both sectors. Taking first the case in which we have a pure
land surplus in agriculture $(\gamma = 1)$, the model can be reduced
to the following set of equations:

$$Y_m = e^{\theta t}K_m$$
$$L_m = e^{(\theta-\phi)t}K_m$$
$$L_a = L - L_m$$
$$Y_a = b(0)e^{\epsilon t}L_a, \qquad t < t_1$$
$$X_a = Y_a - gL$$
$$X_e = X_e(0)e^{\xi t}, \qquad t < t_2$$
$$M = X_a + X_e$$
$$I^* = M$$
$$K_m = I^*$$
$$G(L) = r$$

In these ten equations, the variables can be determined suc-
cessively given an initial total employment $L(0)$ and capital
stock $K_m(0)$. The coefficient g and the various growth rates $(\theta,
\phi, \epsilon, \xi, r)$ are constant by assumption. We note that neither the
wage nor the domestic terms of trade now enter: the equations
involving them are in fact redundant. Domestic commodity
exchanges are completely determined by the foreign sector
flows, while with fixed factors the wage is assumed to adjust in
such a way as to maintain full employment.

The solution of this system involves basically the integration
of the rate of capital accumulation over time. Substituting for
I^*, we have:

$$\dot{K}_m = M = X_a + X_e$$
$$= Y_a - gL + X_e$$
$$= (b-g)L + X_e - bL_m,$$

where $b = b(0) e^{rt}$. Thus we obtain the fundamental differential equation for this open dual economy:

$$\dot{K}_m = b(0)L(0)e^{(\epsilon+r)t} - gL(0)e^{rt} \\ + X_e(0)e^{\xi t} - b(0)e^{(\epsilon+\theta-\phi)t}K_m. \quad (38)$$

This is of the standard form $dy/dt + yg(t) = f(t)$, a first order linear differential equation which has the formal integral:

$$y = e^{-\int g \, dt} \int e^{\int g \, dt} f \, dt.$$

It is not necessary, however, for us to evaluate this solution explicitly, since most of its important characteristics can be deduced directly from equation (38).

The main features of (38) are readily explained. The increment to capital stock varies directly with the level of extractive exports and the exportable agricultural surplus. The latter is an increasing function of population size and of the innovation intensity in agriculture, and a decreasing function of the rate of labor absorption by the modern sector. Labor absorption in turn depends on the size of capital stock and the bias in modern sector technical progress. Considerations of this sort explain the direction of influence that a change in any variable or parameter has on $\dot{K}_m$. For example, a larger initial capital stock has the paradoxical effect (*ceteris paribus*) of *lowering* the rate of increase of K_m, since more labor is then required in the modern sector and this detracts from agricultural exports and import capacity. A larger initial population $L(0)$ has the opposite effect on $\dot{K}_m$ by increasing exports.

Because of its assumption of fixed coefficients in industry, this model makes no statement on the trend in the capital/labor ratio. However, if we suppose that the direction of bias in technical progress is in effect determined by factors such as government wage and tariff policies, then we can trace the implications of that bias through the model. With a labor-saving bias in the modern sector ($\phi > \theta$) the demand for labor is lessened and agricultural exports are enabled to reach a higher level than before. The long-run growth rate of capital stock is given by Max $(\xi, \epsilon + r)$, provided that $\phi - \theta > \epsilon$.[23] If the latter condition does not hold then there is no steady state solution. It would be similar to the empirically less probable case of capital-saving technology in which it would be possible for labor to be withdrawn from agriculture at a rate such that the exportable agricultural surplus was steadily diminished. A sufficiently high rate of technical change in agriculture could of course maintain the level of exports.

Asymptotic trends in growth paths have little meaning in view of our assumed dependence on finite stocks of cultivable land and natural resources. After some period t_1 the rate of land expansion slows and we would have the conventional case of diminishing returns to labor. After another period t_2 the reserves of minerals and forests are no longer sufficient (or, more precisely, their exploitation is no longer as profitable) to permit continued growth of extractive exports at a constant rate ξ. With the rigid linkages which characterize this naive model a falling growth rate of exports is translated immediately into a slower growth of real investment in industry and thus into a slowdown for the whole economy. If substitution of labor for capital is not technologically feasible then the only escape from stagnation is to maintain export growth by means of technical progress in agriculture. (Obviously other possibilities exist in the more general model.) Average productivity in agriculture is given by:

$$Y_a/L_a = b(0)e^{\epsilon t}L_a^{\omega-1},$$

where ω $(\alpha + \beta\gamma$ in the notation of equation 6) is the composite elasticity of output with respect to labor, and the condition for the exportable surplus to rise is therefore that $G(Y_a/L_a)$ is positive, i.e.,

$$\epsilon > (1 - \omega)G(L_a).$$

---

[23] This may be seen by dividing both sides of equation (38) by K_m and deducing a contradiction for any other possible outcome.

When this condition holds over a long period (presumably as a consequence of capitalization in agriculture) we have the case of successful development. Real wages rise and there is an expanding market for modern sector output. Reduced costs and the development of greater technical and marketing skills improve the chances for exporting manufactured products. At the same time the level of import dependence may be reduced by the growth of a domestic capital goods industry. The model in this simple form, however, is inappropriate for tracing this outcome formally. The assumptions we have made that technical progress proceeds at a constant rate in each sector become less realistic in the long term. An endogenous explanation of technical change, perhaps involving feedback mechanisms of the kind introduced by Fei and Ranis,[24] would then be desirable. More fundamentally, the concomitant growth of new intersectoral and intrasectoral flows makes the structural simplifications of the model increasingly inadequate.

PHILIPPINE PARAMETERS

To provide some concreteness to a fairly abstract discussion it is of interest to assemble the various parameters and growth rates which apply to the Philippines in the postwar period. Most of these can be taken directly from Chapter 2. As we have previously noted, there is no question of testing the model against these data.

[24] Their assumption is that a shift in the domestic terms of trade in favor of agriculture (as would tend to occur if industrial output were increasing at a rapid rate relative to food) by making agriculture more profitable would stimulate landlords to introduce technological innovations. Such a mechanism tends to equilibrate the rates of productivity change in the two sectors. Fei and Ranis, "Agrarianism, Dualism, and Economic Development," in *The Theory and Design of Economic Development,* ed. Irma Adelman and Eric Thorbecke (Baltimore: The Johns Hopkins Press, 1966), p. 34. The open model presented by Hornby also has a terms of trade effect giving an endogenous explanation of productivity increases in agriculture. J. M. Hornby, "Investment and Trade Policy in the Dual Economy," *Economic Journal,* 78 (1968), 96–107.

Table 22 presents the average growth rates of the model variables over the period 1950–1968. In a few instances the averages obscure a significant change in the rate of increase in the course of these years, but over-all the table serves to summarize and sharpen the descriptive analysis of Chapter 2. Omitted from the table are the four parameters ϵ, ζ, ν, and δ (respectively, the

Table 22. Philippine growth and structural change in the framework of the open dual economy model (annual geometric rates of change, average 1950–1968)

Variable	Rate of change	Variable	Rate of change
Production:		Investment:	
Y_a	0.040	I^*	0.085
Y_m	0.068	Wages:	
Factor inputs:		w^*	0.005
L_a	0.029	w	0.026
R	0.030	Domestic terms	
L_m	0.044	of trade:	
K	0.068	τ	0.021
		Food consumption	
Foreign trade:		per capita:	
X_a	0.016	g	0.013
X_e	0.134	Population:	
X_m	0.115	L	0.032
M	0.056		
M_K	0.091		
π	−0.012		

Source: Chapter 2.

innovation intensity in agriculture, the proportion of manufacturing output exported, the share of capital goods in total imports, and the rate of depreciation). While their values are formally implied by the variables given, each deserves some further comment.

Let us suppose that the traditional sector is described by a Cobb-Douglas production function with constant returns to scale, i.e., equation (2) with $\beta = 1 - \alpha$. Then the relationship between the growth rates of labor and output is obtained from equations (6) and (7):

$$G(Y_a) = \epsilon + [\alpha + (1 - \alpha)\gamma]G(L_a).$$

For the postwar period γ, the elasticity of the land input with respect to labor, was estimated to average 1.04, and from Table 22, $G(Y_a) = 0.040$ and $G(L_a) = 0.029$. Hence we have the innovation intensity ϵ given by:

$$\epsilon = 0.010 + 0.001\alpha \cong 0.010.$$

In this case the output elasticity with respect to labor has a negligible effect on ϵ, but in a situation in which γ was substantially less than one the influence of α would be important. This calculation of the average innovation intensity is very sensitive to the output and labor series chosen—both of which are among the weaker parts of Philippine data. However, we have no evidence that ϵ is any greater than 1 per cent, and even that may be an overestimate.[25]

The rate of increase of the proportion of manufacturing output exported is obtained formally as $G(\zeta) = G(X_m) - G(Y_m)$. The data in Table 22 would suggest that $G(\zeta)$ was at the very satisfactory level of 4.7 per cent per year. As we saw in the previous chapter, however, the exports included in this category are largely made up of highly processed extractive industry products with the same reliance on the natural resource base that characterizes extractives. Excluding those items, $G(X_m)$ is reduced to 0.032, giving a value for $G(\zeta)$ of -0.036. In the context of the present analysis it is the latter figure which more nearly reflects the Philippine performance in exporting manufactures.

A different correction needs to be applied to the aggregate data on the share of capital goods in imports. For the whole period 1950–1968, the average figures show $G(\nu) = G(M_K) - G(M) = 0.035$. But this increase is accounted for almost entirely by the shifting composition of imports in the 1950's. For

[25] In Chapter 4, the data on productivity in agriculture are disaggregated, and it is seen that a single value for ϵ must obscure a complex set of compositional shifts and individual crop yield changes. The above computation is of more formal than practical significance.

1950–1960, G (ν) averaged 0.055, whereas for 1960–1968 it was only 0.005. Since total imports increased at a fairly steady rate, the implication was that the change indicated a marked slowing of the process of import substitution for consumer manufactures.

Little can be said on two other characteristics of modern sector growth, the rate of capital depreciation and the capital/output ratio. We can observe that the growth of real (gross) investment, G (I^*) (which is very close to that of capital goods imports), is greater than the growth of modern sector output. The difference between the two rates is 0.017. Although in Table 22 we have assumed a constant average capital output ratio, the actual relationships between the incremental ratio and depreciation are not obtainable with the data available. We have similarly to admit ignorance on the allocation of investment between the two major components of the modern sector, extractives and nonextractives, except to the extent that this can be inferred from the resulting production levels and growth rates.

One of the few areas in which the model data can be checked for consistency is in their prediction of the trend in the intersectoral terms of trade (equation 36). According to the model, τ can move in either direction depending upon the volumes of commodities entering the market, which in turn depend on variables such as the level of wages and the labor transfer. Transforming equation (36) into a relationship between growth rates, we have:

$$G(\tau) \cong G(\Upsilon_m) - kG(X_a) - (1 - k)[G(w^*) + G(L_m)], \quad (39)$$

where k is the weighting factor $X_a/(X_a + w^*L_m)$. (The term $(1 - \zeta)$ makes no appreciable contribution since ζ is less than 0.01 and has changed little.) Taking the data for the years 1959–1961, k is found to be 0.15.[26] The right hand side of equa-

[26] The appropriate value for w^* is the estimate of average payrolls per paid employee, given in Table 10 as ₱1,780 in 1961 prices (₱1,570 in 1955 prices), rather than the wage for unskilled workers.

tion (39) can therefore be evaluated, and gives the predicted value of G (τ) of 0.024. Considering the crudities of our assumptions, this is remarkably close to the direct estimate of 0.021 for G (τ), obtained from the entirely independent price data underlying Table 13.

A simple aggregative model has some utility in giving quantitative indications of the effects of changes in the parameters on subsequent growth. In the present case two areas are of

Table 23. Effect of bias in modern sector technical progress and level of innovation intensity in agriculture on modern sector growth and labor absorption: hypothetical data using naive model* (values after 20 years; variables are indices with time zero = 100)

Variable or growth rate	Harrod neutrality ($\theta = 0$, $\phi = 0.03$)		Hicks neutrality ($\theta = \phi = 0.015$)		Solow neutrality ($\theta = 0.03$, $\phi = 0$)	
	$\epsilon = 0$	$\epsilon = 0.03$	$\epsilon = 0$	$\epsilon = 0.03$	$\epsilon = 0$	$\epsilon = 0.03$
K_m/L_m	182	182	100	100	54	54
L_m/L	98	142	125	173	142	188
K_m	325	473	227	312	142	188
Y_m	325	473	306	421	258	342
$G(Y_m)$	.053	.073	.046	.059	.030	.041

Source: Numerical solution of equation (38), taking single year intervals.
* Parameters and initial values from Philippines, 1950.

special interest: the nature of bias in modern sector technical progress and the level of innovation intensity in agriculture. As a means of studying these in numerical terms we have used the Philippine data in the naive model represented by equation (38). However, to isolate the effects of primary interest, exports were assumed to originate only from the traditional sector. Table 23 gives some results from this model for three extreme cases of technical progress in industry and two in agriculture. The Philippines most closely resembles the case of Harrod-neutrality in its modern sector, with a constant capital/output ratio and rising labor productivity. After some twenty years of this growth pattern, it is seen that the absolute level and the growth rate of output are the highest of the three cases, but that labor absorption is the least satisfactory. The importance of rising labor productivity in agriculture is obviously very great in determining the outcome. Equation (38) assumes a pure land surplus, and tracing the solution further through time it is very clear that growth under Harrod neutrality is more sharply curtailed as land expansion slows and ceases than under the other cases.

ECONOMIC IMPLICATIONS OF THE MODEL

While the open dual economy model described in this chapter has been largely drawn inductively from the earlier analysis of the Philippines, the development problems it emphasizes are of very wide interest. The two most important areas in which it touches established growth theory are first, the recognition of capital specificity and all that this entails, and second, the theory of dualistic growth for a closed economy. In attempting to spell out the economic implications of the model it will be helpful to relate it where possible to the literature in these fields.

Capital Specificity

In the closed economy models of Fei-Ranis and Jorgenson it is assumed that intended savings are automatically translated into realized investment and so induce growth.[27] This is also of course a familiar assumption in models of the Harrod-Domar type. In wishing to relax it we accept the contention that it views too simplistically the relationship between savings, investment, and growth. The simplest generalization is to distinguish two categories of industrial output, consumer goods

[27] Fei and Ranis, *Development of the Labor Surplus Economy;* Jorgenson, "Development of a Dual Economy." The Fei-Ranis model is found in its most accessible form (although somewhat modified from its original presentation) in the authors' 1966 article "Agrarianism, Dualism, and Economic Development."

and capital goods, and postulate a low (or zero) rate of transformation between them.

The model structure thus formed is that characterizing the so-called unorthodox Soviet or neo-Marxist growth model, associated with the names of Feldman, Domar, and Mahalanobis[28] and subsequently elaborated by many other writers.[29] Most of this literature is directed toward finding the correct allocation of investment between consumer and capital goods industries to obtain optimum growth under various conditions in a closed economy. The best known result is the "Mahalanobis paradox," that total output will eventually be greater if a relatively high proportion of resources are allocated to capital goods production even if the capital/output ratio in this sector is very much lower than in consumer goods production.

In our present open model, we have assumed that there is no domestic capital goods industry. We do, however, have two major export industries—the modern extractive sector and traditional agriculture—the output of which is transformable into capital goods through trade. If consumer manufactures could also be traded, then capital specificity disappears in the open economy, but we have argued that this is not generally possible.[30] Since we take investment in traditional agriculture

[28] See Evsey D. Domar, "A Soviet Model of Growth," in his *Essays in the Theory of Economic Growth* (New York: Oxford University Press, 1957); and P. C. Mahalanobis, "Some Observations on the Process of Growth of National Income," *Sankhya,* 12 (1952), 307–312.

[29] Including Ronald Findlay, Gordon C. Winston, and Donald J. Harris. See especially Ronald Findlay, "Capital Theory and Developmental Planning," *Review of Economic Studies,* 29 (1962), 85–98; and "Optimal Investment Allocation between Consumer Goods and Capital Goods," *Economic Journal,* 76 (1966), 70–83.

[30] A more precise statement would be that manufactures cannot be exported at world prices. Whatever the reasons, however, whether very high production costs or foreign import quotas, it is a fact that in most underdeveloped countries the nonextractive output of the modern sector is characterized by an extremely low transformation capacity through trade.

to be negligible (for noneconomic reasons), the investment allocation choice is between extractives, a quasi-capital goods sector, and manufacturing industry, which produces only consumer goods. The allocation coefficient was denoted by μ in equation (19). Applying the Mahalanobis result, it might then be expected that most rapid growth would be achieved by making μ as large as possible. While formally correct, this would ignore several highly important considerations. Thus, for example, extractive industries often have few linkages with the rest of the economy and so the benefits from externalities associated with them may be much less than would follow from an equal investment in other parts of the modern sector. Again, the foreign exchange generated is not automatically used to finance capital goods imports—part may be lost through repatriation of profits, capital flight, or import of luxury consumer goods. Perhaps most important of all, the resource base of the extractive sector is often severely limited while its corporate structure may be such that no account is taken of depletion. A careful analysis of these points highlights a number of crucial differences between extractives and a domestic capital goods industry. (Some of these issues are examined with reference to the Philippines in the following chapter.)

A more fruitful analogy could be made between the closed two-sector (consumer goods and capital goods) model with specificity of capital and the open dual economy in which traditional agriculture was conceived of as a capital goods industry. The stress on growth by the development of the capital goods sector in the former case would then correspond to an emphasis on raising agricultural productivity in the dual model. There is no need to pursue the argument, however, since in this context the open dual economy does not differ from the closed dual model with the latter's usual assumption that modern sector output is nonspecific.

Capital specificity in the present model should not be confused with the identification of independent constraints on growth as in the two-gap model introduced by McKinnon.[31] The foreign exchange constraint does not appear as an independent constraint in the open dual economy model. This is not just because we have a market determined foreign exchange rate. If the exchange rate were undervalued, for example, and reserves were large the economy could not usefully be viewed as pressing against a savings-investment ceiling, but rather savings and investment are taking the form of holding foreign assets. Bruton has noted that the constraint on growth imposed by import capacity is more properly described as a "transformation capacity" constraint, referring to limitations on reallocating domestic resources to capital goods production, export growth, or import substituting industries.[32]

Is it realistic to assume that entrepreneurs as a group cannot invest more (in real terms) even if they want to? In the early stages of the typical development program imports of consumer goods can be reduced by import substitution, thus making it possible for entrepreneurs to raise the level of savings and investment. When this potential is exhausted, and assuming away foreign loans, aid and other windfalls, it is reasonable to argue that capital specificity sharply curtails the potential to increase investment. The result of entrepreneurs deciding to raise the share of profits invested may not be to increase the increment to capital stock but instead to shift the intersectoral terms of trade against industry. (This could be traced through a progressively greater overvaluation of the exchange rate—with consequent incentives for smuggling or underdeclaration of exports—leading eventually to devaluation. This sequence was observed in the Philippines.)

---

[31] Ronald I. McKinnon, "Foreign Exchange Constraints in Economic Development and Efficient Aid Allocation," *Economic Journal,* 74 (1964), 388–409. See also Hollis B. Chenery and Alan M. Strout, "Foreign Assistance and Economic Development," *American Economic Review,* 56 (1966), 679–733.

[32] Henry J. Bruton, "On the Role of Import Substitution in Development Planning," *Philippine Economic Journal,* 4 (1965), 18.

The practical consequences of this are important. With capital specificity of this nature it is futile to pursue policies to encourage greater investment if exports cannot simultaneously be increased. If it is possible to increase extractive exports then all is well—at least in the short run—but if not, the alternatives remaining are to raise traditional sector production or reduce food consumption. In these last two cases it is likely that an intersectoral transfer of savings from agriculture to industry will have to play an important role, with either landlords or the government acting as intermediary. (There is little evidence of much intersectoral transfer in the Philippines which took the "short run" path of expanding extractive exports.)

The alternative (or complementary) policy indicated is of course to attack capital specificity itself. The two possibilities are the establishment of a domestic capital goods industry—machines to make machines, or second-order capital goods—or the development of an export industry in manufactures. Our initial assumption in the model, represented by equation (25), permitted the growth of domestic capital goods production, but for sharpness in the later analysis we used the extreme case of equation (26) : $I^* = M_K$.[33] In the more general case these structural constraints would have to be relaxed to allow for a domestic source of durable equipment.[34] An important model developed by Winston, generalizing the two-gap approach, incorporates this possibility and provides an integrated theoretical frame-

[33] A similar assumption is made in the UNCTAD model (known also as the Mosak model), a simple one-sector model designed to predict foreign exchange requirements to attain target growth rates of output. United Nations, Department of Economic and Social Affairs, *Studies in Long-Term Economic Projections for the World Economy: Aggregative Models* (New York, 1964), Chapter 3.

[34] A model similar to the one cited in the preceding note which includes this extension has been developed by ECAFE. See United Nations, Economic Commission for Asia and the Far East, *Problems of Long-Term Economic Projections, with Special Reference to Economic Planning in Asia and the Far East;* Report of the Third Group of Experts on Programming Techniques (New York, 1963), pp. 7–15, 18–21.

work for analyzing investment and trade policies.[35] The major difficulty an economy faces in producing capital equipment appears to be related to economies of scale, a point examined in Chapter 1. The other possibility, of reducing the specificity of domestically produced manufactures through trade, has also proved extremely difficult if not impossible, for reasons which we take up in detail in the following chapter.

Significance of Land Rather Than Labor Surplus

The usual labor surplus model assumes that labor can be withdrawn from the agricultural sector without adversely affecting production, or in its more sophisticated form, that wage levels do not reflect the opportunity cost of employing additional labor in industry. These models also generally assume that the area of cultivated land is constant over time. For a large number of countries empirical evidence shows that cultivated land has expanded and is expanding steadily, and we have therefore preferred to assume this and make the associated assumption that a significant amount of labor cannot be drawn off the land without reducing the level of output. We are in a sense reversing the time dimension from the surplus labor case, taking the initial situation as one where wages were equal to marginal productivity in agriculture while supposing that surplus labor could emerge in the course of time as in the classical Malthusian model of stagnation. Our approach was discussed at some length in Chapter 2 with reference to the Philippines.

The theoretical significance of this distinction is a closer link between industrial growth and the agricultural surplus, while policy implications derive from emphasizing that labor, like the other factors of production, involves a cost. In contrast with the idea (adduced by Nurkse and others) that workers can move to the industrial sector and produce capital goods by labor alone, under a land surplus regime these same workers

[35] Gordon C. Winston, "Consumer Goods or Capital Goods: Supply Consistency in Development Planning," *Pakistan Development Review,* 7 (1967), 348–378.

could remain in agriculture and create capital by generating additional exports—subject of course to an elastic demand. Finally, as a simple explanatory mechanism, a land surplus accounts for the constancy of real wages despite the absence of appreciable technical progress in agriculture without the need to hypothesize institutional determinants of wages.[36]

Effective Demand

The Keynesian revolution made clear the important role of effective demand in analyzing the ills of the advanced economies of the West. By and large the Keynesian analysis is inadequate for underdeveloped countries where the problem is not so much the underutilization of capital equipment but an absolute shortage of capital. The problem is one of capital accumulation rather than lack of effective demand.[37] The major constraints on growth lying on the side of supply are rooted in low productivity which makes it difficult to save, in capital specificity which prevents the transformation of intended savings into realized investment, and in the related problem of balancing the output of commodities.

Accepting this view, the present model of an open dual economy—as also with most other models of dual economy growth—is quite frankly supply-oriented. By assuming that all prices adjust to clear all markets we in effect disregard the possibility of demand constraints.

Nevertheless we should not let an absence of effective demand in the model lead us to deny its existence. Wage rates are some-

[36] The schizophrenic behavior of the dualistic landlord in the Fei-Ranis model—who pays an institutionally determined wage to redundant workers in agriculture while at the same time acting as a financial intermediary, saving and investing in industry, and being innovative and responsive to markets—is commented on by Dixit. Avinash Dixit, "Theories of the Dual Economy: A Survey," mimeographed (Berkeley: University of California, Institute of International Studies, 1969), p. 38.

[37] On this point see, for example, L. R. Klein, "What Kind of Macroeconomic Model for Developing Economies?" *Indian Economic Journal,* 13 (1966), 313–324.

times sticky as in the Keynesian model and some of the under-utilized capital in the Philippines appears to be a consequence of enforcing a minimum wage higher than the market level. More often, however, underutilization of capital is caused by other factors such as poor investment decisions, shifts in demand, erratic policy shifts, and administration of existing policies.[38] Thus, for example, an important factor in under-utilization of capital in the Philippine textile industry has been the smuggling of textiles into that country.

Lack of effective demand should not be confused with in-ability to produce because of high costs. With a small market it may not pay to produce many products. This is a consequence of large economies of scale or inefficiencies in production, not a failure of demand.

Development Alternatives

One of the lessons of history which makes the study of eco-nomic development so complex is that no two countries de-velop in the same way. "Leading" sectors in one country may be "lagging" in another. Some countries grow by becoming increasingly open, while others such as the Soviet Union have stressed self-sufficiency, and foreign trade has played a declining role in their development. But despite these diverse patterns, certain features are almost always present. These include a movement of population out of agriculture, increasing produc-tivity in both sectors, a narrowing of sectoral productivity differ-entials, the growth of manufactured or at least processed agricultural exports, and some progress in domestic capital goods production. These elements can be combined in signif-

---

[38] Undercapacity utilization is not very significant for most Southeast Asian economies, but it has plagued the Indian economy. In India, how-ever, it is not due to lack of effective demand in the Keynesian sense; Bruton ("Import Substitution in Development Planning," pp. 20–22) blames most of it on poor planning which results in inadequate overhead facilities and shortages of imported materials and spare parts.

icantly different proportions according to the size of the country, its natural resources, and the policies followed.

It is not possible then to lay down a prescribed development path, but it is desirable to identify at least a few of the possible patterns. The closed dual economy approach captures one important element of the development process that is a part of virtually every development pattern: the important role played by the agricultural surplus, and (in the usual case of fixed land) particularly surpluses achieved through increases in yields. Yield increases permit the release of labor from agriculture and can make possible the saving to finance industrial investment. This same role is seen in the open economy. The only real difference, and it is an unimportant one insofar as growth relies on the transfer of agricultural savings, is that in the open economy, part of the agricultural surplus is transformed into capital equipment via foreign trade and not directly.

The closed dual economy approach, however, places almost exclusive emphasis on this development path. The theoretical alternative of the industrial sector growing by reinvestment alone is eventually precluded by the inability of a stagnant agricultural sector to produce sufficient food. By contrast, the essence of the open economy approach is to highlight the alternative patterns that are open to the growing economy. An important role in the over-all growth process is played not only by yield increases, but by venting surpluses through trade, exporting manufactures, and developing a domestic capital goods industry.

The Philippines is evidence enough that a modern sector can grow rapidly without agricultural yield increases. In this case it was made possible primarily through the venting of a surplus of land and forests through trade. It is clear from the model that this type of expansion is to some degree an alternative to modern sector growth based on increasing yields. Although in the long run growth cannot continue to be based on the export of resource-intensive products, where such resources are large they can play a vital role in initiating and sustaining the growth process.

The policy implications of the closed dual economy approach are clear: raise agricultural productivity or all else is impossible. In the open economy the matter is more complex. The economy is in fact faced with a choice between alternative patterns of growth and the model in itself cannot indicate the appropriate policy.[39] Some combination of yield increases, land expansion, extractive industry exports, manufactured exports, and capital goods production must be followed, but the appropriate emphasis will vary with conditions from economy to economy. What can be said, however, is that if the open economy is small to medium in size it will not be able to produce many capital goods, and therefore if it is to have sustained development it must depend less on venting surpluses and more on a combination of yield increases and manufactured exports.

The convention of thinking in terms of a closed labor surplus economy and largely abstracting from the implications of population growth and the limited natural resource base has encouraged the simplistic view that the rates of growth of GNP and the other major aggregates are a reliable guide both to past progress and to probable future growth. In fact, of course, the sources of this growth are of crucial importance in making any such evaluation. Growth which derives from "static expansion" or a simple using up of reserves is qualitatively different from that based on productivity increases, and the difference decisively affects future potential. If the past sources of growth

[39] The present descriptive model could of course be recast as an optimization model, seeking investment allocation time-trajectories which maximize some prescribed objective criterion. But the contribution that optimal growth strategies derived from a simple aggregative model can offer toward real policy decisions is probably quite limited, even if there were agreement on the criterion. For a discussion of this dynamic investment allocation problem in conjunction with the closely related issue of choice of techniques (the latter not arising in the present study), see A. K. Sen, "Some Notes on the Choice of Capital-Intensity in Development Planning," *Quarterly Journal of Economics,* 71 (1957), 561–584.

largely exclude manufactured exports and agricultural productivity increases then it is unlikely that an economy is laying a firm basis for future development. Indeed, it may be enjoying short-run growth at the expense of long-run development. There is no such thing as an economy "marking time" because the ratio of population to resources changes.

CHAPTER 4

Exports and Resources: Some Modern Dilemmas of Growth

The simple model of an open dual economy that we have analyzed in the previous chapter we believe describes in broad terms the postwar growth experience of the Philippines and, by implication, of other countries in similar situations. The picture that emerges is of an economy with a modern sector enabled to grow rapidly because of a rising ability to import capital goods but with little evidence of progress in reducing dependence on these imports. Moreover, this rapid growth is achieved without significant transfer of labor from agriculture to industry. The foreign exchange necessary to finance capital goods imports is generated by a relatively stagnant traditional sector surplus and by the export of resource-intensive extractive industry products. Exports of manufactures have been almost negligible.

This linking of modern sector growth to export capacity we see not as a necessary (accounting) relationship but rather as a particular pattern of development that has been followed. We have nevertheless argued that alternatives to it are not easily or quickly to be found: for the Philippines at least, it has become effectively a "rule of growth." It is evident, therefore, that the export sector plays the crucial role in determining prospects for future growth.

In this chapter we shall study the dynamics of export growth once again taking the Philippine case to illustrate a more gen eral thesis. The Philippines provides an instructive example in that its export industries are located in both sectors of the economy. In the terminology used in Chapter 1 it is neither traditional sector dominant nor modern sector dominant, unlike most other Southeast Asian countries. The topics in which we are chiefly interested relate to the relative importance of resource inputs compared to nonresource inputs in exports: the past trends in these relative shares, the problems connected with altering them, and the magnitudes of the exploitable reserves of resources. On the basis of the discussion of these points we are able to make some tentative statements concerning the likely future growth path of exports—and, implicitly, of the whole economy.

For some purposes our broad division between modern and traditional sector exports can be retained, but in most of the analysis we must work at a less aggregated level. We recall, however, our definition of the exportable agricultural surplus as aggregate output (Y_a) less the total food consumption of the population (gL). For given food consumption, any increase in output (whatever the type of crop causing it) will raise traditional sector exports. Thus the whole traditional sector may be regarded as belonging to the export sector and all parts of its output are relevant to this analysis. The changing composition of crops and the interactions between hectarage and yields mean that emphasis on individual crop performances may often give misleading results.

DUALISTIC ANALYSIS OF EXPORT SECTOR

The distinction between the modern and traditional sectors as applied to exports is useful for an analysis of their growth and relation to the development of the economy as a whole. The fundamentally different form of the production function in the two sectors lies at the root of their contrasting growth dynamics and differing impact on the economy. Before exploring the major implications of this dualistic structure, however, it is instructive to contrast our categories with the more conventional distinction between commercial (export) crops and food (subsistence) crops.

Commercial and food crops are the usual broad categories employed in discussing agriculture in underdeveloped countries.[1] In the Southeast Asian context, subsistence crops include rice, corn, cassava, and fruits and vegetables, while commercial crops cover rubber, coconuts, sugar, oil palm, and tobacco. The distinction between them appears at first sight to be both obvious and useful, implying a contrast between traditional, non-monetary farming and price-responsive, monetized commercial farming. The stereotype of this dichotomy is that of "noneconomic" subsistence farmers who grow rice and corn primarily to satisfy their own needs with the secondary aim of marketing the small surplus above these requirements, contrasted with the commercial farmers—"economic men" who practice comparative advantage through specialization in the production of crops which are sold on the world market.[2]

The research of the last two decades has, of course, thoroughly destroyed this straw man. Subsistence farmers as well as commercial farmers have been shown to be responsive to price incentives.[3] On the side of supply there now seems to be no significant distinction between commercial crops and subsistence crops, a conclusion which is not very surprising as most farmers who grow the former also grow the latter. The fact that a large part of the subsistence crops are retained for home consumption is of limited analytical importance.

It might be argued, however, that there remains a difference

[1] See, for example, Richard W. Hooley and Vernon W. Ruttan, "The Agricultural Development of the Philippines, 1902–1965," in *Agricultural Development in Asia*, ed. R. T. Shand (Canberra: Australian National University Press, 1969).

[2] In this usage, subsistence farming implies self-sufficiency rather than the minimum level compatible with survival.

[3] There is a general agreement that price incentives effectively allocate resources among crops but that productivity is much less responsive to price changes. See the discussion of the Philippine case in Chapter 2 and below.

on the demand side: for commercial crops, the world price is basically effective, whereas for food crops, the price is determined by domestic supply and demand. In a fully open economy, such a distinction could not exist because trade in, say, rice and corn (either exports or imports) would be as free as that in coconuts and sugar, and all prices would therefore be determined by world prices. In the Philippines, for example, although government control over the rice trade breaks the short-run connection between world prices and domestic prices, nevertheless, over a period of more than a few years, the average Philippine rice price has remained close to the average world price. Substantial imports are made in times of shortage and high prices, and small exports in times of surplus.[4] If yields of rice increased markedly, then there would seem to be little difficulty under present world conditions in expanding exports—or, if difficulties were to arise in the future, in reallocating rice land to crops more in demand on the world market. Effectively, therefore, food crops are similar to commercial crops on the side of demand as well as supply, and it is surely difficult to argue, as Hooley and Ruttan do, that "it is possible . . . that the heavy dependence of rice or corn on a relatively stagnant domestic market has dampened incentives to achieve rapid productivity growth while the significance of export markets in the case of copra and sugar has encouraged technical change and innovation leading to productivity growth."[5] Once we recognize the basic similarity of subsistence and commercial crops on the side of demand as well as supply, then there is little to be gained by continuing to define them as separate categories.

[4] Some 30,000 tons were exported to Indonesia in 1967–1968.
[5] Hooley and Ruttan, "Agricultural Development of the Philippines." The commercial/subsistence dichotomy is useful, however, to the extent that government policies cause a sustained price discrepancy between food crops and export crops. In the Philippines, this occurred, for example, over 1960–1965 when the prices of export products increased relative to food products and production shifts responded accordingly.

In our dual economy approach, we identify only one category of exports from the traditional sector, drawing no distinction between food and nonfood crops. Moreover, the definition $(X_a = Y_a - gL)$ makes allowance for the fact that some countries specialize in producing nonfood crops while importing part of their food requirements. A rapid increase in commercial crop output, resulting, for example, from a price-induced hectarage shift in favor of these crops at the expense of food crop production, may necessitate a corresponding rise in cereal imports. In such an instance, X_a would not record a rapid rate of growth.

The two broad categories of exports we consider, classified according to the sector contributing most to their value, are distinguished by their different production functions.[6] Exports from the traditional sector by and large involve little capital but are land and labor using. In contrast, modern sector exports (extractive industry products and manufactures) make heavy demands on the scarce factor, capital, but on average generate little employment for the abundant factor, labor.[7] The consequences of this difference in the production functions are similar to those analyzed by Baldwin in his Rhodesia study.[8] For traditional exports the factor requirements fit the existing relative factor conditions and a substantial volume of employment is generated for an essentially unskilled labor force. Most of the traditional sector income can be expected to be spent domestically. The opposite holds true for modern sector export industries such as mining and logging (but to a lesser extent

[6] For a discussion of the actual allocation of export commodities between sectors in the Philippine case, see the section on categorization problems in Chapter 2.

[7] It is conventional to argue that capital is the scarce factor in underdeveloped countries, but the claim that it is scarce in the modern sector must be reconciled with rising capital/labor ratios and the access of this sector to foreign capital.

[8] Robert E. Baldwin, *Economic Development and Export Growth: A Study of Northern Rhodesia, 1920–1960* (Berkeley: University of California Press, 1966).

plantations) where the input requirements do not fit the existing factor supplies and require, for example, considerable training and upgrading of a small labor force.[9] The technological
nature of the modern sector production function induces an
improvement in the quality of the input labor, but the total
employment generated is not substantial. As a result, the modern export industries may have relatively little impact on domestic demand.

Another aspect of dualism which has economic significance is
the different role played by foreign enterprise in the two sectors. The greater skill and capital requirements of the modern
sector are closely associated with the much greater role played
in it by foreign enterprise. In the Philippines, foreign enterprise is of greatest importance in mining where the skill and
capital requirements are the most demanding.[10] It is also significant in the logging industry.[11] In the traditional sector as we
have defined it, however, foreign enterprise plays a very limited role, largely restricted to the processing of agricultural
products where the levels of skills and capital intensity are
closer to those of the modern sector.[12] Foreign management is

[9] For readers unfamiliar with the modern logging industry it should
be stressed that the skill requirements, while not generally as demanding
as those of mining, are quite considerable. Felling, bucking, scaling,
yarding, loading, and especially skylining, require skilled labor—as, of
course, does the processing of plywood and veneer.

[10] The large mining companies are either American or part American.
(The Philippine constitution prohibits foreign interests other than
American from exploiting natural resources.)

[11] In 1965–1966, timber license agreements by area totaled 1.2 million
hectares. Fourteen per cent of the licensed area was held by American
interests and 28% by joint American-Filipino companies. (Source:
Forest Management and Sawmills and Licenses Division, Bureau of
Forestry.)

[12] We have noted earlier the virtual absence in the Philippines of a
plantation economy such as is found in Malaysia and Indonesia—a
consequence, in part, of U.S. colonial policy. A law dating from 1902
restricts corporate holdings to a maximum of 1,024 hectares. Foreign
enterprise in agriculture is essentially limited to two pineapple

more frequently found than foreign capital, particularly in the mining, logging, and sugar milling industries. Partly this is a consequence of government policies, but it also reflects a greater scarcity of domestic skills than of domestic capital.

Foreign enterprise reinforces the tendency noted above for the modern sector export industries to generate relatively little domestic expenditure. Where profits accrue to foreign owners, it is reasonable to expect that a greater share will be remitted abroad than in the case of domestically owned profits. Similarly, income accruing to the salaried foreign labor force adds little to domestic demand because of high propensities to save and to consume imported goods. Thus, foreign enterprise lowers the domestic multiplier associated with the modern sector. Extractive industry exports generate the supply of foreign exchange needed by the modern sector but make less contribution to the demand for domestic industrial output. The extractive sector has some of the characteristics of true enclave dualism with its substantial independence of the domestic economy.

A further contrast between modern and traditional sector exports is the much greater import dependence of the former. Extractive exports are dependent not only on the import of capital goods but also on intermediate products such as chemicals and fuels. In a previous study of Philippine export industries, we have estimated that every $100 of traditional exports required imported inputs of $5 or less. The import component of extractive exports, however, ranged from 14 per cent to 24 per cent.[13] The net contribution of extractives to foreign ex-

---

plantations, two rubber plantations, and one coconut plantation. Among the agricultural processing industries, foreign (American and Spanish) enterprise in sugar milling lost its early dominance in the 1920's and has declined greatly in the postwar period; in coconut processing, however, American, British, and Chinese interests continue to dominate.

[13] George L. Hicks, "The Growing Import Dependence of Philippine Exports," mimeographed (Washington: National Planning Association, Center for Development Planning, 1967). The percentage import component of the various products was estimated as follows: copra,

change earnings is therefore considerably less than the level indicated by the gross figures.

DYNAMICS OF EXPORT GROWTH

The growth dynamics of extractive and traditional exports differ in many respects, but they share the common feature of resource-intensive growth. Essentially, export growth is based on the progressive exploitation of previously unemployed natural resources—land in the case of traditional and plantation agriculture, and forests and minerals for the rest of the extractive sector. Before turning to the key question of the future of this vent-for-surplus type of growth, however, we should again stress the differences in the growth engines of traditional and modern sector exports.

A characteristic of modern sector growth is its dynamism in contrast to the "static expansion" of the traditional sector. Growth in the modern sector is based on investment. Expansion is a function of prices, costs, and profits, and takes place within a largely corporate structure. Capital is a major factor of production, and technology and productivity improve in response to the import of improved equipment and the learning of new skills. One role of capital and advanced technology is to make possible rapid increases in output in response to flexible, profit-oriented resource flows. In contrast to this, the traditional sector appears static and inflexible. Given surplus land, growth of output need depend less on profits, capital accumulation, and technical change than on the increase in the agricultural labor force. Little capital is used in production, and the stable land/labor ratios are a reflection of the static technology. The composition of traditional sector output is responsive to relative price changes, but the ceiling on aggregate output is to a large degree set by the size of the employed labor force.[14]

One consequence of these different growth mechanisms is

---

zero; coconut oil, 0.7; desiccated coconut, 1.4; sugar, 5.7; logs, 14.0; plywood, 18.8; minerals, 23.6.

[14] The evidence relating to the price elasticity of output in traditional agriculture is discussed in Chapter 2.

that total output in the traditional sector tends to rise at a steady rate, little influenced by changes in prices. In the Philippines, despite the great changes in the relative prices of food and manufactured goods between 1920 and 1935, the total output of traditional agriculture and total traditional exports both increased steadily.[15] In sharp contrast, production and export of gold (the major prewar extractive export) responded dramatically to price incentives. Gold production climbed slowly prior to 1929 and then rose rapidly until 1939.[16] The price of Philippine gold relative to other commodities began to rise in 1930 as a result of the collapse in the general price level.

Sustained demand for minerals and logs in the postwar period has induced a rate of increase in output far in excess of that of traditional agriculture and an increase in their exports exceeding that of modern sector production as a whole (see Chapter 2). Plantation industries have generally faced a much less favorable world market situation with sharp price fluctuations and for some commodities a secular decline in prices. The example of the Malaysian rubber industry, however, demonstrates that these factors need not prevent a substantial growth rate of production, both by land expansion and by improvements in productivity.[17] Whether modern sector exports will continue to expand rapidly in the future depends partly on

[15] In 1921–1922 and from 1929 to 1934 the domestic terms of trade moved catastrophically against agriculture. The period 1915-1940 was marked by great agricultural price changes in contrast to relatively stable prices in the postwar period.

[16] Production in 1915 was 63,000 oz.; in 1929, 163,000 oz.; and in 1939, one million oz. C. P. Roa, *The Gold Mining Industry in the Philippines* (Manila: Bureau of Mines, 1967).

[17] As a result of new planting and replanting with improved varieties, estate rubber production in Malaysia has increased steadily since 1951 at an average rate of over 2.5% per year. Rubber prices in the same period have shown both strong fluctuations and a long-run decline. Indonesia's estate rubber industry has regressed through much of the postwar period, but this is part of the poor performance of the entire Indonesian plantation sector and is largely accounted for by domestic political factors such as the consequences of the nationalization of foreign-owned estates and by dysfunctional government regulatory policies.

imponderables such as world prices for the relevant commodities, but it also depends on forest and mineral resources. Future expansion of traditional exports, if land productivity remains stable, will be a function of the quantity and quality of the currently unutilized land.

PROBLEMS OF REDUCING RESOURCE CONTENT OF EXPORTS

In order to reduce this dependence on limited natural resources, two main avenues of approach are possible. So long as the same products are exported, the only possibility is to increase the efficiency of natural resource use. This implies raising the productivity of land and forests. The alternative, which we examine in the present section, is to change the composition of exports, either by exporting manufactured goods which have a low natural resource content or by subjecting existing exports to a greater degree of industrial processing.

Manufactured Exports

The Philippines, in common with many open economies, has been unable to develop a substantial export market for manufactured goods. The share of manufactured products in total exports rose throughout the postwar period, but by the mid-sixties it had reached only 8 per cent. Moreover, if we exclude the categories of plywood and veneer, manufactured exports then represent an insignificant 2 to 3 per cent of total exports with an average annual growth rate of only 3 per cent (see Table 5 and Figure 4). Easily the most important of this residual amount of manufactures is the category "chemical elements and compounds," which consists almost entirely of glycerine. This product is made by foreign firms from coconut oil and essentially reflects Philippine comparative advantage in coconut production. Beer is the only other manufactured export of any significance.[18]

[18] See Bureau of the Census and Statistics, *Foreign Trade Statistics of the Philippines* (Manila, published annually). It may be recalled that exports of processed agricultural products were assigned to the tra-

The advantages to the underdeveloped dual economy of exporting manufactures are both numerous and weighty, but they are more than matched by the difficulties. The major advantages are as follows:

1. An increase in the share of manufactured exports will lower the resource content of total exports. This may be desirable in order to prevent serious depletion of limited natural resources. (See the following section.)

2. Exports enable an industry's growth rate to exceed the ceiling otherwise imposed by the limited size and slow rate of growth of the domestic market.

3. Manufactured exports would raise the ceiling on growth imposed by the foreign exchange constraint.

4. Manufactures are generally thought to have a variety of favorable linkage effects. Their production stimulates demand for a wide variety of commodities and services.

5. Competition in world markets is conducive to efficiency.

These are the usual arguments, but Sicat has added the interesting proposition that:

6. Competition among foreign and domestic producers for a given domestic market results in a conflict situation which induces "negative nationalism." Emphasis on export expansion may channel restrictive nationalism in more constructive directions.[19]

Despite these potential advantages, the practical difficulties are such that there is little immediate prospect for large numbers of underdeveloped countries—and specifically for the open dual economies of Southeast Asia—developing exports of manufactures on a significant scale. The list of these difficulties is also well-known, since they apply to most of the economies that have gone through the process of "successful" import substitu-

---

ditional sector if, as is generally the case, processing adds less than 50% of their export value.

[19] Gerardo P. Sicat, "A Design for Export Oriented Industrial Development," mimeographed (Quezon City: University of the Philippines, School of Economics, 1967).

tion. (As described in Chapter 1, such success tends to be associated with an inability to export manufactures.) Hirschman has summarized some of the arguments in an article referring to the Latin American experience:

The new industries have been set up exclusively to substitute imports, without any export horizon on the part of either the industrialists themselves or of the government; the foreign branch plants and subsidiaries, which have taken an important part in the process, often are under specific instructions not to compete abroad with the products of the parent company; even more decisive than these obstacles deriving from attitudes and institutions is the fact that the new industries, set up behind tariff walls, usually suffer from high production costs in countries that are, moreover, permanently subject to strong inflationary pressures—hence, there is no real possibility of these industries competing successfully in international markets even if they were disposed to do so.[20]

Except for the reference to strong inflationary pressures, these arguments apply equally well to the Philippines. Sicat has described the consequences of the postwar pattern of rapid import substitution with very high rates of effective protection for manufacturing in terms of "the growth of interest groups which fed upon this protection mechanism." Specifically: "This policy pattern fostered a highly protection-minded entrepreneurial class, which is predisposed to seeking protection from competition and thereby shies away from the competitive challenge, especially in new export activities."[21] Elsewhere, he has noted that the import substitution policy "caused Philippines industrialists to be unwillingly drawn into highly restrictive

[20] Albert O. Hirschman, "The Political Economy of Import-Substituting Industrialization in Latin America," *Quarterly Journal of Economics,* 82 (1968), 25. See also the indictment of industrialization policies based on import substitution by Raúl Prebisch, *Towards a New Trade Policy for Development* (New York: United Nations, 1964), pp. 21–22.

[21] Gerardo P. Sicat, "Labor Policies and Philippine Economic Development," mimeographed (Quezon City: University of the Philippines, School of Economics, 1969), pp. 28–29.

contracts covering the use of foreign trademarks and manufacturing processes. These restrictions prevented Filipino manufacturers from exporting these products or from developing their own.''[22] Power has argued at length that import substitution has caused high costs and inefficiency.[23]

In the Philippine context, the incentive to export manufactures was further discouraged by the long period of exchange control, associated with a substantially overvalued exchange rate. Moreover, even after the virtual ending of exchange control in 1962, it is evident that high tariffs have caused the peso to continue to be overvalued.[24] That this overvaluation is an important factor in the apparent inability to export manufactures is strongly indicated by the fact that even foreign companies with good entrepreneurship and actively seeking export opportunities have had negligible success.

In addition to these conventional points Hirschman has argued that perhaps of even greater significance is the reluctance of industrialists to commit substantial resources to an export drive because exporting manufactures involves special risks and new costs which cannot be recovered in the short run. Therefore, he suggests, an industrialist will consider exporting only when he is confident that the basic institutions and policies which affect his interests are stable and responsive to these interests. In practice, industrialists do not "feel securely in control of vital economic policies affecting them. Policy-makers positively cultivate unpredictability and distance from interest groups; at the same time, they are highly manipulative."[25] This description is equally relevant to the Philippines and other Southeast Asian countries and provides an additional forceful

[22] Sicat, "A Design for Export Oriented Industrial Development," p. 7.
[23] John H. Power, "Import Substitution as an Industrialization Strategy," *Philippine Economic Journal*, 5 (1966), 167–204.
[24] John H. Power, "A Note on Estimation of Overvaluation of the Philippines Peso," mimeographed (Quezon City: University of the Philippines, School of Economics, 1967).
[25] Hirschman, "Import-Substituting Industrialization," pp. 28–29.

reason for their demonstrated failure to export manufactures.

It may be countered that, on the basis of the historical experience of a few countries (notably Australia and New Zealand), the capacity to export a significant quantity of manufactures is not an essential requirement for development. The alternative, however, is to base export expansion on products where the comparative advantage is substantial. This issue as it relates to the Philippines will be discussed later in this chapter. At this point we merely emphasize once again that the barriers to exporting manufactures are quite formidable and give a priori plausibility to a growth model like that of Chapter 3 which largely ignores such exports.[26]

Processing of Exports

Processing is a form of manufacturing and a highly processed product such as plywood is for most purposes best classed as a manufactured good. Thus the catalog of arguments listing the advantages that follow from the export of manufactured goods may equally be applied to the gains from the processing of primary products. But, as many examples of "hothouse" import substitution have shown, the costs of certain forms of industrialization are high and may even result in negative value added. The same range of possibilities applies to processing.

The processing of exports increases the industrial value-added component and lowers their resource content. Assuming that natural resources are limited, a movement away from the vent-for-surplus pattern of growth is to that extent advantageous. In addition, it has been argued that large gains in income

[26] The arguments summarized in the preceding paragraphs have all been related to conditions in the exporting country. There are also, of course, many barriers set up in importing countries, in the form especially of tariffs and quotas, which have highly important effects on the level of trade in manufactures. (We take account of some of these in the study of processing industries below.) For a useful discussion, see Harry G. Johnson, *Economic Policies toward Less Developed Countries* (Washington: The Brookings Institution, 1967), pp. 94–107.

and employment are possible by this means. In fact, however, the issues involved are exceedingly complex, and it is often far from certain that a country stands, on balance, to gain from the greater processing of primary products. We shall examine some of these issues with reference to the Philippines.

Plans, policies, and recommendations for greater processing of Philippine exports are frequently advocated, on the general grounds that "the more a product undergoes processing prior to its export, the greater is the gain of the domestic economy."[27] The facts indicate, however, that exports today are as little processed as they were ten or perhaps fifty years ago. The technical potential for greater processing is very substantial: copra can be converted into coconut oil; centrifugal sugar into refined sugar; logs into plywood; and mineral ores can be refined. The economics of realizing this potential is another matter.

On the demand side, the problems of greater processing can be reduced to an analysis of the effect of processing on prices. Many processed products—e.g., coconut oil, plywood, and refined sugar—face tariffs and quantitative restrictions in the importing countries which are not applied to the primary product. It is possible, therefore, that the value of a processed export may be *less* than the value of the primary input. Even if this is not the case, the value of domestic resources absorbed in processing may result in the net value added being negative. This could be caused by a number of problems on the side of supply. Economies of scale, inefficient labor, and the whole complex of factors that cause costs to be high, may well mean that the gains from processing are outweighed by the costs. Decisive examples of potential loss from greater processing occur in the cases of sugar, minerals, and plywood.

Since 1934, the Philippines has had an annual U.S. quota for

[27] Gerardo P. Sicat, "Domestic Economic Gains Foregone by Exports of Logs and Lumber," mimeographed (Quezon City: University of the Philippines, School of Economics, 1968), p. 1.

refined sugar of 74,483 short tons.[28] Refined sugar exported in excess of this quota could only be sold as part of the raw sugar quota. In this example the potential loss associated with greater exports would be equal to the additional cost of processing.

The processing of minerals is an example of a loss induced from the supply rather than the demand side. The Philippines exports a wide range of mineral ores which include copper, iron ore, and manganese. With the possible exception of copper, the scale of production does not justify the smelting of the ores, and the attempt to do so would increase the value of output but yield a negative product.

Similar forces operate on the side both of supply and demand for plywood production. Japan takes some 80 per cent of Philippine log exports but virtually no plywood. Log exports are more profitable partly because there is no tariff, whereas the rate on plywood is 20 per cent.[29] The attempt to export plywood rather than logs to Japan would therefore result in a worsening of relative prices. On the supply side, while Philippine labor costs as measured by wage rates are lower than in Japan, the effect of lower wages is largely negated by the generally lower productivity of labor.[30] Other elements in the cost structure are also higher than in Japan. For example, the lack of a large domestic market for plywood means that small pieces and "odd ends" cannot be used in the Philippines and the recovery rate is therefore lower than in Japan.[31]

The high cost of producing plywood in the Philippines causes

[28] J. Bernhardt, *The Sugar Industry and the Federal Government, a Thirty-Year Record (1917–47)* (Washington: Sugar Statistics Service, 1948), pp. 162–165.

[29] Japan Tariff Association, *Customs Tariffs Schedules of Japan, 1966* (Tokyo, 1967).

[30] J. G. Landgrebe, "The Philippine Textile and Timber Trades," *Philippine Economic Journal*, 5 (1966), 160. In 1962, according to Landgrebe, Japanese labor engaged in plywood manufacture earned U.S. $55 per month compared with $34 in the Philippines, $23 in South Korea, and $21 in Taiwan.   [31] *Ibid.*, p. 153.

profit rates to be low and usually very much lower than the prevailing rates in logging.[32] It could be argued, however, that there is a conflict between private and social gain. Social gains from processing include external economies associated with linkages and labor training, while social costs include the effects of the more rapid denudation of the forests caused by specialization in logging. The question of the gains and losses from the processing of logs is a complex one that cannot be answered without further study.

The coconut industry is perhaps the best illustration of the absence of a long-run tendency for Philippine exports to be subject to more processing and of our thesis that it is not possible to advance, as a firm proposition, that more processing is desirable. The argument—where it can be made—that more processing should take place during the course of development, does not of itself support policies to induce greater processing. In the case of the coconut industry, however, we would argue that there is a close coincidence of private and social gain, that the industry is responsive to profit opportunities, and that the processing that occurs is approximately the optimum.[33]

The extraction of coconut oil from copra has always been the major form of processing of coconut products.[34] Both the oil and the copra are mostly exported, and it is the world price that determines the domestic price of both products. The incentive to extract and export oil rather than copra depends on the cost of extraction and the relative price of copra and oil. Extraction costs are fairly stable, but the relative oil/copra price has shown substantial fluctuations in response to both domestic and international changes.

[32] This statement is based on interviews in 1966–1967 with company managers and officials of various logging enterprises in Mindanao.

[33] The following paragraphs are based on the study by George L. Hicks, "The Philippine Coconut Industry: Growth and Change, 1900–65," mimeographed (Washington: National Planning Association, Center for Development Planning, 1967), pp. 117–165.

[34] The only other significant processing is the manufacture of desiccated coconut directly from fresh nuts.

During and immediately after the first world war, the oil price was highly favorable relative to copra. Not surprisingly, the industry responded by exporting most of the copra in the form of oil. The situation was reversed in the 1950's. American and European tariffs on oil discouraged processing. Of even greater importance was the discrepancy between the official and free market rate for the peso during the period of exchange control. It was relatively easy to smuggle or underdeclare copra and thus obtain an effective exchange rate higher than the official rate. Oil exports, on the other hand, were easy to control and suffered severely from the overvaluation of the peso. Consequently, little copra was processed prior to export.

Between 1960 and 1965, oil processing experienced a remarkable recovery. Oil exports rose from $15 million to $68 million, although the *share* of copra output processed in the mid-sixties was still well below the level of 1919–1920. The increase in processing was partly the result of decontrol in 1960–1962, which virtually eliminated the gap between the official and free exchange rate. More important, however, was the fall in ocean freight rates for coconut oil caused by the introduction of bulk tankers which broke the shipping conference monopoly. The fall in the freight rate for oil, but not for copra, raised the effective oil/copra price.

This case study is an example of the way essentially fortuitous factors have influenced the structure of incentives and the actual degree of processing of coconut products. Unpredictable external forces as well as the vagaries of domestic policies explain the observed course of processing more than do the internal forces of the growth process.

PRODUCTIVITY AND NATURAL RESOURCES

We have argued above that countries pursuing the familiar patterns of growth exemplified by the Philippines are unlikely in the near future to be able to export a significant volume of manufactures or to subject existing exports to much increased processing. While our examples of export industries were restricted to those of a single country, it would be possible to adduce similar or related arguments for many of the other major exports from the Southeast Asian region: rubber, tin, petroleum, palm oil, tobacco, and of course cereals. Some additional processing of copra in the Philippines or rubber in Indonesia may well occur, but simple processing of this type adds relatively little to final value. When substantial processing is involved, as in the manufacture of plywood, then both domestic and international obstacles intervene to preclude any dramatic increase in output. If the future export of manufactures and processed products is at best uncertain, then the possibility of reducing the resource content of exports depends on success in increasing efficiency in the use of the primary inputs. Specifically, unless the productivity of land and forests rises, there is no escape from dependence on vent-for-surplus expansion and the inevitable eventual decline in exports that this implies.

Productivity and Traditional Agriculture

The historical constancy of yields in agriculture was discussed on the aggregate level in Chapters 1 and 2. Before we can evaluate the prospects for future increases in yields we must examine the past performance of the major crops individually. Again we take the Philippine case, with the knowledge that, in this field especially, the Philippines typifies the region as a whole.

Indices of country-wide average yields for six major crops for the three-year prewar average 1939–1941 and annually for 1954–1968 are given in Table 24.[35] Rice, corn, coconuts, and sugar cane have accounted for about 37, 8, 24, and 5 per cent, respectively, of total crop value in recent years. Abaca and tobacco make up a further 4 per cent.[36] Together these crops take up nearly nine-tenths of the total cultivated area. Over the fifteen-year period 1954–1968, rice and corn show only negligible yield increases until the most recent years, and coconuts and sugar have no clear trend. Only the two relatively unimportant com-

[35] Data for the postwar years prior to 1954 are considered much less reliable.   [36] *Statistical Reporter*, 11, no. 2 (1967), 8.

Table 24. Average yield indices for major crops, Philippines, 1939/1941 and 1954–1968 (average yields 1954/1956 = 100)

Year*	Food crops		Commercial crops			
	Rice (1)	Corn (2)	Coconuts† (3)	Sugar‡ (4)	Abaca (5)	Tobacco (6)
1939/1941	94.1	104.8	n.a.	88.4	119.6	100.5
1954	100.1	116.6	90	101.3	90.1	103.8
1955	100.4	92.8	103	97.8	97.5	103.7
1956	99.4	90.6	108	100.9	112.4	92.4
1957	100.6	83.8	115	100.0	112.4	114.5
1958	84.6	103.2	115	116.8	130.9	106.0
1959	92.1	80.6	115	121.5	117.3	103.0
1960	94.2	105.6	110	115.2	109.2	121.1
1961	96.4	98.9	103	107.6	133.1	119.4
1962	102.4	105.0	110	116.3	129.0	125.7
1963	104.5	109.2	105	108.4	142.3	125.8
1964	103.7	113.9	93	102.3	129.2	123.4
1965	103.9	114.2	94	81.6	136.1	109.1
1966	109.1	109.6	95	80.9	138.4	122.9
1967	110.2	115.5	104	93.0	127.9	112.3
1968	115.0	120.5	99	89.6	122.8	125.6

Sources: Columns 1, 2, 5, 6: implicit average yields computed from Department of Agriculture and Natural Resources data on harvested areas and production; column 3: George L. Hicks, "The Philippine Coconut Industry," p. 175, and DANR unpublished data (1966–1968); column 4: Philippine Sugar Association.
* Crop year ending June 30.
† Nuts per bearing tree.
‡ Piculs of sugar per hectare.

mercial crops, abaca and tobacco, evinced any sustained increase during most of the period—averaging at most about 2.5 per cent a year.

Rice yields in the Philippines have been remarkably stable over the greater part of the present century.[37] One important

[37] In the decade 1920–1929, aggregate yield averaged 1.19 metric tons of rough rice (paddy) per hectare; in 1960–1968 it was 1.25. Department of Agriculture and Natural Resources, *Philippine Agricultural Statistics* (Manila, 1954), volume 1, pp. 26–27; and Bureau of Agricultural Economics, DANR, mimeographed releases.

reason for the constancy in the postwar years has been the combination of yield increases in established, irrigated areas (due to new varieties and improved technical inputs such as fertilizer) and yield decreases resulting from the expansion of rice land into poorer upland areas. Moreover, part of the local yield increases observed in the 1960's are merely caused by improvement in the average quality of the land cultivated as some of the marginal land is transferred to other crops. Barker has shown a strong negative correlation between rice hectarage and yield both in the long run and the short run.[38] Thus, for example, the decline in the rice hectarage in Central Luzon and the Western Visayas, which resulted from the expansion of sugar cane into marginal rice growing areas, led to higher average rice yields, while the rapid expansion of hectarage in Mindanao and the Cagayan Valley was associated with marked falls in yields.[39] The yield fluctuations observed in the Western Visayas, the major sugar producing region, mesh closely with the changing fortunes of the sugar industry. Because of the importance of these yield trends, we present the data in some detail in Table 25. Clearly, the aggregate yield data must be intrepreted with great caution if they are to be used to measure technical progress.

Yields of corn have also shown little change over a long period. The average level during 1960–1968, for example, was 0.65 metric tons (shelled corn) per hectare, compared with 0.68 tons in 1925–1930.[40] Unlike rice, corn shows higher yields on newly opened land, but these tend to decline after a period of several years as the natural soil fertility becomes exhausted. (If

[38] Randolph Barker, "The Response of Production to a Change in Rice Price," *Philippine Economic Journal*, 5 (1966), 267–269. In the long-run case, he uses regional cross-section data on area and yield changes over 1952/1954–1960/1962, fitting the function $(y + k) = a (x + k)^b$, where y is percentage change in harvested area; x, percentage change in yield; and k is a scale constant. The estimate of b is -1.76. A doubling of harvested area over this period was associated with an absolute decline in yield of 18%, or 22% below the yield that would have been attained with no change in area.   [39] *Ibid.*, p. 267.

[40] From the sources given in Note 37.

Table 25. Rice yields for selected regions, Philippines, 1950–1968
(metric tons rough price per hectare harvested area)

Year*	Central Luzon	Cagayan Valley	Western Visayas	Southern & Western Mindanao	Philippine average
1950	1.33	1.32	1.08	1.27	1.18
1951	1.33	1.06	1.14	1.32	1.16
1952	1.04	1.33	1.11	1.59	1.15
1953	1.32	1.32	1.09	1.32	1.18
1954	1.33	1.59	1.13	3.18	1.21
1955	1.50	1.30	0.98	1.93	1.19
1956	1.61	1.25	0.88	1.35	1.21
1957	1.61	1.25	0.91	1.36	1.21
1958	1.41	1.08	0.82	1.03	1.02
1959	1.51	1.28	0.86	1.04	1.12
1960	1.39	1.38	1.07	1.03	1.13
1961	1.57	1.09	1.26	1.13	1.16
1962	1.79	1.21	1.24	1.14	1.23
1963	1.82	1.28	1.16	1.27	1.25
1964	1.86	1.13	1.19	1.26	1.24
1965	1.82	1.21	1.28	1.04	1.25
1966	1.98	1.52	1.09	1.05	1.31
1967	2.05	1.54	1.20	1.08	1.35
1968	2.14	1.63	1.20	1.16	1.43

Source: Bureau of Agricultural Economics, DANR data, assembled by International Rice Research Institute.
* Crop year ending June 30.

the land can eventually be irrigated for rice growing, of course, yields are sustained by means of the nutrients contained in the water rather than in the soil.) The relative constancy of corn yields which has been observed results from high yields in areas where cultivation is expanding rapidly, offset by declining yields elsewhere.

Coconuts have apparently experienced a long-term increase in yield (as measured in nuts per bearing tree) between 1918 and 1960 of nearly 30 per cent, or 0.6 per cent per year.[41] Almost

[41] Hicks, "The Philippine Coconut Industry," p. 175. Strictly, a more suitable indicator is nuts per hectare of bearing trees, since production per tree is inversely related to the number of trees per hectare. With

a quarter of the increase, however, is accounted for by the south-
ward shift in the geographical distribution of trees from Luzon
to the higher yielding regions in Mindanao.[42]

Sugar cane, as with rice and to a lesser extent with coconuts,
shows a pronounced negative association between hectarage expansion and yields. The transfer of marginal rice lands in
Central Luzon and the Western Visayas to sugar cane in the
1960's had the effect not only of raising average rice yields on
the remaining land, as we have already seen, but also of depress-
ing cane yields. There is evidence that technological improvements in cane growing—new varieties, wider use of fertilizer,
and some degree of mechanization—were responsible for the
yield increases in the 1950's and thus it is possible that the
slowing of hectarage expansion after 1965 will be followed by
renewed gains in aggregate productivity.[43] Some recovery is
noticeable in the 1967–1968 yields given in Table 24.

Even from this brief survey of the major crops, it is clear that
there are difficult problems of measurement inherent in any
index of agricultural land productivity. Nevertheless, we have
found little evidence that would contradict the general picture
of stagnation described in earlier chapters. Rice yield increases
on the good quality land would appear to be largely offset by
diminishing returns on the poorer land being brought under
cultivation. For corn, the offsetting trends are different but
have had an equivalent effect. In the final years of the period,
however, both rice and corn have shown signs of a significant
upswing in yields; we will discuss these further below. Yield
measurement for coconuts is particularly intractable, but there

---

this measure we observe a rise of 13% over the years 1948–1960 (*ibid.*,
p. 177). Data for other than these census years are not available.

[42] *Ibid.*, p. 176. Mindanao more than doubled its share of coconut trees
between 1948 and 1960. Note, however, that a major reason for the
high output per tree in Mindanao is the low density of trees.

[43] See Hooley and Ruttan, "Agricultural Development of the Philippines." The yield measured in piculs of sugar per hectare depends both
on cane yields and on the recovery rate in processing. Both segments
declined in the 1960's.

have not been any sustained increases according to our data. Finally, for sugar, although rises in yields have apparently been accounted for mainly by technical inputs, again there has been an offsetting trend of diminishing returns which in this instance has more than negated the increase.

If average yields were to remain close to their present levels in the future, then a drastic decline in the rate of growth of agricultural output could not be postponed for long. The imminent closing of the land frontier has been pointed out by many observers.[44] The marked decline in the rate of increase in cultivated area that has occurred since 1959 (see Table 8 and Figure 6) suggests that the land surplus may be almost exhausted. Lower yields in the new areas for all the main crops except coconut (and corn for the first few seasons) indicate that the Philippines has entered the phase of diminishing returns at the extensive margin.[45]

The evidence of the virtual exhaustion of the land surplus is clearest for Luzon and the Visayas. It is frequently argued that there are still large reserves of potential agricultural land in Mindanao. This, however, is questionable. A study by Huke concludes that the potential cultivable area in Mindanao is 4.44 million hectares.[46] This figure is based on the total area of Mindanao of 9.87 million hectares, less the 2.11 million hectares

[44] See, for example, Robert E. Huke, *Shadows on the Land: An Economic Geography of the Philippines* (Manila: Bookmark, 1963); Frederick L. Wernstedt and J. E. Spencer, *The Philippine Island World: A Physical, Cultural, and Regional Geography* (Berkeley: University of California Press, 1967); Frank H. Golay and Marvin E. Goodstein, *Rice and People in 1990* (Manila: U.S. Agency for International Development, 1967); and International Rice Research Institute, Department of Agricultural Economics, "Annual Report 1965," mimeographed (Los Baños, 1966).

[45] As a tree crop, coconuts can grow on slopes of from 10 to 20%, land which is too steep for rice, corn, or sugar (without elaborate terracing). There is still a relative surplus of this type of land, especially in Mindanao where coconut yields are higher than in Luzon and the Visayas.   [46] Huke, *Shadows on the Land*, pp. 150–152.

with slopes of over 20 per cent, less the estimated area which is unsuitable for farming because of swamps, rock outcrops, and thin or eroded soils. A further 5 per cent of the gross area of the island is deducted for land that will be required for nonagricultural uses. The 1948 census showed that the total farm area in Mindanao was 1.5 million hectares. By the 1960 census, the farm area had risen to 2.5 million hectares, an average annual increase of 4.9 per cent. Moreover, even this high rate was considerably lower than Mindanao's population growth rate, which averaged 6.5 per cent over the same period. If the farm area continued to grow at 4.9 per cent a year, then the land surplus based on Huke's estimate would be exhausted by 1972.

In practice, however, the land frontier is approached asymptotically, with a progressive decline in the rate of increase of cultivated area. The area under cultivation is certain to expand —probably for many decades—but necessarily much more slowly than the rates observed in the past. From 1902 to 1938 and from 1938 to 1960 the cultivated area expanded at an average rate of about 3 per cent a year. Golay and Goodstein base their projections of future rice supplies on an assumed expansion rate over the period 1965–1990 of only 1 per cent per year.[47] From data in the U.S. Department of the Interior's River Basin Surveys, these writers estimate that the total potential agricultural area in the Philippines is about three times the 3.1 million hectares available in the major river basins.[48] The average area under cultivation in 1964–1966 was 7.5 million hectares.[49]

[47] Golay and Goodstein, *Rice and People in 1990*, pp. 65–66.

[48] *Ibid.*, p. 65. These reports, based on recent surveys, are a valuable addition to the literature on Philippine land resources. They cover the following river basins: Central Luzon, Cagayan River, Cotabato River, Agusan River, Bicol River, and Ilog-Hilabanyan River.

[49] The 1964–1966 estimated surplus land, according to Golay, is therefore about 2 million hectares. If this is compared with our estimate, based on Huke and the agricultural census, of a 1960 surplus in Mindanao of 1.9 million hectares, it is clear that almost all the remaining land must be in Mindanao.

Assessing a 1 per cent growth rate, this will reach 9.6 million hectares by 1990.

It is not necessary to accept any particular prediction concerning the future rate of expansion of cultivated area in order to draw one main conclusion: that exhaustion of the remaining land surplus will expand the agricultural base by little more than 25 per cent. Without land productivity increases, the combination of a continued high rate of population growth and a limited land surplus implies an inevitable decline in the exportable surplus of traditional agriculture, followed in turn by a rising demand for imported foodstuffs.

It is sometimes suggested that the existence of a land surplus is closely linked with the failure to raise agricultural productivity. Myint, for example, argues as follows:

The fact that peasant export production has not shown any technical improvements in the past does not mean that it is inherently incapable of improvement if adequate resources are ploughed back into it. The past pattern merely shows that these opportunities for improvements have been neglected because, with unused land easily available, it was so much easier to expand along existing lines than to try to introduce improved methods of production.[50]

The implication of this argument is that, with the exhaustion of the land surplus, opportunities for land improvements are less likely to be neglected than in the past. There is little historical evidence, however, to suggest that the closing of the land frontier has been a turning point with respect to productivity trends. In Taiwan, for example, yields began to rise in the early 1920's, but the area under cultivation expanded substantially until the land frontier was effectively closed in 1950.[51] Java, on the other hand, had effectively "filled up" by the beginning of

[50] Hla Myint, *The Economics of the Developing Countries* (London: Hutchinson, 1964), p. 52. See also E. Boserup, *The Conditions of Agricultural Growth* (London: George Allen and Unwin, 1965).

[51] International Rice Research Institute, Department of Agricultural Economics, "Annual Report for 1966," mimeographed (Los Baños, 1967).

the present century; and although yields on the irrigated rice fields have risen slowly, this has been in response to factor substitution brought about by a rising ratio of labor to land. In effect, this has involved technical change, but of a wholly labor-intensive type.[52]

It could well be argued, with perhaps better historical support, that, if the yield take-off is to be achieved at all, it should begin prior to the exhaustion of the land surplus. As long as there is a surplus, the agricultural economy has a certain amount of slack and the per capita output above the minimum subsistence level is still significant. The approach of the land frontier causes output of labor to fall and, with it, the potential to invest and raise productivity.

Despite arguments of this sort, a satisfactory connection between productivity and a land surplus has yet to be demonstrated. Modern research suggests that institutional and technological factors are of major importance.[53] In the opinion of the leading authorities, the prospects for the Philippines of raising productivity in the future depend on scientific advance and the possibility of changes in cultural practices, infrastructure, and institutions.[54] Recent interest has focused on the development and introduction of improved varieties of rice and substantial research has been directed toward the complex of factors needed to complement the new strains. Very much less research has been done on the other major crops—corn, sugar, and coconuts.

Rice and corn differ significantly from sugar and probably

[52] Clifford Geertz, *Agricultural Involution: The Processes of Ecological Change in Indonesia* (Berkeley: University of California Press, 1963).

[53] See, for example, S. C. Hsieh and Vernon W. Ruttan, "Environmental, Technological, and Institutional Factors in the Growth of Rice Production: Philippines, Thailand, and Taiwan," *Food Research Institute Studies*, 7 (1967), 307–341.

[54] Cultural practices here refer primarily to the use of insecticides and fertilizer, weed control, and water management. See IRRI, "Annual Report for 1966." The IRRI annual reports and the Hsieh-Ruttan paper cited in the preceding note form the basis of our discussion relating to rice.

coconuts inasmuch as their technology is highly location specific; that is, agricultural research and development must be done "where the biological and economic environment approximates that where the innovation will be employed."[55] An International Rice Research Institute (IRRI) report notes that "it is increasingly recognized that there is little if any improved rice production technology from the United States or Japan or even Taiwan that can be immediately transferred to Southeast Asia."[56] This inability to transfer technology is one of the major factors explaining the prolonged failure to raise rice yields in contrast to the long-term success in raising sugar yields. Sugar technology is not location specific and much, if not most, of the increase in yields has been in response to the improved varieties developed outside of the Philippines.[57] The POJ (Proefstation Oost Java) varieties developed by the Dutch in Java in the 1920's revolutionized sugar yields not only in Java but also in the Philippines and in much of the sugar producing world. Postwar yields have responded to varieties introduced from Hawaii. Sugar is one of the few cases in Philippine agriculture where it has proved possible to import technical change.

Coconut technology, as with that of other tree crops such as oil palm and rubber, is also universal rather than location specific. Unlike these other tree crops, however, practically no basic research has been directed toward developing a higher yielding coconut palm.[58] The limited research effort of the Philippines has been almost entirely directed toward combatting the major

[55] Hsieh and Ruttan, "Growth of Rice Production," p. 2.

[56] IRRI, "Annual Report for 1966," p. 9.

[57] The relatively "tight" structure of the sugar industry with mill supervision, geographic concentration, and large farms is more favorable to technical advance than most of traditional agriculture.

[58] The classic study in this area is K. P. V. Menon and K. M. Pandalai, *The Coconut Palm: A Monograph* (Ernakulan, S. India: Indian Central Coconut Committee, 1960). Ceylon and India have been the leaders in coconut research since the 1920's. A summary of Philippine research is found in *Compilation of Research and Development on Coconut Conducted in the Philippines* (Manila: National Science Development Board, 1967).

diseases. The successful research on rubber and oil palm is largely because of direct European and American interests in the growing side of these crops. Coconuts, in contrast, have always been mainly a smallholders' crop, and few growing interests are large enough to justify expensive research.

Unlike the other major crops, an integrated intensive research effort has been focused on rice since the early 1960's. A number of new varieties, markedly superior to the traditional ones, have been bred for specific Philippine conditions. The first large-scale planting of the leading new variety (IR8) took place in the wet season (second half) of 1967. This was the first time that enough seed was available to make possible widespread planting. It is still too early to assess the full implications of the new varieties on the national (and international) rice scene. The effects on the limited number of farms which adopted IR8 in 1966 and the dry season of 1967 have been analyzed by IRRI.[59] The results are important because they show for the first time the impact of the new varieties under actual farming conditions in contrast to the "test tube" or at best simulated environment under which the seeds were first tested. The three surveys reported all show conclusively that the yield from IR8 is substantially higher than that of the traditional varieties. The other major finding is that both the net return and expenditure on inputs are also very much higher for the improved varieties.

Table 26 summarizes the results obtained from a sample of lowland rice farms in Rizal Province. The yields, costs, and returns for IR8 approach twice that for the local variety. All the major components of total cost are higher for IR8. Fertilizer expenditure, for example, averaged ₱146 per hectare for IR8 and only ₱39 for the local variety. The absolute difference in costs was even higher for costs in kind, which include harvesting, threshing, and seeds.

A survey in the provinces of Pampanga and Bataan yielded

[59] IRRI, "Annual Report for 1967."

similar conclusions. This survey covered the 1966 wet season and the 1967 dry season. It also distinguished between owner-operated and tenant farmers. Yields on the owner-operated farms were considerably higher than on tenant farms, but in both cases yields were close to twice as high for the IR8 variety.

A further test was conducted in Laguna Province among 155 predominantly tenant-operated farms which had changed from

Table 26. Rice yields, costs, and returns: improved and traditional varieties, Rizal Province, Philippines, 1967 dry season

Yields, costs, and returns	IR8	Local variety*
Number of farms in sample	200	127
Yield (metric tons rough rice per hectare)	5.9	3.2
Gross return (₱1000)	2.13	1.15
Total costs† (₱1000)	0.78	0.38
Net return (₱1000)	1.35	0.77

Source: International Rice Research Institute, Department of Agricultural Economics, "Annual Report for 1967," mimeographed (Los Baños, 1968), p. 8.

* Local variety is Binato, known also as Thailand.

† Includes fertilizers, chemicals, other cash costs, and costs in kind.

the local to the IR8 variety. Yields which had averaged 2.4 metric tons per hectare in the 1966 wet season rose to 4.2 metric tons in 1967. An interesting result of this survey was the data on costs, which showed an increase from ₱106 to ₱277. The farmers who switched to IR8 began to spend four to five times the amount they had previously spent on fertilizer, weedicides, and insecticides. The farmers who made this change are clearly relatively progressive and able to accept not only the new variety but a whole new "package" of inputs. Without these increased inputs the yield differential is very much less.[60]

[60] Even the yields for local rice varieties obtained in these IRRI surveys were well above the Philippine average, indicating that the

The total area planted to new varieties in the Philippines during the first large-scale planting in the 1967/1968 crop year was estimated by a government survey to be about 428,000 hectares, or some 13 per cent of the total rice area planted.[61] This was a tenfold increase over the previous year—a remarkable rate of dissemination, achieved with the help of an intensive educational and distribution campaign. Future gains, however, are likely to be harder to win as the campaign is thought to have already reached a substantial share of the more progressive farmers. There is also evidence that initial enthusiasm can easily turn to disillusion. Some 44 per cent of the farmers growing IR8 rice in the Laguna sample said that they would not plant that variety again. IR8 is certainly more prone to typhoon damage than the local varieties. Even more important to the farmers were complaints of its low price, high cost of production, lack of disease resistance, and inferior eating quality.[62]

A narrow emphasis on one aspect of technical change, in this case varietal improvement, gives an unbalanced view of the potential for future yield increases. Technical change without changes in infrastructure, institutions, and cultural practices is likely to prove of limited value. Admittedly, little is known of the effect on yield of using improved varieties without increased

---

farmers in the sample were either more innovative and skillful or had superior resources. The Philippine Department of Agriculture and Natural Resources undertook wider-ranging surveys of yield increases in the wet season of 1967, finding that the average differential between IR8 and local varieties was about 30% rather than the 50–100% estimates from IRRI. Randolph Barker, "The Role of the International Rice Research Institute in the Development and Dissemination of New Rice Varieties," mimeographed (Los Baños: IRRI, 1969), p. 28.

[61] Randolph Barker, "Economic Aspects of High Yielding Varieties of Rice with Special Reference to National Price Policies: IRRI Report," (Paper presented to the Thirteenth Session of the FAO Study Group on Rice, Manila, March 20–27, 1969), p. 7. The Philippines was well ahead of the other countries of Southeast Asia in adopting the improved seeds.

[62] IRRI, "Annual Report for 1967," pp. 13–16. Susceptibility to typhoon damage, disease resistance, and eating quality are characteristics which further breeding can be expected to improve.

inputs. An IRRI report notes cautiously that if improved varieties are used with existing practices then "the limited available evidence suggests that yields would be no worse than for local varieties under most conditions."[63] In the broader historical context, the experience of countries which have raised yields is that this one of a complex of mutually reinforcing changes. Thus, for example, in the case of Taiwan the yield increases, beginning in the 1920's, were closely associated not only with technical change but also with the development of a modern transportation system, large investment in irrigation works, growth of farmers' associations and rural cooperatives, and a rapid increase in consumption of chemical fertilizers.[64] In the Philippines, as in most other countries of the region, the potential benefit from varietal improvement is greatly limited by the capacity of the irrigation system. Only 15 per cent of Philippine rice land is presently irrigated. Many other technological and institutional factors are likely also to play a restraining role in the realizing of these potential benefits.

Notwithstanding our caveats above, it is nearly certain that a number of countries in Southeast Asia, including the Philippines, will shortly be faced (at least for a limited period) with significant rice surpluses.[65] This situation raises its own problems, notably those concerned with appropriate pricing policies if, as expected, world demand is inelastic.[66] In the longer run

[63] *Ibid.,* p. 17.

[64] This argument is elaborated in Hsieh and Ruttan, "Growth of Rice Production."

[65] Official Philippine forecasts presented to the FAO Study Group on Rice in March 1969 show the exportable rice surplus increasing to over one million tons (rough rice) by 1975. Clearly, however, such forecasts are highly sensitive to the government price support policies assumed.

[66] Most rice importing countries in Southeast Asia were not far from self-sufficiency even before the development of the new varieties. Less than 2% of world rice production is traded internationally. For a discussion of some of the issues raised by prospective surpluses, see Randolph Barker, "Economic Problems Associated with Increased Rice Supplies" (Paper presented to the International Rice Research Conference, IRRI, Los Baños, April 28–May 2, 1969).

the alternative of course exists of transfering resources from rice production to other uses.

Perhaps the present situation can best be summed up by stressing that investment in research and development has not opened up a new low cost route to achieving higher yields. Further yield increases will probably occur in the near future, but they will require a complex of dynamic changes inconsistent with the historic pattern of "static expansion." Moreover, there is as yet no certainty that these increases will have a continuing impact on rice production in Southeast Asia. The 1968 IRRI Annual Report concludes: "There is thus no question that a 'breathing spell' has been gained in the food-population race. . . . However, it remains to be seen how these initial gains in rice production will be translated into sustained growth."[67]

The potential for raising productivity in traditional agriculture may be summarized as follows. Among the crops with a location-specific technology there has been a major advance in the development of improved rice varieties. Technical change, however, is only one of the requirements for sustained yield advances. No similar technical advance has been made for corn although the Mexican example shows that it is undoubtedly feasible. For crops such as coconuts and sugar, where imported technical change is possible, there is little indication of any past break with historical trends. Genetic research with a tree crop such as coconut takes a decade or more to affect output appreciably, and as yet nothing has been started. Sugar yields may well continue their slow upward trend, but this crop now accounts for a very small part of traditional agriculture. For the sector as

[67] IRRI, Department of Agricultural Economics, "Annual Report for 1968," mimeographed (Los Baños, 1969), p. 64.

An immensely important set of issues, largely ignored by the IRRI studies (as in most writing on agricultural development), concerns the consequences—economic, social, and ecological—of rapid expansion of irrigation and intensive application of chemical fertilizers and pesticides. Barker ("Increased Rice Supplies," p. 15) has noted the lack of basic research on the problems raised by new irrigation schemes even as construction of dams presses forward.

a whole, the chances of substantial, nation-wide yield increases over the next decade do not appear to be very favorable. Yield increases for rice in the lowland irrigated areas are almost certain to occur, but there may also be offsetting yield declines on the extensive margin.

Extractives: Resources and Utilization

Forest Resources. The rapid growth in the export of wood products (mainly logs) explains about half of the absolute growth in total exports since 1950. Accounting for less than 5 per cent of exports in the early 1950's, wood products grew to 27 per cent by 1966/1968. If this growth rate is maintained in the future, then the rate of growth of total exports and the potential rate of growth of the economy will rise. Since we see no reason to expect any lessening of world demand for wood products, we shall concentrate on the determinants of supply.

On the supply side, the continued growth of wood products will depend largely on the quantity and quality of forest resources. Based on estimates for 1963/1965, Philippine commercial forests total about 12.6 million hectares, of which 6.3 million are in Mindanao and 3.8 million in Northern Luzon. The average quality and density of the forest reserves in Mindanao are very much higher than in the rest of the country so that, in terms of volume of standing timber, some 60 per cent of reserves are in Mindanao.[68] Production, and especially exports, are overwhelmingly concentrated in that island. The future of Philippine wood production and, in particular, the future of log exports, will thus be determined primarily by Mindanao's reserves.

These reserves are subject to several forms of depletion apart from authorized logging. Included are losses through illegal logging and clearing for shifting cultivation, squatting, and authorized extension of the agricultural area for permanent

[68] Of the total reserves of 1.8 billion cubic meters, 1.1 billion are in Mindanao. (Unless otherwise stated, the statistics in this section are from unpublished reports of the Bureau of Forestry, Manila.)

settlement. Statistics based on legal logging are therefore quite inadequate as a measure of the rate of decline of forest area. Reliable estimates of the rate of decline of forest area can be based only on aerial photography. Such photography is available for Mindanao but as yet not for the other major forest areas. Although it was long thought that Mindanao did not suffer severely from illegal logging, this illusion was destroyed by the aerial surveys which clearly expose the gravity of the situation. Photographs taken in 1952 and again in 1963 show that the commercial forest area declined from 7.3 million hectares in the former year to 6.3 million hectares in 1963.[69] This is an average annual decline of 92,000 hectares, or a timber drain of 20.1 million cubic meters. Of this annual decrement, only 4.8 million cubic meters (24 per cent) was a consequence of authorized logging. Land clearing, shifting cultivation and illegal logging therefore accounted for 15.3 million cubic meters.[70]

Although we do not have similarly accurate data for Luzon, it is thought that the illegal drain on forests in Northern Luzon is as severe as in Mindanao. Both shifting cultivation and illegal logging are widespread. Some 60 per cent of the Luzon forests have been cut-over, and it is believed that more than half of this area will not regenerate to high forest. Farquhar estimates the annual loss of forest area in Northern Luzon at 40,000 hectares.[71]

The land that has been deforested has almost all been converted to cropland and pasture, and only an insignificant part to open land or other uses. Basically, this rapid deforestation is caused by the increase in the agricultural population. In response to this pressure the authorities have released large areas of forested lands for agriculture. Official releases of land have frequently exceeded 100,000 hectares per year. Even without

[69] B. C. Agaloos, *Forest Resources of Mindanao* (Manila: Bureau of Forestry, USAID/NEC Forest Development Project, 1965), p. 15.

[70] *Ibid.*, p. 17.

[71] J. D. Farquhar, *Demonstration and Training in Forest, Forest Range, and Watershed Management* (Manila: United Nations Development Programme, 1967), pp. 24–25.

.uch authorized sanction it is very doubtful if the demand for
1ew farming land could be resisted.

Not only has much forest land been turned into farm land
out also most of the increases in farm land were at the expense of forest. This is shown clearly by the data (from aerial
photography) in Table 27. The increase in cropland and pasture of 1.095 million hectares is closely matched by the decline
.n forest area of 1.007 million hectares. Farm land expanded

Table 27. Land utilization in Mindanao, 1952 and 1963 (thousand hectares)

Land utilization	1952	1963	Change
Forest	7,320	6,313	−1,007
Nonforest			
Cropland and pasture	1,126	2,221	+1,095
Open land	990	874	− 116
Marsh and small water	82	78	− 4
Urban and other areas	25	57	+ 32
Total	2,223	3,230	+1,007

Source: B. C. Agaloos, Forest Resources of Mindanao, p. 15.

.lightly more than the forest area declined because a small
amount of open land was converted to cropland and pasture.
The open land declined slowly because much of it is marginal
for agricultural uses, with eroded soils, rock outcrops, and other
deficiencies. Most of the remaining potential farm land is forested area. Based on Huke's estimate, which we noted earlier,
of a potential cultivable area in Mindanao of 4.4 million hectares, it follows that the remaining potential cropland and pasture in 1963 was some 2.2 million hectares, or double the area
then cultivated.[72] About 2 million hectares of this must consist
of forest area.

It is likely that the rate of decline in the forested area ob-

[72] This is not inconsistent with the 1960 census estimate of 2.5 million
hectares of farm area. The latter includes about 300,000 hectares of
forest area and some "other land."

served over the period 1952–1963 increased in the years which followed. If the rate of growth in the farm population remained constant, then the annual absolute decline in the forested area would show an upward trend. The cutting and export of logs in the period 1963–1968 was at a rate almost twice as high as that in the period 1952–1963. However, as we have seen, authorized logging accounts for only about one-quarter of the cutting drain. The remainder is caused basically by the extension of farming area, and part of this extension takes place in areas that have been cut over by authorized loggers. Another factor that may have operated to reduce the forest drain is the possible decline in migration into Mindanao in recent years. If the cropland and pasture only increased at the same rate after 1963 as it did in the earlier period and this increase took place mostly at the expense of forests, then the forest reserves would be reduced by about 2 million hectares between 1963 and 1973. This would exhaust the forest land suitable for agriculture while still leaving two-thirds of the 1963 forest area intact.

The depletion of the remaining forested areas would take longer and depend on the growth in log production and exports. Well before the whole forested area was destroyed, however, the ecological consequences of massive deforestation—e.g., erosion and watershed destruction—would probably reduce the cultivable area and adversely affect the productivity of much of the remaining farm area. If the full consequences of this ecological deterioration are to be avoided, then, at the very least, the expansion of cultivated area and the growth of log production must slow drastically in the near future. It is not possible for logs to continue in their role as the mainspring of Philippine export expansion.

The actual level of future log exports depends not only on the realities of the resource situation but also on policy decisions and the other unpredictable forces discussed earlier in this chapter. Projections are therefore difficult. Nevertheless, Farquhar, who in his capacity as United Nations Food and Agriculture Organization forestry expert in Manila is perhaps best qualified to do so, has made projections of log exports in 1975 and 1985.[73] He bases these on a number of assumptions regarding allowable timber cuts and domestic demand. Principally, he assumes that commercial forest area can be stabilized at a minimum of six million hectares and that the demands of domestic industry are met before logs are exported. His three projections (high, medium, and low estimates) for 1965–1985 are given in Table 28, converted to average annual rates. Although the

Table 28. Past and projected average annual growth rates of Philippine log exports, 1955–1985* (per cent)

Period	Average growth rate		
1955–1965	11.5		
	High	Medium	Low
1965–1975	5.0	2.4	−1.0
1975–1985	1.0	−3.3	−15.0

Source: Computed from estimates and projections by J. D. Farquhar, *Forest, Forest Range, and Watershed Management*, table 3.4 and pp. 43–44.
* Based on data in physical units.

range of estimates is necessarily wide, a drastic decline in the growth rate is clearly predicted and, by the late 1970's, a probable cessation of growth.

Minerals. Mineral exports, mainly of gold, copper, iron ore, and chromite, have grown considerably in the postwar period but have not markedly increased their share in total exports, which has fluctuated around 10 per cent. Assuming that world prices remain generally favorable, the future expansion of Philippine mineral exports, as with logs, will mainly depend on the size and quality of reserves. The geology of much of the Philippines is moderately favorable for the occurrence of minerals, but only a little more than 10 per cent of the total area has

[73] Farquhar, *Forest, Forest Range, and Watershed Management*, pp. 43–44.

been systematically surveyed. However, the mining companies have generally surveyed their own concessions and most of the regions where known geological formations are particularly favorable.

One estimate of economic reserves is that made by the mining companies as reported in the census. The 1961 census of mining and quarrying estimated the value of total reserves of metallic minerals at ₱3,693 million. This was equal only to about 18 years' production at the 1961 level or 9 years' output at the 1966 level. This estimate has since been proved too conservative, but there is little evidence to suggest that the Philippines has vast mineral resources. The known reserves of gold, the mainstay of Philippine mineral production for over a century, have been considerably depleted.

A survey of the company reports of all major mining companies does not suggest a period of great expansion in the near future, with the partial exception of copper production which may for some years maintain its rapid growth under the stimulus of high world prices. Easily the largest mining establishment is the Atlas Consolidated Mining and Development Corporation, which produced 40 million pounds of copper in 1958, rising to 66 million in 1967. The company planned to raise this to a maximum of 100 million pounds by 1969. Having reached this ceiling, no further expansion is planned or, indeed, would be possible without massive new investment with a gestation period of five years or more. This company accounts for about 30 per cent of Philippine mineral output and is considered by many to be the dynamic production leader. Few other companies are in a position to initiate a period of sustained expansion such as would be needed to make Philippine minerals an engine of rapid export growth, although foreign investment (especially from Japan) is likely to play a significant role in this area in the future. Important developments in nickel and iron ore production are in prospect, but on the other hand a fairly extensive oil search has so far not yielded very promising results. Moreover, starting from a small base, even a growth rate of as much as 10 per cent per year would have little impact over the next decade on the rate of increase of total exports. Presently known reserves and the production plans of companies do not suggest that such a high and sustained growth rate is likely. While major new discoveries could radically change the outlook, it is most probable that the past steady but not sensational rate of growth will be maintained.

PAST GROWTH AND THE FUTURE OF PHILIPPINE EXPORTS

Analysis of the postwar period shows that the Philippines failed to develop an export market for manufactures or to increase the processing of primary exports. The evidence points to a likely continued inability to develop along these lines. The only remaining way to reduce the resource content of exports is to increase the productivity of the primary inputs. The two major inputs for present exports are land and forests. The more important input is land where productivity has remained fairly constant for decades. There are exciting prospects for raising the productivity of rice-growing land, which in the mid-sixties accounted for about one-third of the total farmed area. These prospects, however, are based on technical advances (varietal improvements) which will have only a limited impact unless they are accompanied by changes in infrastructure, institutions, and cultural practices. There is little prospect of significantly raising the productivity of coconuts and most of the other crops (with the probable exception of corn) which account for the bulk of the cultivated area. The increases in rice yields, moreover, may well be partly offset by the already observed diminishing returns at the extensive margin.

The rate of expansion of the cultivated area is certain to be very much slower in the future than in the past, and total cultivated area can only increase by about 2 million hectares over the 7.5 million reached in the mid-sixties. Most of the increase in the cultivated area will continue to take place at the expense of forest land, further narrowing the base of the other major export product. With the severe and continuing depletion of forest reserves under this pressure for agricultural land, the past growth rate of log exports must fall dramatically in the near future. Mineral exports may well maintain their past upward trend, but the resource base is probably not large enough to support a high sustained rate of growth.

In determining the future growth rates of both traditional sector exports and exports of forest products a key factor is the rate of natural increase of the population. With a land surplus, a higher growth rate of population will mean (*ceteris paribus*) a higher growth rate of traditional exports and a faster diminution of forest reserves. As the land frontier closes the effect of rapid population growth may be seen principally in greater absolute food consumption and a correspondingly smaller exported agricultural surplus. Over the intercensal interval 1948–1960, the Philippines showed an average rate of natural increase of 3.2 per cent, equivalent to a doubling time of 22 years. This was substantially higher than most other parts of Southeast Asia, chiefly because of the relatively low death rate. With an extremely young population and continued improvement in mortality it is to be expected that the growth rate will increase in future decades. (There would seem to be no reason not to expect fertility to remain close to its present high level.) Table 29 shows the growth rates underlying the official NEC population projections. By 1980 under the "low" assumption the population would be 53.9 million; under the "medium" assumption, 55.3 million; and under the "high" assumption, 58.1 million. In the latter case, the growth rate would be at the startling level of 4 per cent in the 1970's—a doubling time of 17 years. And official population projections, it should be noted, are notoriously apt to be conservative.

It is clear that, on balance, it is most unlikely that the postwar rate of growth of exports can be maintained for long. The following assumptions appear to be realistic for projecting factors affecting future Philippine export growth:

1. Population growth remains very high (above 3.4 per cent per annum) and per capita food consumption is stable.

2. No dramatic change in the share of the labor force in agriculture.

3. Increasing yields for rice and possibly for corn, but partly offset by diminishing returns at the margin. Stagnation for

Table 29. Crude rates of natural increase of population implied in official population projections, Philippines, 1960–1980 (per cent per year)

Period	Natural increase		
	Low*	Medium†	High‡
1960–1965	3.29	3.29	3.43
1965–1970	3.36	3.46	3.73
1970–1975	3.44	3.61	3.99
1975–1980	3.49	3.73	4.05

Source: National Economic Council, Office of Statistical Coordination and Standards, "The Population and Other Demographic Facts of the Philippines," Philippine Economy Bulletin, 2, no. 4 (1964), 15.
* Normal mortality decline; slowly declining fertility after 1965.
† Normal mortality decline; continued high fertility.
‡ Rapidly declining mortality; continued high fertility.

other crops. The outcome may be that over-all average yields remain approximately constant as in postwar years.

4. An increase in the already rapid rate of diminution of forested area.

If these predicted forces are correct, then the rate of growth of both traditional and extractive exports must decline substantially in the future, the former in response to slowing land expansion and the latter with the exhaustion of forest reserves.

This analysis is supply-oriented since virtually nothing has been said about likely future trends in world demand. Any softening of commodity prices will, of course, impede the growth in the total value of exports. Predicting prices is even more hazardous than predicting supply, but a serious worsening in the terms of trade does not appear very likely. World demand for extractives, in particular, is likely to remain strong, and there are no overwhelming reasons to expect falling prices for coconuts and sugar. Rather, the crucial problems are on the side of supply, where traditional resources exploited through trade are approaching exhaustion.

In the following chapter we shall combine these features of the export sector with the findings from Chapter 2 on the structure and characteristics of other parts of the domestic economy, particularly those relating to import dependence and modern sector productivity changes. We shall then be in a position to draw conclusions regarding future Philippine development on the basis of the open dual economy model.

CHAPTER 5

Toward Stagnation?

In their classic survey of the field, Hahn and Matthews characterize the basic problem of aggregative growth theory as being "to find theoretical constructs which, without being downright misleading, are crude enough to bear the weight of crude evidence."[1] The growth model presented and used in this study is clearly not disqualified by a lack of crudeness; the extent to which it may be misleading is a more difficult question.

The model does not of course capture the intricate and highly important changes which necessarily accompany economic development—the growth of a skilled labor force, gradual increase in efficiency of management and administration both in private enterprise and in government, the development of infrastructure such as communications which improve the working of factor and product markets, and so on. Nevertheless, by greatly simplifying reality, it provides a means for distinguishing essential interrelationships among important features of the economy—in the present case, trade, agricultural productivity, capital specificity, the foreign and domestic terms of trade, technical change in industry, and intersectoral transfers of labor, goods, and savings. Without some such model theoretical problems such as the determination of the domestic terms of trade in an open economy may be difficult to solve,

---

[1] F. H. Hahn and R. C. O. Matthews, "The Theory of Economic Growth: A Survey," in *Surveys of Economic Theory: Growth and Development* (New York: St. Martin's Press, 1965), p. 110.

while there would be almost no way of drawing out the wide implications of a given policy change. With a model which attempts to approach the real world by disaggregation we may lose both in elegance and even perhaps in insight.

The focus of attention in this model is the integration of trade and growth in the context of dualism. The relationship between trade and growth is a mutual one, with a simple endogenous theory being introduced to "explain" exports and show how trade responds to the growth of the economy. (This contrasts with most one-sector open models, which direct attention to the effect on growth of an exogenously given increase in trade or, in the planning version, postulate a target rate of growth and ask how fast trade must rise in order to reach this objective.) Exports are in a sense a surplus and their level is changed by agricultural productivity increases, population shifts—in part a consequence of industrial technical progress —and investment allocation. Trade in turn plays a key role in the growth process through its transformation capacity, enabling an economy to overcome capital specificity in industry or to bypass it by converting the output of primary industries into capital goods. If all goods could be traded, the problem of the open economy would be no different in essence from that of the closed economy with zero capital specificity. But in practice not all goods can be traded and as a result the growth dynamics of the open economy differ in several essential ways.

The extreme assumptions we have made concerning the level of import dependence in industry serve to dramatize a real situation, but they may also exaggerate it. In a more policy-oriented study we should obviously not take as simple constraints on the system the conditions which it will be a major policy objective to change. The analysis would instead make use of the conceptual tools of standard economics related to dynamic comparative advantage and intertemporal allocation of resources to derive optimal growth strategies. The present study, however, is to a large degree concerned with a descriptive analysis of the past (and continuing) experience of certain open dual economies. Where unfavorable development patterns have been routinized if not institutionalized it may require a major policy shift to change the rules of growth.

If the application of this model to the Philippines is accepted as generally valid then it follows, as we concluded in Chapter 3, that in many respects the Philippines has enjoyed short-run growth at the expense of long-run development. Its growth has been generated by a combination of import substitution and resource-intensive exports. Although we studied this pattern in some detail in Chapter 2, it is useful to review our findings against the conventional measures which are usually taken to indicate development performance. Such indicators include aggregate measures of income and its distribution, trends in productivity, sectoral distribution of labor, the composition of exports, and the import content of investment.

Both gross national product and real per capita income rose significantly over the period 1950–1968. GNP at constant prices increased at an average annual rate of 6.1 per cent, population at 3.2 per cent, and per capita income at 2.9 per cent. The performance, however, was less satisfactory in the second half of the period. In manufacturing, the share of income accruing to labor showed a slight but appreciable downward trend over the years for which we have data (1956–1966). This in itself cannot be regarded as a favorable sign,[2] although in the early stages of development it is consistent with having wages determined by agricultural productivity. Two offsetting trends in the modern sector have been a shift in the domestic terms of trade in favor of agriculture, which raises the wage measured in indus-

[2] Kuznets notes, on the basis of a longitudinal study of development in a group of European countries, that "if any general conclusion is justified, it is that the share in national income of the returns on capital declined over time in almost all countries—in some from almost a half to about a fifth or a quarter; and the share of 'labor' must correspondingly have risen." Simon Kuznets, *Modern Economic Growth: Rate, Structure, and Spread* (New Haven: Yale University Press, 1966), p. 180.

trial goods, and increasing average skill levels which raise the differential between average and base level wages.

The average productivity of labor in the traditional sector showed a rate of increase of at most about 1.1 per cent, while in the modern sector it grew at twice this rate. There was therefore a divergence in the intersectoral differential, which conflicts with the historical pattern in developed countries.[3] In the late 1960's there was some evidence of a reversal in this trend.

The share of GNP originating in the traditional sector fell from 30 per cent in the early 1950's to 22 per cent by the mid-1960's. This important structural shift was accompanied by only a very modest reallocation of labor—a fall from 62 per cent to 56 per cent over the same period. This again is not consistent with historical trends in the course of development which show more rapid reallocation of labor than of output.[4] It is of course both a consequence of the extremely high rate of population growth in the postwar period and of the nature of industrial technical change.

Two highly important changes generally associated with development in the open economy are a rising share of manufactures in exports and a decline in the import content of investment. The first of these is not without exceptions: a few underdeveloped countries such as India export a high proportion of manufactures while some developed countries—those with a strong comparative advantage in primary products—have not had to develop manufacturing exports.[5] Import dependence, on the other hand, is a function both of the size of

---

[3] *Ibid.*, p. 64.

[4] Cross-section data show the proportion of labor force in agriculture ranging from 70–80% in the low income countries such as Thailand, India, and Pakistan, to about 20% at an income level of $1000. Charles P. Kindleberger, *Economic Development* (New York: McGraw Hill, 1965), p. 172.

[5] See Alfred Maizels, *Industrial Growth and World Trade* (Cambridge: Cambridge University Press, 1963), pp. 59–64.

the country and its level of development (the evidence was reviewed in Chapter 1). For a country of the Philippines' size we should expect steady though not rapid progress in reducing the import content of investment. In fact, however, we have seen that in both these respects the Philippines has not performed well. The growth in manufactured exports recorded in Table 5 was almost entirely accounted for by extractive industry derivatives. The evidence on the import content of investment is not very satisfactory, but such as it is it indicated a high and nondecreasing level.

We can sum up the Philippine performance, then, by concluding that it was a very uneven one. Average per capita income grew significantly over the period, but it was associated with only some of the changes which usually occur during the development process. These simple indices do not, however, tell the whole story. It is not only the observed changes and the rates of growth which are important but the sources of growth and the quality of the growth process. Analysis of some of these further dimensions suggested that the Philippine performance and the outlook for the future are much less promising than the past aggregate trends imply.

On the side of imports, we saw in Chapter 2 that one direct result of the Philippines' policy of rapid import substitution was to enable capital goods imports to grow much more rapidly than total imports. Over 50 per cent of the 1950–1968 rise in the level of capital goods imports could be accounted for by this shift in composition. To the extent that the import content of investment has been relatively constant, which the evidence indicated, the modern sector was enabled to grow much more rapidly than would otherwise have been possible. Since the share of capital goods in imports probably cannot increase much further (in the 1960's it has fluctuated around a level of 60 per cent) the average growth rate of capital imports is bound to be closer to the growth of total imports in the future. If the latter maintained its past level, capital goods imports would grow not at 9 per cent but at 5 to 6 per cent. It is more likely, however, that total imports will grow less fast in the future; this follows from our analysis of the export sector in Chapter 4. While attempts to forecast future growth trends almost inevitably involve errors which range from the large to the spectacular, the relatively simple structure of Philippine exports makes possible the projection of past trends with some degree of assurance.

In Chapter 4, we estimated the size of the surplus of cultivable land and forests remaining to be vented through trade. The total remaining agricultural area in 1966 was of the order of two million hectares, a little over 25 per cent of the area then being cultivated. Total reserves of commercial forests were estimated at the same time to be about 12.6 million hectares, of which a significant proportion was on potential agricultural land. The rate at which this surplus will be depleted can only be conjectured. However, only a major departure from this historical and postwar pattern of agricultural and export expansion can prevent a decline in export growth over the next decade.

On the basis of the assumptions listed at the end of Chapter 4, we might expect that growth of traditional sector output could be maintained close to its average postwar rate of 4.0 per cent. Whether or not exports from this sector can be raised from their very low average growth rate of 1.6 per cent would then depend critically on domestic food consumption which absorbs the bulk of sectoral output. From the formal equation $X_a = Y_a - gL$ (equation 13 of Chapter 3), G (g) was found to have an average value of 0.013 during 1950–1968. If per capita domestic absorption continues to rise at this rate then exports would roughly maintain their past trend. A rise in the natural increase of population would exert a further drag on export growth.

It is not altogether unlikely that incipient productivity improvements in agriculture could induce a higher aggregate output growth, or that domestic absorption could slow appreciably in the future. In either case exports would increase more rapidly, although probably not at a rate any greater than that of population, say 3.4 per cent. We shall take this figure as an optimistic assumption.

Extractive industry exports can be projected more simply with the data given in Chapter 4. The medium projection for the growth of log exports is 2.4 per cent for 1965–1975 and −3.3 per cent for 1975–1985, reflecting the painful transition to a stabilized, replenishable forest base (see Table 28). Little can be said on the future growth of mineral exports; we argued that, on the basis of known reserves and the production plans of major companies, little change was likely in the past rate of growth. Over 1950–1968, this averaged 9.1 per cent and for 1960–1968, 7.6 per cent. Taking the intermediate value of 8 per cent for minerals and the medium log projection, the category of extractive exports would show a growth rate of 4.6 per cent over 1966/1968–1975 and 3.3 per cent over 1975–1985. In the late 1970's, minerals would overtake logs as the major component of extractives.

Exports of manufactures, mainly plywood and veneer, increased at an average rate of 11.5 per cent in the period 1950–1968. Taking into account the depletion of forests, the growth of the domestic market, and the obstacles to greater exports discussed in Chapter 4, it seems unlikely that plywood and veneer can for long sustain manufactured exports at this rate. As an extremely optimistic assumption, however, we might suppose that other manufactures could progressively take their place and maintain the same over-all growth rate.

Combining the rates suggested in the preceding paragraphs, we find that they imply that total exports would grow at a rate of 4.7 per cent over 1966/1968–1975 and 4.8 per cent over 1975–1985 if traditional exports maintained the constant rate of 3.4 per cent. If traditional output increased at only 1.6 per cent, total exports would grow at 4.0 per cent in 1966/1968–1975 and 4.3 per cent in 1975–1985.

The purpose of computations of this sort is not to predict future growth rates but rather to draw out the consequences of the pattern of export development which has been followed in the past. A decline in the growth rate of total exports is clearly implied in this pattern, even in the unlikely event that exports of manufactures can continue to increase at their past average rate.

This study is focused on theory and analysis rather than development strategy and policy. Analysis must lay the basis for policy, but the highly aggregated and selective approach that we have adopted can do little more than point in the general direction of an appropriate development strategy. Detailed lines of policy with operational relevance require disaggregation, short-run analysis, and constant reference to the economic, political, and institutional framework. Despite the obvious limitations of the present study, we believe that a long-run, growth-oriented approach clarifies the underlying dynamics of an economy such as the Philippines. An understanding of these fundamental relationships at least indicates the outlines within which a detailed strategy of development must be evolved. In this case study, therefore, a broad strategy outline is implicit in the analysis of the growth process.

In essence, the Philippines in the period 1950–1968 sought and found an "easy" path to growth. The considerable growth in total output and per capita income was based largely on the exploitation of previously unutilized natural resources and the policy of import substitution. The using of the surplus of land and forests was an easy process in that it did not basically require productivity increases, technical change, or substantial upgrading of skills. In short, growth was not accompanied by the difficult, dynamic, and surely indispensable changes associated with successful development.

The growth of modern manufacturing was to a large extent based on import substitution of consumer goods. There was little backward integration towards capital goods and the import content of investment remained high. Import substitution, by causing a large shift in the composition of imports, made it possible for capital goods imports and therefore industrial output to rise rapidly. This, too, is now well recognized as an essentially easy process, bringing considerable growth with relatively little learning of difficult skills. Labor productivity increased but probably less in response to indigenous innovation than to rising capital/labor ratios and technical change embodied in imported capital equipment.

The venting of natural resources through trade and import substitution are both of a nonrepeatable nature and lay the basis for future stagnation rather than sustained growth. A development strategy for the Philippines must therefore seek a radical break with this ultimately self-defeating growth pattern. A successful strategy deriving from the present analysis should be directed toward the following four major areas:

1. Natural resource content of exports and agricultural output.

2. The import dependence of investment.

3. Bias in technical change.

4. Population growth.

The natural resource content of exports can be lowered through increasing the basic productivity of land and forests, increased processing of exports, and diversification through the growth of manufactured exports. Raising basic agricultural and forest productivity is probably the most urgent priority, but the other alternatives are also important. The highly successful albeit belated research effort devoted to improving the technology of rice production has perhaps led to underestimation of the many complex but nontechnological obstacles which can stand in the way of sustained yield increases. Some of the problems associated with greater processing of agricultural and extractive exports and with the exporting of manufactures were discussed in Chapter 4.

The lowering of the import dependence of investment

through domestic manufacture of a wider range of industrial intermediate goods and producers' durables would raise the ceiling on growth imposed by the level of imports and exports. There may also be many other favorable effects associated with extending import substitution backward to nonconsumer goods, stemming from the rising level of skills and interindustry demand.

The postwar labor-saving bias in the industrial sector's technical change has severely restricted the flow of labor from agriculture to industry. Detailed research needs to be directed toward an analysis and evaluation of this bias—especially to discover the degree to which it can and should be reversed by government action to correct factor price distortions. Although the undesirable consequences of extreme labor-saving technical change are easily recognized, we know little about alternative patterns. Outside the immediate field of economics, an understanding of the social and political factors underlying the emergence of these distortions is also clearly of the greatest importance.

The advantages of a lower rate of population growth are well known, but in terms of this analysis they center on the slowing down of the rate of exhaustion of a limited natural resource surplus. Until very recently the Philippines has been able to absorb much of its population increase by expansion of cultivated land, and it has even derived (short-run) advantages from doing so through the effect on traditional exports. Indeed, indirectly a considerable part of the postwar economic growth can be regarded as having been generated by rapid population increase. The full costs of the very great momentum that has been built up are not yet quantifiable. What is certain, however, is that the tremendous burden of a population growth rate approaching 4 per cent will be ever more seriously felt as stocks of land and other natural resources diminish.

To state objectives in such general terms is very far from articulating a workable development strategy. It can help to set broad criteria by which policy can be evaluated, however.

A strategy which conflicted with these major objectives would perpetuate the past growth patterns and make more probable the ultimate stagnation that those patterns imply. One which succeeded by the same criteria would transform the basic dynamics of growth and the outlook for the Philippine economy.

Bibliography

(This bibliography encompasses the main theoretical and empirical literature relevant to Chapters 2 and 3. It is not coincident with the footnote references.)

Agaloos, B. C. *Forest Resources of Mindanao.* Manila: Bureau of Forestry, USAID/NEC Forest Development Project, 1965.

Asian Development Bank. *Asian Agricultural Survey.* N.p.: University of Tokyo Press and University of Washington Press, 1969.

Barker, Randolph. "Economic Aspects of High Yielding Varieties of Rice with Special Reference to National Price Policies: IRRI Report." Paper presented to the Thirteenth Session of the FAO Study Group on Rice, Manila, March 20–27, 1969.

——. "Economic Problems Associated with Increased Rice Supplies." Paper presented to the International Rice Research Conference, IRRI, Los Baños, April 28–May 2, 1969.

——. "The Response of Production to a Change in Rice Price." *Philippine Economic Journal,* 5 (1966), 260–276.

Bruton, Henry J. "On the Role of Import Substitution in Development Planning." *Philippine Economic Journal,* 4 (1965), 14–28.

——. "The Two Gap Approach to Aid and Development: Comment." *American Economic Review,* 59 (1969), 439–446.

Castro, Amado A. "Import Substitution and Export Promotion: Trade and Development." In *The Structure and Development in Asian Economies;* Proceedings of a conference held by Japan Economic Research Center. Tokyo: Japan Economic Research Center, 1968.

Chenery, Hollis B. "The Two Gap Approach to Aid and Development: A Reply to Bruton." *American Economic Review*, 59 (1969), 446–449.

Dixit, Avinash. "Theories of the Dual Economy: A Survey." Mimeographed. Berkeley: University of California, Institute of International Studies, 1969. (Project for the Explanation and Optimization of Economic Growth, technical report no. 30.)

Dobb, Maurice. *An Essay on Economic Growth and Planning.* London: Routledge and Kegan Paul, 1960.

Domar, Evsey D. "A Soviet Model of Growth." In his *Essays in the Theory of Economic Growth.* New York: Oxford University Press, 1957.

"Family Income Distribution and Expenditure Patterns in the Philippines: 1965." *Journal of Philippine Statistics*, vol. 19, no. 2 (1968).

Farquhar, J. D. *Demonstration and Training in Forest, Forest Range, and Watershed Management.* Manila: United Nations Development Programme, 1967.

Fei, John C. H., and Gustav Ranis. "Agrarianism, Dualism, and Economic Development." In *The Theory and Design of Economic Development,* edited by Irma Adelman and Eric Thorbecke. Baltimore: The Johns Hopkins Press, 1966.

——. *Development of the Labor Surplus Economy: Theory and Policy.* Homewood, Ill.: Richard D. Irwin, 1964.

Findlay, Ronald. "Capital Theory and Developmental Planning." *Review of Economic Studies*, 29 (1962), 85–98.

——. "Optimal Investment Allocation between Consumer Goods and Capital Goods." *Economic Journal,* 76 (1966), 70–83.

Fonollera, Raymundo E. "Labor and Land Resources in Philippine Agriculture: Trends and Projections." Paper presented to an International Rice Research Institute seminar, Los Baños, May 28, 1966.

Golay, Frank H. "The Environment of Philippine Economic Planning." *Philippine Economic Journal*, 4 (1965), 284–309.

——. *The Philippines: Public Policy and National Economic Development.* Ithaca: Cornell University Press, 1961.

Golay, Frank H., and Marvin E. Goodstein. *Rice and People in 1990.* Manila: U.S. Agency for International Development, 1967.

Goodstein, Marvin E. *The Pace and Pattern of Philippine Economic Growth: 1938, 1948, and 1956.* Southeast Asia Program

Data Paper, no. 48. Ithaca: Cornell University, Department of Asian Studies, 1962.

Hicks, George L. "The Growing Import Dependence of Philippine Exports." Mimeographed. Washington: National Planning Association, Center for Development Planning, 1967.

———. "The Philippine Coconut Industry: Growth and Change, 1900–65." Mimeographed. Washington: National Planning Association, Center for Development Planning, 1967.

———. "Philippine Foreign Trade, 1950–1965: Basic Data and Major Characteristics." Mimeographed. Washington: National Planning Association, Center for Development Planning, 1966.

———. "Philippine Foreign Trade Statistics: Supplementary Data and Interpretations, 1954–1966." Mimeographed. Washington: National Planning Association, Center for Development Planning, 1967.

Hirschman, Albert O. "The Political Economy of Import-Substituting Industrialization in Latin America." *Quarterly Journal of Economics,* 82 (1968), 1–32.

Hooley, Richard W. "The Concept of Dualism in the Theory of Development." Mimeographed. Washington: National Planning Association, Center for Development Planning, 1968.

———. "Implications of Saving Structure for Economic Development." *Philippine Economic Journal,* 1 (1962), 105–130.

———. "Long Term Economic Growth in the Philippines, 1902–1961." In *Growth of Output in the Philippines,* edited by Richard W. Hooley and Randolph Barker. Manila: University of the Philippines, School of Economics, and International Rice Research Institute, 1967.

———. *Saving in the Philippines, 1951–1960.* Quezon City: University of the Philippines, Institute of Economic Development and Research, 1963.

Hooley, Richard W., and Vernon W. Ruttan. "The Agricultural Development of the Philippines, 1902–1965." In *Agricultural Development in Asia,* edited by R. T. Shand. Canberra: Australian National University Press, 1969.

Hooley, Richard W., and Gerardo P. Sicat. "Investment Demand in Philippine Manufacturing." Mimeographed. Quezon City: University of the Philippines, School of Economics, 1967.

Hornby, J. M. "Investment and Trade Policy in the Dual Economy." *Economic Journal,* 78 (1968), 96–107.

Hsieh, S. C., and Vernon W. Ruttan. "Environmental, Technological, and Institutional Factors in the Growth of Rice Production: Philippines, Thailand and Taiwan." *Food Research Institute Studies,* 7 (1967), 307–341.

Huke, Robert E. *Shadows on the Land: An Economic Geography of the Philippines.* Manila: Bookmark, 1963.

Inter-industry Relations Study of the Philippine Economy: Partial Report. Manila: University of the Philippines, School of Economics, and Bureau of the Census and Statistics, 1968.

International Rice Research Institute, Department of Agricultural Economics. "Annual Report." Mimeographed. Los Baños, annual.

Johnston, Bruce F. "Sectoral Interdependence, Structural Transformation, and Agricultural Growth." In *Subsistence Agriculture and Economic Development,* edited by Clifton R. Wharton. Chicago: Aldine, 1969.

Jorgenson, Dale W. "The Development of a Dual Economy." *Economic Journal,* 71 (1961), 309–334.

——. "The Role of Agriculture in Economic Development: Classical versus Neoclassical Models of Growth." In *Subsistence Agriculture and Economic Development,* edited by Clifton R. Wharton. Chicago: Aldine, 1969.

——. "Surplus Agricultural Labour and the Development of a Dual Economy." *Oxford Economic Papers,* 19 (1967), 288–312.

——. "Testing Alternative Theories of the Development of a Dual Economy." In *The Theory and Design of Economic Development,* edited by Irma Adelman and Eric Thorbecke. Baltimore: The Johns Hopkins Press, 1966.

Journal of Philippine Statistics. Manila: Bureau of the Census and Statistics, quarterly (vol. 1, 1941).

Lampman, Robert J. "Some Interactions between Economic Growth and Population Change in the Philippines." *Philippine Economic Journal,* 6 (1967), 1–20.

——. "The Sources of Post-War Economic Growth in the Philippines." *Philippine Economic Journal,* 6 (1967), 170–188.

Lawas, José M. "Output Growth, Technical Change, and Employment of Resources in Philippine Agriculture: 1948–1975." Ph.D. dissertation, Purdue University, 1960.

Levy, Emanuel. "Review of Economic Statistics in the Philippines: Interim Report." Mimeographed. Manila: World Bank Resident Mission, 1964.

———. "Review of Economic Statistics in the Philippines: Interim Report-B." Mimeographed. Manila: World Bank Resident Mission, 1965.

———. "The Usefulness of Existing National Accounts for the Analysis of the Philippine Economy." *Philippine Economic Journal,* 5 (1966), 134–145.

McKinnon, Ronald I. "Foreign Exchange Constraints in Economic Development and Efficient Aid Allocation." *Economic Journal,* 74 (1964), 388–409.

Mahalanobis, P. C. "Some Observations on the Process of Growth of National Income." *Sankhya,* 12 (1952), 307–312.

Maizels, Alfred. *Exports and Economic Growth of Developing Countries.* Cambridge: Cambridge University Press, 1968.

———. *Industrial Growth and World Trade.* Cambridge: Cambridge University Press, 1963.

Mangahas, Mahar, Aida E. Recto, and Vernon W. Ruttan. "Market Relationships for Rice and Corn in the Philippines." *Philippine Economic Journal,* 5 (1966), 1–27.

Mears, Leon A., and Randolph Barker. "Effects of Rice Price Policy on Growth of the Philippine Economy: An Analytical Framework." In *Growth of Output in the Philippines,* edited by Richard W. Hooley and Randolph Barker. Manila: University of the Philippines, School of Economics, and International Rice Research Institute, 1967.

Myint, Hla. "The 'Classical Theory' of International Trade and the Underdeveloped Countries." *Economic Journal,* 68 (1958), 317–337.

———. *The Economics of the Developing Countries.* London: Hutchinson, 1964.

Paauw, Douglas S. "The Philippines: Estimates of Flows in the Open, Dualistic Economy Framework, 1949–1965." Mimeographed. Washington: National Planning Association, Center for Development Planning, 1968.

Paauw, Douglas S., and John C. H. Fei. "The Transition in Open

Dualistic Economies." Mimeographed. Washington: National Planning Association, Center for Development Planning, 1970. 2 vols.

Paauw, Douglas S., and Joseph L. Tryon. "Agriculture-Industry Interrelationships in an Open Dualistic Economy: The Philippines, 1949–1964." In *Growth of Output in the Philippines,* edited by Richard W. Hooley and Randolph Barker. Manila: University of the Philippines, School of Economics, and International Rice Research Institute, 1967.

The Philippine Economy Bulletin. Manila: National Economic Council, bimonthly (vol. 1, 1963).

Philippines, Bureau of the Census and Statistics. *The BCS Survey of Households: Bulletin.* Manila, irregular (no. 1, 1957). Title varies: *Philippine Statistical Survey of Households.*

——. *BCS Survey of Manufactures.* Manila, annual (since 1956). Title varies: *Annual Survey of Manufactures.*

——. *Census of the Philippines, 1960: Agriculture.* Manila, 1963.

——. *Census of the Philippines, 1960: Population and Housing.* Manila, 1962–63.

——. *Economic Census of the Philippines, 1961.* Manila, 1965.

Philippines, Central Bank. *Annual Report.* Manila, annual.

——. *Statistical Bulletin.* Manila, quarterly.

Philippines, National Economic Council, Office of Statistical Coordination and Standards. "The National Income of the Philippines for CY 1946 to 1967 and the National Accounts: Overall Revision (as of August 30, 1968)." Mimeographed. Manila, 1968.

——. "The Philippine Economy in 1968 and the National Accounts, CY 1966 to 1968, with Supporting and Analysis Tables." Mimeographed. Manila, 1969.

Philippines, Program Implementation Agency. "Trend and Structure of Philippine Manufactures, 1953–1963." Mimeographed. OPS Monograph Series. Manila, n.d.

"The Population and Other Demographic Facts of the Philippines." *The Philippine Economy Bulletin,* 2, no. 4 (1964), 5–19.

Power, John H. "Import Substitution as an Industrialization Strategy." *Philippine Economic Journal,* 5 (1966), 167–204.

——. "A Note on Estimation of Overvaluation of the Philippines Peso." Mimeographed. Quezon City: University of the Philippines, School of Economics, 1967.

Power, John H. "The Structure of Protection in the Philippines." Mimeographed. Quezon City: University of the Philippines, School of Economics, 1969.

Prebisch, Raúl. *Towards a New Trade Policy for Development.* New York: United Nations, 1964.

Qayum, A. "Models of Balanced and Maximum Growth in Dualistic Economies." In *Towards Balanced International Growth;* Essays presented to J. Tinbergen, edited by H. C. Bos. Amsterdam: North Holland, 1969.

Raj, K. N. "Role of the 'Machine-Tools Sector' in Economic Growth: A Comment on Indian and Chinese Experience." In *Socialism, Capitalism, and Economic Growth;* Essays presented to Maurice Dobb, edited by C. H. Feinstein. Cambridge: Cambridge University Press, 1967.

Raj, K. N., and A. K. Sen. "Alternative Patterns of Growth under Conditions of Stagnant Export Earnings." *Oxford Economic Papers,* 13 (1961), 43–52.

Reyes, Peregrino S., and Teresita L. Chan. "Family Income Distribution in the Philippines." *Statistical Reporter,* 9, no. 2 (1965), 30–36.

Roa, C. P. *The Gold Mining Industry in the Philippines.* Manila: Bureau of Mines, 1967.

Ruprecht, Theodore K. "Labor Absorption Problems and Economic Development in the Philippines." *Philippine Economic Journal,* 5 (1966), 289–312.

——. "Output Stimulation and Employment Stagnation: Policy By-Products in the Philippines." *Economic Development and Cultural Change,* 17 (1968), 77–89.

Ruttan, Vernon W. "Two Sector Models and Development Policy." In *Subsistence Agriculture and Economic Development,* edited by Clifton R. Wharton. Chicago: Aldine, 1969.

Ruttan, Vernon W., A. Soothipan, and E. C. Venegas. "Changes in Rice Production, Area, and Yield in the Philippines and Thailand." *Economic Research Journal* (Manila), 12 (1965), 181–201.

Sen, A. K. "Some Notes on the Choice of Capital-Intensity in Development Planning." *Quarterly Journal of Economics,* 71 (1957), 561–584.

Sicat, Gerardo P. "Analytical Aspects of Two Current Economic Policies." *Philippine Economic Journal,* 4 (1965), 107–119.

——. "A Design for Export Oriented Industrial Development."

Mimeographed. Quezon City: University of the Philippines, School of Economics, 1967.

———. "Import Demand and Import Substitution in the Philippines, 1953–1963." Mimeographed. Quezon City: University of the Philippines, School of Economics, 1969.

———. "Labor Policies and Philippine Economic Development." Mimeographed. Quezon City: University of the Philippines, School of Economics, 1969.

———. "The Manufacturing Sector after Decontrol." Mimeographed. Quezon City: University of the Philippines, School of Economics, 1967.

———. "Production Functions in Philippine Manufacturing: Cross-Section Estimates, 1956–59." *Philippine Economic Journal, 2* (1963), 107–131.

———. "Some Aspects of Capital Formation in the Philippines." Ph.D. dissertation, Massachusetts Institute of Technology, 1963.

Sicat, Gerardo P. *et al. Economics and Development: An Introduction.* Prepublication issue. Quezon City: University of the Philippines Press, 1965.

Simkins, Paul D., and Frederick L. Wernstedt. "Growth and Internal Migrations of the Philippine Population, 1948 to 1960." *Journal of Tropical Geography,* 17 (1963), 197–202.

Spencer, J. E. *Land and People in the Philippines: Geographic Problems in Rural Economy.* Berkeley and Los Angeles: University of California Press, 1952.

The Statistical Reporter. Manila: National Economic Council, Office of Statistical Coordination and Standards, quarterly (vol. 1, 1957).

Treadgold, Malcolm, and Richard W. Hooley. "Decontrol and the Redirection of Income Flows: A Second Look." *Philippine Economic Journal,* 6 (1967), 109–128.

"The Trend of the Labor Force." In *First Conference on Population, 1965.* Quezon City: University of the Philippines Press, 1966.

Tryon, Joseph L. "The Behavior of Production, Prices and Productivity in Philippine Agriculture, 1949–1964." Mimeographed. Washington: National Planning Association, Center for Development Planning, 1968.

———. "Internal and External Terms of Trade in Post-War Philippines." *Philippine Economic Journal,* 6 (1967), 189–209.

Umaña, Salvador C. "Growth of Output of Philippine Manufacturing: 1902–60." In *Growth of Output in the Philippines,* edited by Richard W. Hooley and Randolph Barker. Manila: University of the Philippines, School of Economics, and International Rice Research Institute, 1967. Also published in *Economic Research Journal* (Manila), 13 (1966), 146–160.

United Nations, Department of Economic and Social Affairs. *Studies in Long-Term Economic Projections for the World Economy: Aggregative Models.* New York, 1964.

United Nations, Economic Commission for Asia and the Far East. *Problems of Long-Term Economic Projections, with Special Reference to Economic Planning in Asia and the Far East;* Report of the Third Group of Experts on Programming Techniques. New York, 1963.

———. "Reclassification of Imports and Exports from the SITC." Mimeographed. Bangkok, 1967.

Verdoorn, P. J. "Complementarity and Long-Range Projections." *Econometrica,* 24 (1956), 429–450.

Wall, David. "Import Capacity, Imports and Economic Growth." *Economica,* 35 (1968), 157–168.

Wernstedt, Frederick L., and J. E. Spencer. *The Philippine Island World: A Physical, Cultural, and Regional Geography.* Berkeley: University of California Press, 1967.

Williamson, Jeffrey G. "Dimensions of Postwar Philippine Economic Progress." *Quarterly Journal of Economics,* 83 (1969), 93–109.

———. "Economic Growth in the Philippines: 1947–1965: The Role of Traditional Inputs, Education and Technical Change." Mimeographed. Quezon City: University of the Philippines, School of Economics, 1967.

Winston, Gordon C. "Consumer Goods or Capital Goods: Supply Consistency in Development Planning." *Pakistan Development Review,* 7 (1967), 348–378.

Index

Adams, Nassau A., 25–26, 27–28
Agricultural surplus: exportable, 47, 60–61, 132–135, 179; supply elasticity of, 100–104, 186; total, 59–60, 132, 134
Annual Survey of Manufactures, 64, 92
Atlas Consolidated Mining and Development Corporation, 216

Balance of payments, 105–107, 146–147
Balance of trade, 106, 146–147
Baldwin, Robert E., 17, 18, 19, 22, 182
Barker, Randolph, 103, 198
Bodkin, Ronald G., 116
Boeke, J. H., 61
Bruton, Henry J., 170, 174
Bureau of the Census and Statistics Survey of Households, see *Philippine Statistical Survey of Households*
Burma, 9, 10, 14, 32, 47

Cairncross, A. K., 23
Capital: in agriculture, 14–15, 124–125; in industry, 62, 63, 67–68; underutilization of, 173–174; *see also* Capital/output ratio
Capital goods, imports of, 50–51, 72, 111, 118, 164–165
Capital goods industry, 109, 171; difficulty of establishing, 28–29
Capital/labor ratio, 68, 88–89, 166
Capital/output ratio, 63, 67–69, 114–115, 165
Capital specificity, 11, 144–145, 167–172

Caves, Richard E., 17, 21
Cereals, *see* Food
Chenery, Hollis B., 25, 28
Coconut: processing, 194–195; research, 205, 210; yields, 197, 199–200, 201
Colonial period, 11–12, 20, 30, 183
Commercial crops, 31, 180–181
Construction industry, 66, 83
Consumer goods, imports of, 50–51
Copper, 216
Copra, *see* Coconut
Corn, 196–197, 198–199, 210
Crop areas, 56–57, 213–214; price responsiveness of, 99, 182
Crop yields, 57, 196–211; price responsiveness of, 99–100
Cultivated area, *see* Crop areas *and* Land expansion

Data quality, 43, 44, 45–46, 51, 56, 68–69, 92
Decontrol of peso, 73, 74, 89, 120, 195
Demand: effective, 173–174; for Philippine exports, 191, 219–220
Department of Agriculture and Natural Resources, Philippines, 56, 208
Devaluation, *see* Decontrol of peso
Development policy, 175–177, 228–231
Dixit, Avinash, 173
Domar, Evsey D., 168
Dovring, Folke, 83
Dual economy model: accounting system, 33–37; general form, 154–157; naive form, 158–160; operation, 157–158, 160–162; Philippine parameters, 162–167

241

Dualism, 2; enclave, 18, 184; and export sector, 10–16, 182–185

Economic Census of the Philippines, 1961, 62, 92
Economies of scale, 28, 193
Elasticity of demand, foreign, *see* Demand, for Philippine exports
Elasticity of factor substitution, 116, 135–136
Employment: modern sector, 52, 62, 148; traditional sector, 52, 56–57, 149; *see also* Labor; Underemployment; *and* Unemployment
Estates, *see* Plantation industry
Exchange rate for peso, 46, 190, 195; *see also* Decontrol of peso
Exportable surplus, *see* Agricultural surplus, exportable
Exports: categorization, 41, 180–183; future growth, 214–215, 217–220, 226–228; import content, 184–185; modern sector, 33, 41–42, 48–50; processing, 191–196; resource content, 187–191, 229; traditional sector, 31, 41, 48–49; understatement, 45–46; *see also individual products*
Extractive industries, 40, 73–75, 141–143, 169, 182–183; exports, 41–42, 49, 227

Factor bias, *see* Technical progress, factor bias
Factor price distortions, 69, 89–90, 230
Factor price ratio, 89
Factor shares, 63–65, 223
Factor substitution, *see* Elasticity of factor substitution
Farquhar, J. D., 212, 214–215
Fei, John C. H., 55, 100, 123, 149, 162, 167
Feldman, G. A., 168
Fertilizer, 72, 206, 207, 210
Findlay, Ronald, 13, 168
Fisheries, 118
Fonollera, Raymundo E., 82
Food: consumption, 100–102, 131, 133, 226; demand elasticities, 102–104; imports, 47, 101
Foreign enterprise, 183–184
Foreign exchange constraint, 13–14, 109–111, 120, 170

Foreign exchange reserves, *see* Balance of payments
Foreign investment, 184, 216
Forests: extent, 211–215; illegal depletion, 211–212; *see also* Logging industry
Frankel, Marvin, 136

Golay, Frank H., 57, 100, 202
Gold, 186, 216
Goodstein, Marvin E., 57, 100, 202
Gross national product: growth, 44, 117, 223; sectoral shares, 44, 224

Haberler, Gottfried, 23–24
Hahn, F. H., 221
Harvested area, *see* Crop areas *and* Land expansion
Hectarage elasticity, *see* Crop areas, price responsiveness of
Higgins, Benjamin, 18
Hirschman, Albert O., 29, 189, 190
Hooley, Richard W., 79, 88, 112–114, 120, 181
Hornby, J. M., 162
Hotelling, Harold, 142
Hsieh, S. C., 204, 205
Huke, Robert E., 201–202, 213

Import constraint on growth, *see* Foreign exchange constraint *and* Investment, import dependence of
Import dependence, *see* Investment, import dependence of
Import substitution, 25–29, 30, 70–72, 107–108, 165, 189–190, 225, 228–229
Imports: categorization, 42–43; demand, 108; export dependence, 105–108; understatement, 46, 47, 106
Income distribution, 64
Indonesia, 9, 31, 32, 40, 57, 125, 186, 203–204, 205
Industry, *see* Manufactures *and* Modern sector
Inflation, 189
Innis, Harold A., 19
Innovation, *see* Technical progress
Intermediate goods, imports of, 42–43
International Rice Research Institute, 31, 205, 206, 209, 210
Intersectoral trade, 72, 151–153; *see also* Terms of trade, intersectoral

Inventories, 66, 111
Investment: allocation, 11–15, 143, 144, 168–169, 176; import dependence of, 25–28, 108–111, 146, 222–223, 224–225, 229–230; rate, 65–66
Investment function, 112–114, 143, 154
Invisibles, 105–107, 146–147
Irrigation, 32, 209, 210
IR8, *see* Rice, new varieties

Jorgenson, Dale W., 123, 167

Klein, L. R., 116
Kuznets, Simon, 25, 27, 223

Labor, 124; intersectoral transfer, 15–16, 52–53, 55, 94, 147–149, 224; productivity, 54, 57, 74, 89, 161, 193, 224; *see also* Employment; Underemployment; *and* Unemployment
Labor force: concept, 51, 82, 87; participation rate, 54
Labor market, 86–87, 94, 148–149
Labor surplus model, 21, 98, 172
Land expansion, 20–21, 56–57, 77–80, 125, 172, 202–203, 212–213; contribution to output growth, 31–32, 117; theory, 77, 124–128; *see also* Crop areas
Land frontier, closing of, 129, 201–204
Land/labor ratio, 57, 76–82
Land surplus, 31, 76, 128; extent, 201–203, 213–214; significance, 1–2, 97–98, 129–131, 172–173; and technical progress in agriculture, 203–204
Land utilization, 213
Lawas, José M., 117
Levy, Emanuel, 43, 56, 109
Lewis, W. Arthur, 21, 87
Logging industry, 74, 183, 212, 214; exports, 193, 211, 214–215
Luzon, 80–82, 94–96, 198, 199, 200, 211, 212

MacBean, A. I., 22
McKinnon, Ronald I., 170
Mahalanobis, P. C., 168–169
Maizels, Alfred, 25, 26, 28–29, 70
Malaysia, 9, 10, 31, 32, 40, 47, 57, 186
Mangahas, Mahar, 99, 102, 103

Manila, 88, 95–96
Manufactures: difficulty of exporting, 29–30, 188–191; exports, 42, 48–50, 145, 164, 187–191, 224–225, 227; production, 67–70
Manufacturing, unorganized, 69–70
Matthews, R. C. O., 221
Mears, Leon A., 103
Migration: to land frontier, 94–97, 125; rural-urban, 87–88, 94–97; *see also* Labor, intersectoral transfer
Mill, John Stuart, 23
Mindanao, 77, 80–82, 95–97, 198, 199, 200, 201–202, 211–214
Minimum wage law, 92, 93
Mining industry, 183; exports, 215; growth, 216–217; processing, 193; reserves, 215–217
Models, role of, 122–123, 221–222; *see also* Dual economy model
Modern sector, 10, 45, 61–75, 135–146, 185; definition, 39–41
Mosak, Jacob L., 171
Multiple cropping, 32, 56–57, 80–81
Myint, Hla, 18, 20–22, 31, 203
Myrdal, Gunnar, 83

National accounts, Philippine, 43–45, 101
National Economic Council, Philippines, 39, 44, 218
National Planning Association, 34, 39, 43
Natural resources, 141, 211, 215–216
NEC, *see* National Economic Council, Philippines
Neo-Marxist growth model, 13, 168–169
Net exportable surplus, *see* Agricultural surplus, exportable
Nonshiftability of capital, *see* Capital specificity
North, Douglass C., 18, 19
NPA, *see* National Planning Association
Nurkse, Ragnar, 17, 172

Open dual economy model, *see* Dual economy model
Openness, significance of, *see* Trade, in dual economy model

Paauw, Douglas S., 39–40, 43, 59
Peso, exchange rate, *see* Exchange rate for peso
Philippine Statistical Survey of Households, 51–52, 58, 83, 91, 102
Pioneer settlement, *see* Migration, to land frontier
Plantation industry, 40, 183, 186
Plywood industry, 193–194
Policy, *see* Development policy
Population growth, 150–151, 218–219, 230
Power, John H., 29, 190
Production function: and impact of trade, 20–22; modern sector, 116–117, 135–139; traditional sector, 76–79, 124–131
Profits, 63, 65, 113, 120
Program Implementation Agency, Philippines, 69, 101, 103
PSSH, see *Philippine Statistical Survey of Households*

Ranis, Gustav, 55, 100, 123, 149, 162, 167
Recto, Aida E., 99, 102
Resettlement, *see* Migration, to land frontier
Returns to factors, *see* Factor shares
Rice, 31, 103, 210; interaction between hectarage and yield, 103, 198; in international trade, 181, 209; new varieties, 206–209; prospective surpluses, 209–210; yields, 196–199, 206–207
Rubber, 186
Ruprecht, Theodore K., 53, 82, 85
Ruttan, Vernon W., 99, 102, 181, 204, 205

Savings: in modern sector, 170; in traditional sector, 153, 171
Savings constraint, 170
Sen, A. K., 176
Services, 41, 86
Shifting cultivation, 211, 212
Sicat, Gerardo P., 89–90, 108, 112–114, 116, 188, 189–190, 192
Smuggling, 47, 170, 174, 195
Soviet growth model, unorthodox, 13, 168–169
Staple theory, 19

Streeten, Paul P., 122
Subsistence crops, 20, 180–181
Sugar: processing, 192–193; yields, 39, 197, 200, 205, 210

Taiwan, 203, 209
"Take-off," 5, 204
Tariffs, 29, 192, 195
Technical progress: in agriculture, 100, 131, 161, 164, 166, 196–201, 203–211; factor bias, 88–89, 137–139, 160–161, 166–167, 230; in industry, 88–89, 136–140, 166–167, 230; and trade, 24; *see also* Capital/output ratio *and* Labor, productivity
Technology, transferability of, 204–205
Terms of trade: foreign, 22, 107, 219–220; intersectoral, 72–73, 120, 151–153, 165–166, 170, 186
Thailand, 9, 10, 14, 31, 32, 47, 57
Trade: and development, 6–7, 16–25; in dual economy model, 175–177, 222; *see also* Balance of trade *and* Intersectoral trade
Traditional sector, 45, 56–61, 123–131, 185–186; definition, 39–41
Tryon, Joseph L., 39–40, 59
Two-gap growth model, 7, 170–172

Umaña, Salvador C., 115
Underemployment, 83, 85–86
Unemployment, 82–84, 85, 150
United Nations Conference on Trade and Development, 7, 171
United Nations Economic Commission for Asia and the Far East, 42, 171
Urbanization, *see* Migration, rural-urban

"Vent-for-surplus" theory, 20–22, 31, 75
Visayas, 80–81, 95–97, 198, 199

Wages, 66–67, 90–94, 119; determination, 149–150, 173; intersectoral differential, 92–93
Wall, David, 111
Welfare legislation, 90, 93–94
Williamson, Jeffrey G., 101, 103
Winston, Gordon C., 171

Yields, agricultural, *see* Crop yields

Trade and Growth
in the Philippines

Designed by R. E. Rosenbaum.
Composed by Kingsport Press, Inc.,
in 11 point Baskerville, 2 points leaded,
with tables in monotype Baskerville, and
display lines in monotype Deepdene.
Printed letterpress from type by Kingsport Press
on 60 pound Warren's No. 66 Antique Text
with the Cornell University Press watermark.
Bound by Kingsport Press
in Joanna Arrestox B book cloth
and stamped in All Purpose imitation gold.